Suhasini L. Kumar, MA, MLS
Editor

The Changing Face of Government Information: Providing Access in the Twenty-First Century

The Changing Face of Government Information: Providing Access in the Twenty-First Century has been co-published simultaneously as *The Reference Librarian*, Number 94 2006.

Pre-publication
REVIEWS,
COMMENTARIES,
EVALUATIONS . . .

"**A** DOCUMENTS INFORMATION POWERHOUSE . . . EXCELLENT INSIGHT. . . . ESSENTIAL READING for anyone serving government documents collections, and a useful read for every librarian involved in collection development and public service."

Cheryl LaGuardia, MLIS
Research Librarian
and Head of Instructional Services
Harvard College Library

The Haworth Information Press®
An Imprint of The Haworth Press, Inc.

The Changing Face of Government Information: Providing Access in the Twenty-First Century

The Changing Face of Government Information: Providing Access in the Twenty-First Century has been co-published simultaneously as *The Reference Librarian*, Number 94 2006.

Monographic Separates from *The Reference Librarian*™

For additional information on these and other Haworth Press titles, including descriptions, tables of contents, reviews, and prices, use the QuickSearch catalog at http://www.HaworthPress.com.

The Changing Face of Government Information: Providing Access in the Twenty-First Century, edited by Suhasini L. Kumar, MA, MLS (No. 94, 2006). *An examination of all aspects of providing current and future electronic access to government information.*

New Directions in Reference, edited by Byron Anderson, MA, MLIS, and Paul T. Webb, MA, MLIS (No. 93, 2006). "*An interesting collection. . . . I was especially intrigued by Harry Meserve's insider's evaluation of San José's merger of public and university library services, and Anderson's activist call for librarians to fight aspects of the Digital Millennium Copyright Act.*" *(Andrew B. Werthheimer, PhD, Assistant Professor, Library & Information Science Program, University of Hawaii at Manoa)*

The Reference Collection: From the Shelf to the Web, edited by William J. Frost (No. 91/92, 2005). *An essential guide to collection development for electronic materials in academic and public libraries.*

Relationships Between Teaching Faculty and Teaching Librarians, edited by Susan B. Kraat (No. 89/90, 2005). *Documents the efforts of teaching librarians to establish effective communication with teaching faculty.*

Research, Reference Service, and Resources for the Study of Africa, edited by Deborah M. LaFond and Gretchen Walsh (No. 87/88, 2004). *Examines reference services in terms of Africa and libraries in both the United States and Africa.*

Animals Are the Issue: Library Resources on Animal Issues, edited by John M. Kistler, MLS, MDiv (No. 86, 2004). *Contains listings of written and electronic resources that focus on the ethics of animal treatment and use.*

Digital versus Non-Digital Reference: Ask a Librarian Online and Offline, edited by Jessamyn West, MLib (No. 85, 2004). *A librarian's guide to commercial Ask A Librarian (AskA) and tutorial services and how they compare to traditional library services.*

Cooperative Reference: Social Interaction in the Workplace, edited by Celia Hales Mabry, PhD (No. 83/84, 2003). *This informative volume focuses on effective social interactions between library co-workers, presenting perspectives, firsthand accounts, and advice from experienced and successful reference librarians.*

Outreach Services in Academic and Special Libraries, edited by Paul Kelsey, MLIS, and Sigrid Kelsey, MLIS (No. 82, 2003). *Presents an array of models and case studies for creating and implementing outreach services in academic and special library settings.*

Managing the Twenty-First Century Reference Department: Challenges and Prospects, edited by Kwasi Sarkodie-Mensah, PhD (No. 81, 2003). *An up-to-date guide on managing and maintaining a reference department in the twenty-first century.*

Digital Reference Services, edited by Bill Katz, PhD (No. 79/80, 2002/2003). *A clear and concise book explaining developments in electronic technology for reference services and their implications for reference librarians.*

The Image and Role of the Librarian, edited by Wendi Arant, MLS, and Candace R. Benefiel, MA, MLIS (No. 78, 2002). *A unique and insightful examination of how librarians are perceived–and how they perceive themselves.*

Distance Learning: Information Access and Services for Virtual Users, edited by Hemalata Iyer, PhD (No. 77, 2002). *Addresses the challenge of providing Web-based library instructional materials in a time of ever-changing technologies.*

Helping the Difficult Library Patron: New Approaches to Examining and Resolving a Long-Standing and Ongoing Problem, edited by Kwasi Sarkodie-Mensah, PhD (No. 75/76, 2002). *"Finally! A book that fills in the information cracks not covered in library school about the ubiquitous problem patron. Required reading for public service librarians." (Cheryl LaGuardia, MLS, Head of Instructional Services for the Harvard College Library, Cambridge, Massachusetts)*

Evolution in Reference and Information Services: The Impact of the Internet, edited by Di Su, MLS (No. 74, 2001). *Helps you make the most of the changes brought to the profession by the Internet.*

Doing the Work of Reference: Practical Tips for Excelling as a Reference Librarian, edited by Celia Hales Mabry, PhD (No. 72 and 73, 2001). *"An excellent handbook for reference librarians who wish to move from novice to expert. Topical coverage is extensive and is presented by the best guides possible: practicing reference librarians." (Rebecca Watson-Boone, PhD, President, Center for the Study of Information Professionals, Inc.)*

New Technologies and Reference Services, edited by Bill Katz, PhD (No. 71, 2000). *This important book explores developing trends in publishing, information literacy in the reference environment, reference provision in adult basic and community education, searching sessions, outreach programs, locating moving image materials for multimedia development, and much more.*

Reference Services for the Adult Learner: Challenging Issues for the Traditional and Technological Era, edited by Kwasi Sarkodie-Mensah, PhD (No. 69/70, 2000). *Containing research from librarians and adult learners from the United States, Canada, and Australia, this comprehensive guide offers you strategies for teaching adult patrons that will enable them to properly use and easily locate all of the materials in your library.*

Library Outreach, Partnerships, and Distance Education: Reference Librarians at the Gateway, edited by Wendi Arant and Pixey Anne Mosley (No. 67/68, 1999). *Focuses on community outreach in libraries toward a broader public by extending services based on recent developments in information technology.*

From Past-Present to Future-Perfect: A Tribute to Charles A. Bunge and the Challenges of Contemporary Reference Service, edited by Chris D. Ferguson, PhD (No. 66, 1999). *Explore reprints of selected articles by Charles Bunge, bibliographies of his published work, and original articles that draw on Bunge's values and ideas in assessing the present and shaping the future of reference service.*

Reference Services and Media, edited by Martha Merrill, PhD (No. 65, 1999). *Gives you valuable information about various aspects of reference services and media, including changes, planning issues, and the use and impact of new technologies.*

Coming of Age in Reference Services: A Case History of the Washington State University Libraries, edited by Christy Zlatos, MSLS (No. 64, 1999). *A celebration of the perseverance, ingenuity, and talent of the librarians who have served, past and present, at the Holland Library reference desk.*

Document Delivery Services: Contrasting Views, edited by Robin Kinder, MLS (No. 63, 1999). *Reviews the planning and process of implementing document delivery in four university libraries–Miami University, University of Colorado at Denver, University of Montana at Missoula, and Purdue University Libraries.*

The Holocaust: Memories, Research, Reference, edited by Robert Hauptman, PhD, and Susan Hubbs Motin (No. 61/62, 1998). *"A wonderful resource for reference librarians, students, and teachers . . . on how to present this painful, historical event." (Ephraim Kaye, PhD, The International School for Holocaust Studies, Yad Vashem, Jerusalem)*

Electronic Resources: Use and User Behavior, edited by Hemalata Iyer, PhD (No. 60, 1998). *Covers electronic resources and their use in libraries, with emphasis on the Internet and the Geographic Information Systems (GIS).*

Philosophies of Reference Service, edited by Celia Hales Mabry (No. 59, 1997). *"Recommended reading for any manager responsible for managing reference services and hiring reference librarians in any type of library." (Charles R. Anderson, MLS, Associate Director for Public Services, King County Library System, Bellevue, Washington)*

Business Reference Services and Sources: How End Users and Librarians Work Together, edited by Katherine M. Shelfer (No. 58, 1997). *"This is an important collection of papers suitable for all business librarians. . . . Highly recommended!" (Lucy Heckman, MLS, MBA, Business and Economics Reference Librarian, St. John's University, Jamaica, New York)*

The Changing Face
of Government Information:
Providing Access
in the Twenty-First Century

Suhasini L. Kumar, MA, MLS
Editor

The Changing Face of Government Information: Providing Access in the Twenty-First Century has been co-published simultaneously as *The Reference Librarian*, Number 94 2006.

The Haworth Information Press®
An Imprint of The Haworth Press, Inc.

New York • London • Victoria (AU)
www.HaworthPress.com

Published by

The Haworth Information Press®, 10 Alice Street, Binghamton, NY 13904-1580 USA

The Haworth Information Press® is an imprint of The Haworth Press, Inc., 10 Alice Street, Binghamton, NY 13904-1580 USA.

The Changing Face of Government Information: Providing Access in the Twenty-First Century has been co-published simultaneously as *The Reference Librarian*, Number 94 2006.

The development, preparation, and publication of this work has been undertaken with great care. However, the publisher, employees, editors, and agents of The Haworth Press and all imprints of The Haworth Press, Inc., including The Haworth Medical Press® and Pharmaceutical Products Press®, are not responsible for any errors contained herein or for consequences that may ensue from use of materials or information contained in this work. With regard to case studies, identities and circumstances of individuals discussed herein have been changed to protect confidentiality. Any resemblance to actual persons, living or dead, is entirely coincidental.

The Haworth Press is committed to the dissemination of ideas and information according to the highest standards of intellectual freedom and the free exchange of ideas. Statements made and opinions expressed in this publication do not necessarily reflect the views of the Publisher, Directors, management, or staff of The Haworth Press, Inc., or an endorsement by them.

Cover design by Jennifer M. Gaska.

Library of Congress Cataloging-in-Publication Data

The changing face of government information : providing access in the twenty-first century / Suhasini L. Kumar, editor.
      p. cm.
    "Co-published simultaneously as The reference librarian, volume 45, number 94 2006."
    Includes bibliographical references and indexes.
    ISBN-13: 978-0-7890-3155-6 (alk. paper)
    ISBN-10: 0-7890-3155-8 (alk. paper)
    ISBN-13: 978-0-7890-3156-3 (pbk. : alk. paper)
    ISBN-10: 0-7890-3156-6 (pbk. : alk. paper)
    1. Libraries–Special collections–Electronic government publications. 2. Electronic government publications–United States. 3. Electronic government information–United States. 4. Depository libraries–Reference services–United States. 5. United States. Government Printing Office. 6. Federal Depository Library Program. 7. Information policy–United States. I. Kumar, Suhasini L. II. Reference librarian.

Z688.G6C46 2006
025.2'84–dc22

2005023973

Indexing, Abstracting & Website/Internet Coverage

The Reference Librarian

This section provides you with a list of major indexing & abstracting services and other tools for bibliographic access. That is to say, each service began covering this periodical during the year noted in the right column. Most Websites which are listed below have indicated that they will either post, disseminate, compile, archive, cite or alert their own Website users with research-based content from this work. (This list is as current as the copyright date of this publication.)

Abstracting, Website/Indexing Coverage . . . . Year When Coverage Began

- *Academic Abstracts/CD-ROM (EBSCO)* 1994
- *Academic Search Complete (EBSCO)* 1996
- *Academic Search Elite (EBSCO)* 1995
- *Academic Search Premier (EBSCO)*
  <http://www.epnet.com/academic/acasearchprem.asp> 1995
- *Advanced Polymers Abstracts (Cambridge Scientific Abstracts) <http://csa.com>* 2006
- *Aluminum Industry Abstracts (Cambridge Scientific Abstracts)*
  <http://www.csa.com> 2006
- *Biomeditaties (Biomedical Information of the Dutch Library Association)*
  <http://www.nvb-online.nl> 2006
- *Business Source Corporate (EBSCO): coverage of nearly 3,350 quality magazines
  and journals; designed to meet the diverse information needs of corporations;
  EBSCO Publishing <http://www.epnet.com/corporate/bsourcecorp.asp>* 1995
- *Cambridge Scientific Abstracts (a leading publisher of scientific information
  in print journals, online databases, CD-ROM, and via the Internet)
  <http://www.csa.com>* 2006
- *Ceramic Abstracts (Cambridge Scientific Abstracts) <http://www.csa.com>* 2006
- *Composites Industry Abstracts (Cambridge Scientific Abstracts) <http://csa.com>* 2006
- *Computer and Information Systems Abstracts (Cambridge Scientific Abstracts)*
  <http://www.csa.com> 2004
- *Corrosion Abstracts (Cambridge Scientific Abstracts) <http://www.csa.com>* 2006
- *CSA Engineering Research Database (Cambridge Scientific Abstracts)*
  <http://csa.com> 2006

(continued)

(continued)

(continued)

Special bibliographic notes related to special journal issues (separates) and indexing/abstracting:

- indexing/abstracting services in this list will also cover material in any "separate" that is co-published simultaneously with Haworth's special thematic journal issue or DocuSerial. Indexing/abstracting usually covers material at the article/chapter level.
- monographic co-editions are intended for either non-subscribers or libraries which intend to purchase a second copy for their circulating collections.
- monographic co-editions are reported to all jobbers/wholesalers/approval plans. The source journal is listed as the "series" to assist the prevention of duplicate purchasing in the same manner utilized for books-in-series.
- to facilitate user/access services all indexing/abstracting services are encouraged to utilize the co-indexing entry note indicated at the bottom of the first page of each article/chapter/contribution.
- this is intended to assist a library user of any reference tool (whether print, electronic, online, or CD-ROM) to locate the monographic version if the library has purchased this version but not a subscription to the source journal.
- individual articles/chapters in any Haworth publication are also available through the Haworth Document Delivery Service (HDDS).

The Changing Face
of Government Information:
Providing Access
in the Twenty-First Century

CONTENTS

ANNOTATED RESOURCES

ABOUT THE EDITOR

Suhasini L. Kumar, MA, MLS, is Associate Professor and Head of the Government Documents Department at the Carlson Library at The University of Toledo. She is also Coordinator of the Information and Instruction Services Division where her areas of expertise include English and Theatre. She has contributed to *The Reference Librarian*, the *Library Instruction Series*, and *Magazines for Libraries* for which she is also a consultant. Her research interests include government information reference and instruction, and designing specialized information literacy sessions for international students.

IN MEMORIAM

William Katz

Dr. William (Bill) Katz passed away on September 12, 2004. Dr. Katz was Editor of the Haworth journals *The Acquisitions Librarian* and *The Reference Librarian* as well as *Magazines for Libraries*, *RQ* (the journal of the Reference and Adult Services Division of the American Library Association), and the "Magazines" column in *Library Journal.* In addition to his contributions to library science as an author and editor, he was a much-beloved professor in the School of Information Science and Policy at the State University of New York at Albany and a mentor to many of his former students in their professional lives. His association with The Haworth Press began in 1980 and lasted more than two decades. His steady hand, friendly guidance, and steadfast leadership will be missed by all of us at *The Acquisitions Librarian*, *The Reference Librarian*, and The Haworth Press.

Introduction

Suhasini L. Kumar

The past few years have radically changed the way government information is created, processed, disseminated, and accessed. The ease with which information could be electronically disseminated over the Internet had a great impact on the Government Printing Office (GPO) and provided it with opportunities to increase open access to the workings of the government and enabled it to transit from a paper-based information policy to an electronic one.

This volume addresses several concerns relating to government documents librarianship in an electronic milieu. Articles focus on the changes that have occurred in the way government documents librarians perform their duties with regard to acquiring, providing access and reference services in the new electronic environment. Issues concerning the effects of 9/11 on the library community, and the preservation and authentication of electronic documents are also addressed here.

As the Government Printing Office moves toward a wholly electronic distribution system for government information, reference services within the Federal Depository Library Program (FDLP) are also undergoing changes. Many depository libraries have opted to consolidate their reference service points with the main reference desk or other areas. Salem's article reports on the results of a survey of FDLP institutions identifying the factors contributing to the reorganization of services. Nicholson, Stave, and Zhang write about how the University of

[Haworth co-indexing entry note]: "Introduction." Kumar, Suhasini L. Co-published simultaneously in *The Reference Librarian* (The Haworth Information Press, an imprint of The Haworth Press, Inc.) No. 94, 2006, pp. 1-3; and: *The Changing Face of Government Information: Providing Access in the Twenty-First Century* (ed: Suhasini L. Kumar) The Haworth Information Press, an imprint of The Haworth Press, Inc., 2006, pp. 1-3. Single or multiple copies of this article are available for a fee from The Haworth Document Delivery Service [1-800-HAWORTH, 9:00 a.m. - 5:00 p.m. (EST). E-mail address: docdelivery@haworthpress.com].

Available online at http://www.haworthpress.com/web/REF
doi:10.1300/J120v45n94_01

Oregon Libraries successfully integrated its business reference service and map collection into its government documents collection.

Rawan and Malone describe the pilot project undertaken by the University of Arizona Library in conjunction with the United States Government Printing Office's Library Programs Service to create a model for a virtual depository library.

Electronic resources have given rise to electronic reference services. Kelly and Hartman indicate that the critical features missing in today's e-government reference service models is the research expertise found in Federal Depository Libraries and propose that these services be coordinated nationally by an AskUS-FDLP Library Portal.

Many are the concerns regarding preservation and perpetual access to government information. Lyons' paper examines how the National Archives and the Government Printing Office are responding to the technical, financial, legal, and political challenges of providing permanent public access to electronic government information. Kumar discusses GPO's plans to provide perpetual access to both electronic and tangible information resources and its endeavors to authenticate electronic government documents.

Myers, who is renowned for her role in establishing the Documents Data Miner, writes about the emergence of the Documents Data Miner products that served to single-handedly move issues of collection development, processing and cataloging of government documents from a 19th century paper-based environment to a 21st century data mining model. Kawula and Weible address cataloging concerns and management of records in an OPAC centering on the use of direct links to online resources.

Access to government sponsored scientific and technical reports has always been elusive. Nickum's article examines the reasons why effective access to federally funded technical reports has been hard to get and illustrates how new technologies have greatly improved access to this important body of literature. Tipton describes how access to government numeric data and statistical information has been made easier resulting in increased patron demand for government data and how this has also changed the role of documents librarians.

The terrorist attacks of September 11 were followed by the USA Patriot Act and other anti-terrorism measures that threatened open access to information, patron privacy, and confidentiality of patron records. The library community was distressed by the threat to these liberties and Martorella carefully examines these issues in her article.

Jorgensen discusses the online government information movement and uses government documents as resources to retrace the events that occurred in federal government agencies during the movement of government information to the Internet.

Annotated subject bibliographies are important to researchers. Cowgill's selective annotated list of print and electronic government resources provides information on Native Americans, and Jobe identifies key local environmental information sites from an increasing amount of state and local environmental resources.

Exciting changes are taking place in the field of government documents' librarianship as GPO advances toward a completely electronic dissemination system. Experts in the field believe that the government documents librarian's role will have to change with the times; librarians will now have to focus more on using their knowledge and expertise to teach users how to skillfully retrieve what they need from this enormous wealth of government information.

GOVERNMENT PRINTING OFFICE'S TRANSITION TO A MORE ELECTRONIC FORMAT AND ITS IMPACT ON THE COLLECTION AND REFERENCE SERVICES

A Virtual Depository: The Arizona Project

Atifa Rawan
Cheryl Knott Malone

SUMMARY. The University of Arizona Library, in conjunction with the United States Government Printing Office's Library Programs Service, worked to create a model for a virtual depository by replacing tangible documents with their online counterparts whenever possible. The

Atifa Rawan is Government Documents Librarian, University of Arizona Library (E-mail: rawana@u.library.arizona.edu); and Cheryl Knott Malone is Associate Professor, School of Information Resources (E-mail: ckmalone@email.arizona.edu), both at the University of Arizona, Tuscon, AZ.

[Haworth co-indexing entry note]: "A Virtual Depository: The Arizona Project." Rawan, Atifa, and Cheryl Knott Malone. Co-published simultaneously in *The Reference Librarian* (The Haworth Information Press, an imprint of The Haworth Press, Inc.) No. 94, 2006, pp. 5-18; and: *The Changing Face of Government Information: Providing Access in the Twenty-First Century* (ed: Suhasini L. Kumar) The Haworth Information Press, an imprint of The Haworth Press, Inc., 2006, pp. 5-18. Single or multiple copies of this article are available for a fee from The Haworth Document Delivery Service [1-800-HAWORTH, 9:00 a.m. - 5:00 p.m. (EST). E-mail address: docdelivery@haworthpress.com].

Available online at http://www.haworthpress.com/web/REF
doi:10.1300/J120v45n94_02

partnership was achieved by dedicated teamwork: the UA team provided the searching and assessment; the GPO team provided the legal and organizational framework as well as the indexing. At the end of the pilot project's year the program was deemed to be a success and GPO and UA worked to make this process a more permanent one with positive long-term effects in terms of costs and human and physical resources. *[Article copies available for a fee from The Haworth Document Delivery Service: 1-800-HAWORTH. E-mail address: <docdelivery@haworthpress.com> Website: <http://www.HaworthPress.com> © 2006 by The Haworth Press, Inc. All rights reserved.]*

KEYWORDS. Federal Depository Library Program, university libraries, government documents, electronic depository collections, virtual depository, electronic resources cataloging, mining

INTRODUCTION

In a partnership spanning more than a century, the Federal Depository Library Program (FDLP) of the Government Printing Office (GPO) has worked with regional and selective depository libraries to provide the public with free access to information produced at government expense. For much of that time, the phrase "government documents" has evoked an image of books, pamphlets, maps, and microfiche tucked into an out-of-the-way corner of the stacks. Since the mid-1990s, however, government agencies and offices have distributed information directly to the public from their own Web sites. And at the same time GPO has taken a number of steps to provide permanent public access to government information accessible over the Internet. FDLP estimates that it now distributes 65% of new government publications in electronic formats.[1] The availability of free information on government Web sites, including GPO's own GPO Access gateway to databases and finding aids, has led some library directors to question the need to stay in the depository program. The question for most government documents librarians and their directors, however, is not whether to stay in the program. The real question is how to ensure that the program's increasing move toward providing indexing of and access to greater online dissemination serves libraries and their users well.

The Depository Library Council, whose 15 members are appointed by the U.S. Public Printer to serve as advisors, recently suggested that

GPO explore the concept of virtual depository collections, and FDLP program managers discussed the idea.[2] Nothing in the statute governing federal depository libraries precludes an all-electronic selection profile for established depositories, which must have at least 10,000 books, other than government publications, to remain in the depository system.[3] This is a requirement even for libraries that adjust their FDLP selection profile to receive only online titles. Further, the *FDLP Guidelines on Substituting Electronic for Tangible Versions of Depository Publications* state that "(a) depository is permitted to replace tangible versions with electronic equivalents provided the electronic version is complete, official, and permanently accessible."[4] Librarians can consult the *Substitution List: Official FDLP Permanent Full-Text Databases*, to verify which electronic items are considered "complete, official, and permanently accessible."[5] The FDLP guidelines also recommend that any selective depository library electing to replace print, microfiche, CD-ROM, and other tangible formats with electronic versions work with the regional depository library to be sure the regional retains tangible versions as a backup collection.

These guidelines have been set in place by the FDLP and the Depository Library Council to lay the groundwork for selective depository libraries to begin systematically replacing tangible with electronic formats. The indexing provided by the GPO's Cataloging Branch has extensively supported this format migration by depository libraries. Without direct experience, though, it is not clear what all the ramifications might be. To gain the needed direct experience, the University of Arizona Library, in partnership with GPO, conducted a year-long pilot project during which the library selected online electronic rather than tangible formats wherever possible. The University of Arizona is a land-grant institution classed in the Carnegie category of Doctoral/Research Universities-Extensive. The library has been in the FDLP since 1907 and operated as a regional depository between 1963 and 1987. It currently selects 59% of the materials available through the Library Program Service (LPS) of GPO and primarily serves the university's faculty, students, and staff as well as residents of the 7th and 8th Congressional Districts. Further, the library is organized on a team, rather than departmental, basis, which facilitates collaboration on special projects. The UA Library's collection policies, in recognition of customer needs and preferences as well as of physical space limitations, emphasize the provision of access to electronic information resources, from full-text databases to aggregations of e-journals to cataloged e-books. The Cataloging Branch of the GPO has been operating under very similar service policies. The pilot project made it possible for the library to begin aligning the depository selection profile with the policies shaping other areas of the collection; at the same time the pilot project helped to establish a preliminary framework for UA library staff to understand the impact of the move toward greater electronic access to government information. It aided GPO's Cataloging Branch in refining its procedures for adding electronic titles to the depository collection and to increase its indexing service to the community. The pilot project also set a precedent for a selective depository that establishes an all-electronic item selection to be evaluated in biennial surveys, self-studies, and inspections on an equal and fair footing with depositories that continue to select tangible formats.

During the pilot project, which ran from September 2002 to September 2003, four key activities were undertaken:

1. Formation of a project team, consisting of GPO and UA staff;
2. Revision of the library's depository selection profile;
3. Recommendations of electronic federal government documents in the library's profile but not available through the FDLP; and
4. Assessment of the experience.

What follows is a discussion of each of these activities and its contribution to the pilot project from the dual perspectives of the UA librarian in charge of the project and GPO's Electronic Collection manager.

FORMATION OF A PROJECT TEAM

Because the pilot touched on aspects of cataloging, collection development, communication, record keeping, and assessment, the library created a project team to guide the various aspects. The UA team was coordinated by the library's government documents librarian and included a social sciences librarian, a science librarian, a faculty advisor from the UA School of Information Resources and Library Science (SIRLS), and three SIRLS graduate student interns. The librarians on the UA project team sent information about the pilot project to all UA Library staff and to other area libraries. The coordinator also provided training and supervision for the SIRLS students and worked with the faculty advisor to assess the project.

The coordinator served as the team's liaison to GPO as well. In preparation for the pilot project, UA Library and GPO's Depository Services staff met in July 2002 and established a process for the depository regulations with planned milestones for the project. The library and GPO agreed to do a baseline initial assessment followed by periodic informal assessments of progress. Assessments were conducted as needed throughout the project and the project coordinator and GPO staff stayed in close contact during the year.

The library did not digitize and load government information products onto its servers, but focused instead on providing reliable access to online resources. The library's Technical Services and Archival Processing (TSAP) team relied on GPO's Cataloging Branch staff to conduct link maintenance and to archive all the materials cataloged for the pilot project as well, ensuring that access to the materials is permanent. TSAP also provided access to all pilot project materials via SABIO, the library's information gateway.

The Arizona State Library, the regional depository in the area, provided assistance with interpreting the legal responsibilities of the UA Library according to the established processes and procedures of the FDLP. In the event the library needed physical copies of specific titles that had been selected in electronic format only, the State Library agreed to provide backup service by providing those needed titles in tangible form.

The pilot project coordinator briefed the UA Library information resource managers on depository selection criteria and processes and worked with them to recommend electronic items for inclusion in the FDLP's electronic collection.

REVISION OF THE LIBRARY'S
DEPOSITORY SELECTION PROFILE

Just before the beginning of the pilot project, the UA Library modified its depository item selection profile to replace tangible format items with available electronic format items. The modifications were made in consultation with the library's information resource managers. The profile for 2002-2003 included 3,509 items, 59% of the total 5,946 depository items available for selection (see Figure 1). The year before, the profile included just over 55% of the total items available (see Figure 2). Out of the 900 initial items available in both formats, the library selected 703 items in electronic format only. In some cases, however, the library made exceptions, choosing both paper and electronic formats of

FIGURE 1. Items Selected: 3,509 (59%) out of 5,946 Offered for Selection

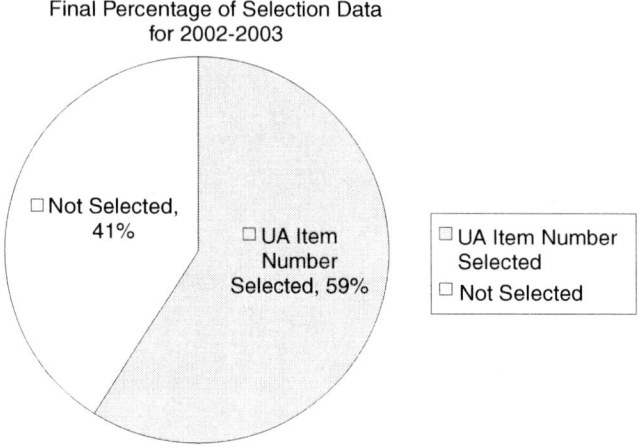

Final Percentage of Selection Data
for 2002-2003

the same item. These exceptions included maps, tangible electronic products that contained large datasets, and highly used titles.

Since May of 2002 the library had received a monthly list of depository items that were available in dual formats (tangible and online) from GPO. The library's information resources managers compared the August list against the library's 2001-2002 GPO selection profile and determined which items were newly available online. From that list, information resource managers identified 25 titles to be received in both paper and e-format, based on heavy use and/or difficulty in using the electronic format (see Appendix A). After the completion of the project, the information resource managers reassessed the list of exceptions. They dropped 4 titles and added 2. The exceptions for 2003-2004 decreased to 23 titles received in dual formats.

The Library staff worked with GPO to maintain a backup process for the deselected tangible products because the 2002-2003 profile heavily favored electronic access for the duration of the pilot year. GPO created two separate profiles labeled UNIV of ARIZ/VLC PILOT PROJ-Library 0023 and UNIV OF ARIZ-Library 1070. Library 0023 was an active profile based on current item selections for the pilot's duration. These documents were processed and cataloged. From October 2002 to August 2003, library staff processed 2,039 paper pieces, including

FIGURE 2. Selection of Items by Format

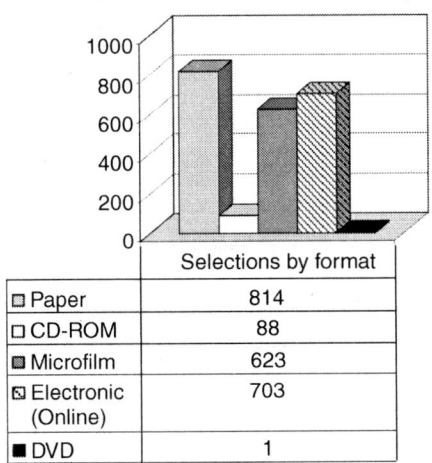

Selections by format	
▢ Paper	814
▫ CD-ROM	88
▩ Microfilm	623
⊠ Electronic (Online)	703
■ DVD	1

maps, and 1,025 microfiche pieces. These pieces included frequent publications such as the *Official Gazette of the United States*, the *Internal Revenue Bulletin*, and *Employment and Earnings* as well as titles the library elected to receive in dual formats such as *CPI Detailed Report*, *Monthly Labor Review*, and *Survey of Current Business*. Library staff also processed 468 pieces issued on CD-ROM and DVD. The number of items processed totaled approximately 10% of the library's depository items received during the year.

Shipments received on the backup profile, Library 1070, were stored unprocessed until after the conclusion of the pilot project. The backup collection was necessary in case the pilot project proved unsuccessful or the UA Library determined the electronic-only resources did not fit well with its mission and services. GPO agreed to allow time to unpack the items at the end of the pilot and to decide whether the backup tangibles needed to be processed for inclusion into the library's depository collection. GPO also agreed to give the library an extension on the July 31 selection profile deadline to allow the library to assess needs based on the pilot experience. Some 400 boxes containing print, 100 packages of microfiche, 200 separate items, and 100 map cylinders remained unprocessed during the pilot year. After the completion of the pilot, these items were re-assessed and none was added to the collection.

IDENTIFICATION OF ELECTRONIC
FEDERAL GOVERNMENT DOCUMENTS

The UA project coordinator and the three graduate student interns checked items on the library's profile to identify those available on the Internet but not disseminated in electronic format through the FDLP. The UA team also submitted titles that had been cataloged by GPO in electronic format prior to GPO's adoption of PURLs. The coordinator and interns notified GPO of these titles by submitting them to lostdocs@ gpo.gov. Cataloging Branch staff reviewed the submitted items for possible inclusion in the program and when possible, resolved any nonworking URLs for older documents. The interns worked from the "List of Classes, May 2002, EL Only" for the UA Library and verified that these documents were accessible via GPO Access. From October 2002 to August 2003, 3,509 items (6,423 titles) from the library's 2002-2003 profile were checked. The library submitted 3,288 titles to GPO; about 25% of these titles had been searched more than once. On the average, it took an experienced intern 15 minutes per title to search and verify; some searches required additional effort. For example, the interns would find a PURL through GPO Access that was supposed to be for a series but that turned out to link to only one of the documents in the series; additional research was required to locate other related items. In one instance, the record for an annual report that was updated every year linked only to the PURL for the 1998 report. The interns also found that the lack of standardization of federal agency Web sites slowed their search times. While some agencies made it easy to find documents with links on their homepages to such things as "Document Libraries" or "Publications" or site maps linked to some agencies' homepages, others did not. Some agencies employ databases that must be queried for documents and reports, such as the Department of Transportation's TRIS Online, which requires users to execute a search to locate publications.[6]

Over the course of the year, the number of discontinued titles from GPO was 12. Currently, the library and GPO are collaborating in the continuation of this project; submissions are now being sent via the Lostdocs submission form at http://www.access.gpo.gov/su_docs/fdlp/ tools/lostdocs.html. As part of this collaboration, GPO and the UA library hired two SIRLS graduate assistants whose main tasks are the verification of titles and the submission of appropriate items to the Lostdocs e-mailbox. A GPO cataloger trained the interns in the GPO process of evaluating electronic resources for addition to the FDLP electronic collection. The minimum information required for submissions to Lostdocs includes the full title or series of the work, item number, full URL associated with a series or titles (e.g., http://pubs.usgs.gov/pp/p1657/), any associated PURL found, and, if possible, OCLC accession numbers. General publications and handbooks, manuals, and guides were not searched. Records with only one issue of a serial title and problematic and broad series were not included. Only URLs leading to full content (not partial or incomplete content) were submitted. From their experience early in the pilot year, the three interns developed a system for searching that utilized the most helpful and easy to navigate sites first (see Figure 3).

Once the submissions were sent to GPO, the submissions were evaluated for their viability for entry into the program. Document fragments that were not full-text, links that were dead ends, and electronic resources that otherwise did not comply with Title 44 and SOD 71 were discarded. The viable submissions were split out among the staff equally and the documents were then classified, PURLed, archived, and cataloged. Many of the submissions included sites that required further mining. At the end of the pilot, approximately 3,349 titles were cataloged by GPO. This number is greater than the number of titles sent, due to mining that GPO did independently following up the submissions from UA.

Under the direction of the UA project coordinator, the interns created an internal master working file. The file listed all of the items in the library's depository selection profile. The file was color coded to show the status of each item. The record for each item included full information regarding its Superintendent of Documents number, title, item number, format, frequency, PURL/URL, and comments. The file was updated whenever the following changes occurred:

- Submissions were sent to lostdocs@gpo.gov;
- A new issue of the List of Classes–all EL including multi-format publications was received from GPO;
- Lists of discontinued items were found in the Administrative Notes Technical Support;
- Dead PURL links were found; or
- The library dropped an item from its profile.

The updated file was uploaded to the Library's Government Documents Web page.[7] The interns created a separate database that included SuDocs numbers, titles, item numbers, and hyperlinks to electronic items. This list was uploaded to the Government Documents Web page

FIGURE 3. Interns' Ordered Preferences for Identifying Government Information Resources Available on the Web but Not Distributed by FDLP

1. GPO Access–http://www.access.gpo.gov/su_docs/index.html

2. WorldCat–Useful for finding cataloging location such as DLC or GPO and looking for PURL addresses

3. Google–advanced search–http://www.google.com

4. Federal Web sites hosted on GPO access– http://www.access.gpo.gov/su_docs/sites.html

5. Catalog of US Government Publications– http://www.access.gpo.gov/su_docs/locators/cgp/index.html

6. US Government Agencies Database (Duke University)– http://www.lib.duke.edu/texis/searchdb/uslinks/uslinks

7. A-Z Index to Government Agencies– http://www.firstgov.gov/Agencies/Federal/All_Agencies/index.shtml

8. University of Denver SuDoc List of Classes–http://www.du.edu/bdld/locinds.htm#gtr00

9. SearchGov–http://www.searchgov.com/

10. FirstGov–http://www.firstgov.gov/ (not highly recommended)

with regular updates.[8] The final item list was given to the TSAP to be forwarded to Marcive to upload cataloging records into the library's on-line catalog. The TSAP staff link bibliographic records directly to the Web-based resources on agency sites or archived copies on the GPO servers.

ASSESSMENT OF THE EXPERIENCE

During the pilot project, faculty, students, and staff were asked about their experiences with and preferences regarding government information.[9] Several assessment tools and methodologies were used to determine users' satisfaction and patterns of use in regard to electronic documents. For the most part, users expressed appreciation for the convenience of being able to locate a broad range of authoritative information any time from any place with a computer and an Internet connection. When seeking government information, library staff tended to begin with the online catalog while students tended to use Internet search engines such as Google. Overall, though, library staff and customers used a variety of access tools, underscoring the importance of such activities as providing persistent links in catalog records, including librarian-created resource guides on the library's Web site, and offering information literacy instruction focused on government publications. There was no known instance of an interlibrary loan request for the tangible version of an online government resource during the pilot year, nor was there a need to approach the State Library for a print or microform backup of an electronic document.

Beyond aspects of users' relative satisfaction with electronic government information were administrative and operational considerations. Because the UA Library is committed to providing access to electronic information, the move toward a virtual depository collection was in keeping with the overall collection management policy. The pilot project coordinator shared information about the pilot throughout the year to ensure that information services staff, technical services staff, and information resources managers understood the project and their role in shaping and completing it.

As a result of the pilot, the UA Library decided to move decisively toward a virtual depository collection for those materials available and archived by GPO. The library's federal depository collection development policy was revised to institutionalize the new approach.[10] Under its newly revised collection development policy, the library systematically substitutes the EL format for the tangible. Further, the library staff reevaluated the selection profile for depository items, making few changes. From the original list of 25 titles in the 2002-2003 profile that the library selected in dual formats, 4 titles were dropped and 2 new titles were added. In addition, the library dropped another 106 paper and microfiche map items from its 2003-2004 profile.

The selection of EL rather than tangible depository products during the pilot project year resulted in significant savings in staff time that would otherwise have gone toward the various activities involved in processing print and microfiche documents. Processing time was cut to 10% of what it was before the change, and this translates to savings of staff and student time. Additionally, the library, already outgrowing its finite space, also saved resources by not having to find room for the tangible products that would have been received and processed under the old selection profile. The library saved 190 linear feet of shelving space, one microfiche cabinet drawer, and one map cabinet. It became apparent that the receipt of tangible formats represented an opportunity in the sense that resources expended on processing and shelving them could now go toward other needed library services and activities. All of these factors–customer satisfaction, collection policy coherence, staff communication and participation, and the freedom to deploy resources elsewhere–made it ultimately possible for the project coordinator to secure support for and endorsement of the move to a virtual depository from the library's Information Resources Council, information resource managers, and TSAP team members.

NOTES AND REFERENCES

1. We use the term "online electronic information" here to distinguish the intangible information distributed over the Internet from tangible electronic formats such as CD-ROM and DVD. In the remainder of the article, when we refer to electronic information we mean the intangible, Internet-based format, which was the focus of the project described.

2. Depository Library Council. *Responses to recommendations.* Fall, 2001. Available from: http://www.access.gpo.gov/su_docs/fdlp/council/rfa01.html.

3. 44 U.S.C. 1909.

4. Federal Depository Library Program, *FDLP Guidelines on Substituting Electronic for Tangible Versions of Depository Publications.* July 18, 2000, Section 3. Available from: http://www.access.gpo.gov/su_docs/fdlp/coll-dev/subguide.html.

5. Federal Depository Library Program, *Substitution List: Official FDLP Permanent Full-Text Databases.* July 11, 2002. Available from: http://www.access.gpo.gov/su_docs/fdlp/coll-dev/substitutions.html.

6. Department of Transportation, TRIS Online. Available from: http://199.79.179.82/sundev/search.cfm.

7. University of Arizona Library, "GPO Profile–UA Holdings." Available from: http://www.library.arizona.edu/library/teams/sst/pol/guide/gpo-profile.htm.

8. University of Arizona Library, "Electronic Depository Documents." Available from: http://www.library.arizona.edu/library/teams/sst/pol/guide/gpo-pilot/gpo-elec.htm.

9. Atifa Rawan, Cheryl Knott Malone, and Laura Bender, "Assessing the Virtual Depository Program: The Arizona Experience," *Journal of Government Information,* forthcoming.

10. University of Arizona Library, "Collection Development Policy and Management for Federal Documents." Revised August 2003. Available from: http://www.library.arizona.edu/library/teams/sst/pol/guide/coll-policyrev.html.

APPENDIX A. Titles Received in Dual Formats

	SuDocs	Title	Item No.	Tangible Form
	A 1.47:	Agricultural Statistics	0001	Paper
***	A 1.76:	Agricultural handbooks	0003	Paper
	A 1.38/2:	Agriculture Fact Book (annual)	0013-A-01	Paper
	A 92.53/3:	Census of agriculture state and county data, geographic area series, vol. 1 (Arizona)	0015-B-02	Paper
	A 92.54:	Census of agriculture, vol. 2, Subject series	0015-B-57	Paper
	A 92.53/57:	Census of agriculture, final volumes (misc.)	0015-B-58	Paper
	C 3.186/14-2:	The Hispanic population in the US (Annual)	0142-C-01	Paper
	C 3.134:	Statistical Abstract of the US (Annual)	0150	Paper
	C 3.277:	Economic and Agriculture Censuses	0154-C	CD-ROM
	C3.277/3:	Company Statistics Series (Economic Series)	0160-E-02	Paper
	C 59.11:	Survey of current business (monthly)	0228	Paper
	C 13.11:	Handbooks (numbered)	0245	Paper
***	HE 1.63:	Trends in the well-being of American children and youth	445-M-01	Paper
	ED 1.109:	The Condition of education	0461-A-12	Paper
**	ED1.310/2:	Digest of Education Statistics	0466-A-03	Paper
	HE 20.7042/6:	Health United States (annual)	483-A-19	Paper
	HE 20.316:	Trends in Indian Health	0486-I-03	Paper
***	HE 20.417/5:	National household survey on drug abuse: Summary of findings	0497-D-39	Paper
**	I 19.3:	USGS Bulletin	0620	Paper
***	I 19.16/2:	Geographic names information system (GNIS)	0621-J	CD-ROM
	I 19.42/4:	Water resources investigations (numbered)	0624-B	Paper
	I 19.13:	Water supply papers	0625	Paper

APPENDIX A (continued)

SuDocs	Title	Item No.	Tangible Form
I 19.165:	Minerals Yearbook	0639	Paper
L 2.3/4:	Occupational outlook handbook	0768-C-02	Paper
L 2.38/3:	CPI detailed report	0768-F	Paper
L 2.38/10:	Summary data from the consumer price index	0768-F	Paper
L 2.6:	Monthly labor review	0770	Paper

** tangible titles added in 2003-2004
*** tangible titles dropped in 2003-2004

The Depository Library Community and Collaborative Participation in E-Government: AskUS (FDLP Librarians) and We Will Answer!

Melody Specht Kelly
Cathy Nelson Hartman

SUMMARY. The continuation of the Federal Depository Library Program's historic information dissemination, access, and preservation roles are now dependent upon multi-agency e-government collaboration. The collections and research expertise of Federal Depository libraries are the critical features missing in current e-government service models. The authors propose that the public service and resource discovery features now available at FDLP libraries be coordinated nationally via an AskUS-FDLP Library Portal. *[Article copies available for a fee from The Haworth Document Delivery Service: 1-800-HAWORTH. E-mail address: <docdelivery@haworthpress.com> Website: <http://www.HaworthPress.com> © 2006 by The Haworth Press, Inc. All rights reserved.]*

Melody Specht Kelly is Associate Dean and Adjunct Professor, School of Library and Information Science (E-mail: mkelly@library.unt.edu); and Cathy Nelson Hartman is Head, Digital Projects Department, and Associate Fellow, Texas Center for Digital Knowledge (E-mail: chartman@library.unt.edu), both at the University of North Texas, Denton, TX.

[Haworth co-indexing entry note]: "The Depository Library Community and Collaborative Participation in E-Government: AskUS (FDLP Librarians) and We Will Answer!" Kelly, Melody Specht, and Cathy Nelson Hartman. Co-published simultaneously in *The Reference Librarian* (The Haworth Information Press, an imprint of The Haworth Press, Inc.) No. 94, 2006, pp. 19-32; and: *The Changing Face of Government Information: Providing Access in the Twenty-First Century* (ed: Suhasini L. Kumar) The Haworth Information Press, an imprint of The Haworth Press, Inc., 2006, pp. 19-32. Single or multiple copies of this article are available for a fee from The Haworth Document Delivery Service [1-800-HAWORTH, 9:00 a.m. - 5:00 p.m. (EST). E-mail address: docdelivery@haworthpress.com].

Available online at http://www.haworthpress.com/web/REF
© 2006 by The Haworth Press, Inc. All rights reserved.
doi:10.1300/J120v45n94_03

KEYWORDS. Federal Depository Library Program, future, Internet portal, Ask a Librarian

INTRODUCTION

This article examines the federal Executive Branch and Congressional vision of e-government and the role of the Government Printing Office's (GPO) Federal Depository Library Program (FDLP) to demonstrate how the FDLP can effectively participate in existing e-government initiatives. The continuation of the FDLP's historic information dissemination, access, and preservation roles is now dependent upon multi-agency e-government collaboration. The collections and research expertise residing in Federal Depository libraries are the critical features missing in current e-government service models. The authors propose that the public service and resource discovery features now available at FDLP libraries be coordinated nationally via an AskUS-FDLP Library Portal. The AskUS Portal would include an enhanced FDLP participant directory, interactive e-mail reference, chat services, and a searchable database to enable discovery of locally digitized collections. To encourage participation and collaboration, the active involvement of professional organizations such as the American Library Association's Government Documents Round Table and the American Association of Law Librarians is important to the success of an AskUS Portal. The authors also propose that these enhanced services be integrated into the "Ask a Librarian" feature offered by FirstGov.gov and the Library of Congress. Furthermore, the authors encourage the Depository Library community to form collaborative partnerships to digitize historical documents collections for discovery through the AskUS Portal.

BACKGROUND

Stakeholders within the Federal Depository Library Program envisioned the future of federal government information during the spring 2003 meeting of the Depository Library Council. In the summary of this endeavor, Council members outlined a vision for the future FDLP. They noted the following elements:

- "The Government Printing Office [GPO], in partnership with federal depository libraries, meets the needs of the public for no-fee access to official government information;

- The new era of partnership between GPO and federal depository libraries should retain the best aspects of the existing system while incorporating new technologies and services to provide a higher degree of dispersion of government information to the public;
- A more flexible internal organizational structure for FDLP must be developed to meet institutional missions of partner libraries [for example: flexibility would allow different institutions to focus on electronic collections only or to share the normal Regional Library services when institutional missions limit full participation];
- GPO should become an aggregator for federal information;
- Partner libraries should become facilitators in the federal information dissemination process rather than repositories of printed government publications; and
- The traditional library role of facilitator to no-fee public access to federal information remains key."[1]

The group also envisioned that GPO would:

- "Expand its partnerships with the Library of Congress, the National Archives and Records Administration, and other federal agencies that can help it achieve its goals in the centralized management of federal government information;
- Explore information product development that is focused on value-added services [such as enhanced no-fee GPO Access databases searching features];
- Provide services for varied communities of users; and
- Focus on marketing and training the use of government information services."[2]

For these stakeholders, the role of FDLP libraries is that of Service Providers and Facilitators who share knowledge about information services with government agencies and the public.[3] But it remains for those individuals concerned with free and open access to government information to translate the principles, not the outdated methods of the traditional FDLP libraries, into a new Service Provider/Facilitator Role.

The challenge is how to incorporate this collective FDLP Libraries' Service Provider/Facilitator Role within the broader context of existing e-government information initiatives. Success will require the acceptance by both GPO and its potential partners of the reality that no one government agency, publisher, or service provider can achieve the goal of broader access to government information by acting alone. Public managers and elected officials seek to build and sustain a process that ensures fairness, accountability, privacy, security, and efficiency, as well as preservation of the public record.[4]

It is evident from *The Information Dissemination Annual Report, Fiscal Year 2003* that GPO and the Superintendent of Documents are well aware of these realities. The *Annual Report* highlighted the progress made in the transition to a more electronic Federal Depository Library Program and that ". . . the Information Dissemination organization [Superintendent of Documents] joined or increased participation in a number of significant groups during FY2003" to better position themselves to "assume a leadership role in the information industry."[5] The Superintendent of Documents now participates in the Book Industry Study Group (http://www.bisg.org/) which sets industry standards and the National Information Standards Organization (NISO) (http://www.niso.org/) which engages in interagency work on electronic resource management, digital reference services, performance measures/statistics for libraries, reference linking, controlled vocabularies and thesauri, interoperability, best practices for electronic journals, and scientific and technical reports.[6]

In the *Annual Report*, the Superintendent of Documents also reported progress on three important initiatives. First, the implementation of a Public Key Infrastructure to allow the use of digital signatures ensuring the protection of publication data against unauthorized modification and guaranteeing authenticity of information downloaded from GPO Access. Secondly, GPO signed an agreement with the National Archives and Records Administration (NARA) to become an official archival affiliate, which now makes GPO Access databases official information archives and allows GPO to continue permanent public access of the contents. Thirdly, a draft collection plan was prepared which establishes a Public Information Collection (print and digital) that will become the collection of last resort for all Federal Depository Libraries. Progress was also made on an Integrated Library System procurement to create and maintain bibliographic information, and GPO partnered in the creation of Regulation.gov, the online rulemaking initiative.[7]

Librarians from the last century understood the essential element required in working with the publishers to ensure future access. They embedded their bibliographic structures into the process of publishing and editing. Their success resulted in the standard Twentieth-Century bibliographic resources we came to rely upon for cataloging and indexing. GPO has worked aggressively to bridge the chasm that divides the Executive and Legislative Branches to create a cooperative system that will embed structures for bibliographic organization, access, and preservation to ensure free, permanent public access to government publications.

Significantly, GPO reached an agreement for a pilot project with the Office of Management and Budget (OMB) that allows GPO to coordinate contracting for Executive Branch printing under Title 44 of the U.S. Code. Under the agreement GPO will receive two print copies and *one electronic copy* of each publication, thus ensuring bibliographic control and public dissemination.[8] The importance of the pilot project and its successful completion can not be overstated. A continuation and expansion of this agreement to include all federal agencies would ensure that GPO and the FDLP could continue their historic missions of organization, dissemination, access, and preservation of government information within the current Executive Branch Citizen-Centered E-government environment.

THE VISION OF CITIZEN-CENTERED E-GOVERNMENT SERVICES

E-Government services trace their beginnings to the early years of the Clinton Administration with the implementation of a few agency Web sites. Then with an Executive Memorandum issued December 1999, President Clinton directed agencies to receive and respond to citizens via e-mail. This was followed six months later on June 24, 2000 with the announcement of FirstGov.gov (www.firstgov.gov) as a single Internet portal to government agencies. President Clinton promised that FirstGov.gov, a project of the President's Management Council, administered by the General Services Administration and cooperatively sponsored with private partnerships, would allow users to search all 27 million federal agency Web pages at one time. The FirstGov.gov portal was a premiere initiative of the Clinton Administration's Reinventing Government and Access America e-government visions.

Taking advantage of technology advances, the Bush Administration announced in 2002 that FirstGov.gov would be re-launched as an interactive site to not only link citizens with government agencies but also provide improved government services and referrals. Included on the FirstGov.gov site are direct links to Federal Executive, Legislative, and Judicial agencies as well as states, local government, and tribal authorities. Visitors may search by broad topic or browse sites designed for specific functions, governmental programs or audiences, including searching the database (http://draco.aspensys.com/fcic/public/searchpub. htm) used by the Federal Consumer Information Center (FCIC) personnel to answer direct inquiries.

To achieve this redesign of FirstGov.gov and upgrade customer services, it was necessary for the General Services Administration to first combine three existing citizen information programs–the National Contact Center (1-800-FED-INFO); FirstGov.gov; and Publications Order Fulfillment (better known as the Federal Consumer Information Center of Pueblo CO) under the Office of Citizen Services and Communications (OCSC). Then in July 2003, the OCSC announced the creation of USA Services as the new centerpiece of Citizen-Centered Government and the umbrella for FirstGov.gov and the other OCSC customer service programs. USA Services pledged to provide citizens with responses to all Internet, e-mail, and telephone inquiries within two business days or less. Under the USA Services program, federal agencies are encouraged to form partnerships to utilize personnel in the Federal Citizen Information Center who are trained to manage customer inquiries using the Searchable Knowledgebase (http://draco.aspensys. com/fcic/public/searchpub.htm).

During a pilot project with the Interior Department's Fish and Wildlife Services, FCIC staff answered approximately 95 percent of the questions referring the remainder back to Fish and Wildlife. Currently twelve agencies have signed agreements with USA Services.[9]

These improvements to FirstGov.gov and the creation of USA Services implement the Congressional vision of e-government (Public Law 107-347, the E-Government Act of 2002) as one of interagency cooperation–an improvement of government performance and outcomes within and across agencies. Under the mission of USA Services, FirstGov.gov is a leader in the Office of Management and Budget's e-government strategy to simplify the delivery of services to citizens[10] and meet President Bush's primary goals to expand e-government to:

- Make it easy for citizens to obtain services and interact with the federal government;
- Improve government efficiency and effectiveness; and
- Improve government's responsiveness to citizens.[11]

Are FirstGov.gov and USA Services fielding inquiries successfully? Peter Meyers of the *Wall Street Journal* endeavored to evaluate their services and reported his findings in his column "Personal Finance–Cranky Consumer: Trying to Reach Uncle Sam by E-mail." Summarizing his experience posing a half-dozen questions ranging from tax deductions, disease statistics by city, and travel restrictions, Meyers complimented the speedy responses he received to his inquiries, but noted that the strength of the service is in finding information "buried on other agencies' Web sites" rather than answering questions that mixed federal, state, or city issues. When Meyers contacted the agency a spokeswoman responded that ". . . its answer was sufficient since their representatives aren't researchers but rather guides to other agencies."[12]

This last comment clearly identifies a future role for librarians and other information professionals in the e-government future of FirstGov. gov. Because the vision of FirstGov.gov's Citizen-Centered E-government Services is anchored to specific government programs and Web sites, this e-government vision does not duplicate the existing Service Provider/Facilitator Role already performed by the Federal Depository Library Program participants. Among these services are: quality research assistance across geographic and governmental agencies, one-on-one information literacy instruction, specialized digital collections, and the ability to assist users to place information within an historical context.

AN FDLP LIBRARIES' SERVICES GATEWAY– THE AskUS PORTAL

"USA Services, and its FirstGov.gov, is the official multi-channel front door to federal information and services for citizens offering a single point of contact where information for all federal agencies can be refined, consolidated and disseminated."[13] Therefore, to bring the FDLP into this cooperative e-government vision, the Service Provider/Facilitator role of the FDLP librarians and their library collections must be placed in a prominent position within the FirstGov.gov referral system.

Currently "Libraries" are listed on the FirstGov.gov site under the sidebar "Reference Center" menu along with such categories as "Abbreviations and Acronyms," "Contacts and Directories," "Data and Statistics, etc." Under the "Libraries" heading are links to the Library of Congress's (LC) "Ask a Librarian" feature (http://www.loc.gov/rr/askalib/), FDLP's "Locate a Federal Depository Library" directory (http://www.gpoaccess.gov/libraries.html), and links to specific federal libraries along with directories for public and state libraries. Other than the LC's "Ask a Librarian" link, no direct interactive library services are offered and this is an obvious void in FirstGov.gov's ability to actually be the *official* multi-channel front door to federal information and services for citizens.

Individually, the members of the Depository Library community already bring skilled research expertise to their local clientele and to the world through online reference forms and e-mail. Yet our "Mother Ship," GPO, has not harnessed this collective wisdom and energy to advantage. The FDLP community remains a hidden talent buried on local library Web sites. The FDLP librarians comprise an important resource now missing in the current Executive Branch Citizen-Centered E-Government Vision. GPO can change this by expanding the concept of FDLP Library Partnerships to include interactive reference and research discovery services and then reach out to other agencies.

The GPO, supported by creative and organizational Partnerships with the FDLP library community, the American Library Association's Government Documents Round Table, and the American Association of Law Libraries must fill this identified "Cooperative Service Provider/Facilitator" void by first restructuring and then redesigning the library services featured on its GPO Access Web site (http://www.access. gpo.gov) to become a true FDLP Library Services Gateway–the AskUS Portal.

This AskUS Portal must include an "Ask a Librarian" feature–Ask FDLP Librarians offering first, e-mail reference services by geographic area and/or subject expertise, and later, an online chat service by time-zone/region/state. To support the Ask FDLP Librarians' services, the current "Locate a Federal Depository Library" directory database should be redesigned to enable the user to not only locate a local library, but identify specific reference and collection strengths and then pose a question to a specific library or group of libraries. Responses to questions provided by librarians could be included in the "knowledge base" that GPO is creating as a resource for librarians and other users.

Having established an Ask FDLP Librarians service, GPO should explore a partnership with the Library of Congress (LC) that will enhance the existing "Ask a Librarian" service via the FirstGov.gov Reference menu to include the new Ask FDLP Librarians service; work with LC to bring these services to a more prominent position on the FirstGov.gov site; and with the assistance of ALA GODORT and AALL take the lead in cooperating with such statewide reference initiatives such as the Massachusetts Trial Court Law Libraries Legal Reference, AskaLibarian: UK's Electronic Reference Library, the California State Libraries' 24/7 Reference, AskColorado, AskFlorida, and the nascent AskTexas project. These services parallel the state and local government links already available on FirstGov.gov.

INFORMATION RESOURCES TO SUPPORT
THE AskUS PORTAL E-GOVERNMENT VISION

In addition to the online *Government Publications Catalog (MoCat)*, GPO Access databases, and other online finding aids, an "access element" for the AskUS Portal should be created to support resource discovery for born digital and digitized copies of government publications on FDLP Libraries' servers. The Portal would then bring centralized access to the primary resources that document America's heritage and culture by providing broadcast searching of born digital and digitized federal documents collections in depository libraries.

Depository libraries hold the most extensive record of U.S. historical publications intended for public use, positioning them uniquely to continue with the creation of digital copies of these historical publications. FDLP libraries around the country began digitizing their collections several years ago, now resulting in a significant, combined Internet resource for the public. However, at this point, the user must search broadly across the Web to determine if the needed resource is digitized and available. The AskUS Portal would bring centralized access to these disbursed collections for search and retrieval by users, a major benefit for the public and for librarians providing reference services. The Portal should also link these resources to the digital collections sponsored by the Library of Congress, the Institute of Museum and Library Services (IMLS), the National Science Foundation (NSF), and other government agencies that assist with funding for digitization of historical, government information collections.

Furthermore, FDLP librarians concerned about continued local access to electronically published government information often choose to build their own electronic collections of publications considered important for local users. Sophisticated software that harvests publications from Web sites is commercially available and enables libraries to select and capture publications, store them locally, and provide access to them on their servers. These collections should also be indexed by the AskUS Portal. This local collection development activity for born digital publications, in combination with the digitized historical collections, would strongly supplement the already existing FDLP Electronic Collection[14] hosted by GPO.

SUCCESSFUL INFORMATION ACCESS SERVICE
DEPENDS UPON COLLABORATION

The success of an access service on the AskUS Portal to search and retrieve both born digital and digitized historical publications from FDLP servers depends on strong collaborative relations among the FDLP libraries, professional organizations such as ALA GODORT and AALL, GPO and other federal agencies. Together, these stakeholders must digitize collections that compliment rather than duplicate, create project standards that ensure interoperability, address issues of authenticity, and plan for long-term preservation.

Projects to digitize historical collections of government publications incur significant costs for institutions. To maximize the number of publications made available to the public for the costs incurred, duplication of effort must be minimized. In 2000, the American Library Association (ALA) Government Documents Round Table (GODORT) members showed strong interest in digitization of government publications and possible collaborative projects by charging an ad hoc committee to investigate these issues. The Ad Hoc Committee on Digitization of Government Information presented its report to the GODORT Steering Committee at the ALA Annual Conference in 2002. Recognizing the high level of interest expressed by many in the depository library community, the Ad Hoc Committee report recommended that GODORT take a leadership role in organizing collaborative projects to digitize large collections of government publications.[15] GODORT is the appropriate group to spearhead collaborative efforts because of its national membership and long-held relationship with GPO and other federal agencies.

The Ad Hoc Committee report recommended that GODORT create a clearinghouse for digitization projects involving government publications, including international, federal, state, and local government publications. Institutions could register their projects so others would know that digitization of specific publications or series was in progress. The clearinghouse would also allow institutions to find collaborators for projects.[16] The Ad Hoc Committee launched the clearinghouse in 2002 and turned over responsibility for its continuing operation to GODORT's Government Information Technology Committee (GITCO). At the 2004 ALA Midwinter meeting, GITCO began exploring ways to move this clearinghouse to GPO to broaden its impact and to increase the level of participation by including federally funded projects.

Moreover, GODORT's GITCO, in collaboration with GPO, is uniquely situated to play a leadership role in bringing the stakeholders together to create project specifications to enable interoperability and support successful search and retrieval of government publications stored on many FDLP library servers. Well-defined project specifications could also ease concerns about authenticity of electronic copies of government publications and facilitate planning efforts for the long-term preservation of the digital copies.

CONCLUSION

As 2004 begins, a defining moment is at hand for the Government Printing Office (GPO), the Federal Depository Library Program (FDLP) libraries, the American Library Association's Government Documents Round Table (ALA GODORT), the American Association of Law Libraries (AALL), and other institutional stakeholders concerned with the future preservation of free and open, permanent public access to government information. Together these groups must seize the opportunity now available to clearly define the future role of the FDLP and its partners within an e-government environment. Unless we agree to work cooperatively and extend this cooperation to the Executive Branch, the effectiveness of our efforts will be limited and the FDLP may gradually become an anachronistic program consisting of legacy collections. The rich knowledge base currently residing with experienced FDLP librarians will be lost as these professionals retire or move into other specializations.

In the past, cooperation across the Legislative and Executive Branch has come at a territorial price and the perceived and/or actual loss of control and funding sources. The creation of an FDLP libraries' AskUS Portal linked to Firstgov.gov and other Executive Branch e-government service initiatives does not pose the same risks. On the contrary, the AskUS Portal will bring to the forefront the long hidden FDLP's librarians' Service Provider/Facilitator role and the FDLP libraries' valuable Research and Digital Collection Services. Included in the AskUS Portal will be:

- Ask FDLP Librarians–enhanced directory, e-mail, reference forms, and chat services organized by geography, time zones, and specializations. Involve FDLP librarians, GPO, ALA-GODORT, and

AALL and partner with the Library of Congress, Firstgov.gov, and other agency portals in their Ask a Librarian services.

- *Catalog of U.S. Government Publications (MoCat)*, GPO Access databases, and other finding aids–located within the FDLP Libraries' AskUS Portal these resources will then be visually connected to the Ask FDLP Librarians' feature and facilitate one-on-one instruction and reference services.
- Search Across FDLP Libraries' Digital Collections–centralized access to the primary resources that document America's heritage and culture now scattered across numerous individual FDLP libraries.
- Facilitate the digitization of collections that compliment rather than duplicate–work cooperatively with funding sources, the Library of Congress, the Institute of Museum and Library Services (IMLS), and the National Science Foundation (NSF).
- Create digital project specifications that ensure interoperability, address issues of authenticity, and plan for long-term preservation that meet international norms.

Our time is short to make an AskUS Portal a reality. We must set aside past differences and embrace our cooperative e-government future.

NOTES

1. Depository Library Council. *Envisioning the Future of Federal Government Information: Summary of the Spring 2003 Meeting of the Depository Library Council to the Public Printer.* [Online] Available: http://www.access.gpo.gov/su_docs/fdlp/council/EnvisioningtheFuture.html.

2. Depository Library Council.

3. Depository Library Council.

4. Shuler, John A. "Libraries and Government Information: The Past Is Not Necessarily Prologue." *Government Information Quarterly*, vol. 19, no. 1, 2002: 1.

5. U.S. Government Printing Office. "Information Dissemination Annual Report Fiscal Year 2003." *Administrative Notes*, vol. 24, no. 12, October 2003: 3.

6. U.S. Government Printing Office: 3-5.

7. U.S. Government Printing Office: 7-8.

8. Russell, Judith C. "The Federal Depository Library Program: Current and Future Challenges of the Electronic Transition." *Administrative Notes*, vol. 24, no. 9, July 15, 2003: 18-19.

9. Hardy, Michael. "GSA Launches Citizen Information Services." *Federal Computer Week*, August 4, 2003. [Online] Available: http://www.fcw.com.

10. Forman, M. A. *E-government strategy, implementing the president's management agenda for e-government-simplified delivery of services to citizens.* Washington, D.C.: Office of Management and Budget, 2002: 1.

11. Forman: 1.

12. Meyers, Peter. "Personal Finance–Cranky Consumer: Trying to Reach Uncle Sam by E-Mail." *Wall Street Journal (Easter Edition),* August 12, 2003: D2.

13. PRNewswire. "GSA Launches USA Services." *EETimes: The Industry Source for Engineers & Technical Managers Worldwide,* July 30, 2003. [Online] Available: http://www.eetimes.com/story/90720.

14. Federal Depository Library Program, U.S. Government Printing Office. *Managing the FDLP electronic collection: A policy and planning document at GPO.* Washington, D.C.: GPO. [Online] Available: http://www.access.gpo.gov/su_docs/fdlp/pubs/ecplan.html.

15. Hartman, C. N., ed. *Report: Digitization of government information.* Chicago: American Library Association, Government Documents Round Table, Ad Hoc Committee on Digitization of Government Information. [Online] Available: http://sunsite.berkeley.edu/GODORT/dgi/report.pdf: 7-9.

16. Hartman, 8.

REFERENCES

Depository Library Council. *Envisioning the Future of Federal Government Information: Summary of the Spring 2003 Meeting of the Depository Library Council to the Public Printer.* [Online] Available: http://www.access.gpo.gov/su_docs/fdlp/council/EnvisioningtheFuture.html.

Federal Depository Library Program, U.S. Government Printing Office. *Managing the FDLP electronic collection: A policy and planning document at GPO.* Washington, D.C.: GPO. [Online] Available: http://www.access.gpo.gov/su_docs/fdlp/pubs/ecplan.html.

Forman, M. A. *E-government strategy, implementing the president's management agenda for e-government–simplified delivery of services to citizens.* Washington, D.C.: Office of Management and Budget, 2002.

Hardy, Michael. "GSA launches citizen information services." *Federal Computer Week,* August 4, 2003. [Online] Available: http://www.fcw.com.

Hartman, C. N., ed. *Report: Digitization of government information.* Chicago: American Library Association, Government Documents Round Table, Ad Hoc Committee on Digitization of Government Information. [Online] Available: http://sunsite.berkeley.edu/GODORT/dgi/report.pdf.

Meyers, Peter. "Personal Finance–Cranky Consumer: Trying to Reach Uncle Sam by E-Mail." *Wall Street Journal (Easter Edition),* August 12, 2003: D2.

PRNewswire. "GSA Launches USA Services." *EETimes: The Industry Source for Engineers & Technical Managers Worldwide,* July 30, 2003. [Online] Available: http://www.eetimes.com/story/90720.

Russell, Judith C. "The Federal Depository Library Program: Current and Future Challenges of the Electronic Transition." *Administrative Notes,* vol. 24, no. 9, July 15, 2003: 16-24.

Shuler, John A. "Libraries and Government Information: The Past Is Not Necessarily Prologue." *Government Information Quarterly*, vol. 19, no. 1, 2002: 1-7.

U.S. Government Printing Office. "Information Dissemination Annual Report Fiscal Year 2003." *Administrative Notes*, vol. 24, no. 12, October 2003: 3-9.

Elusive No Longer?
Increasing Accessibility
to the Federally Funded
Technical Report Literature

Lisa S. Nickum

SUMMARY. Since World War II, the United States has been actively pursuing scientific research and development. Over 50 years later, the federally funded technical report literature, the results from the nation's R&D, has grown extensively. However, this vast technical report literature has not had effective methods of dissemination during these decades to provide easy access to its riches. The technology of the late 20th and early 21st century is enabling more effective access to this literature. This article will examine some of the reasons why effective access to federally funded technical reports has been elusive and will illustrate some new technologies that are greatly improving access to this literature. *[Article copies available for a fee from The Haworth Document Delivery Service: 1-800-HAWORTH. E-mail address: <docdelivery@haworthpress.com> Website: <http://www.HaworthPress.com> © 2006 by The Haworth Press, Inc. All rights reserved.]*

Lisa S. Nickum is Government Publications Librarian, Arthur Lakes Library, Colorado School of Mines, Golden, CO 80401 (E-mail: lnickum@mines.edu).

[Haworth co-indexing entry note]: "Elusive No Longer? Increasing Accessibility to the Federally Funded Technical Report Literature." Nickum, Lisa S. Co-published simultaneously in *The Reference Librarian* (The Haworth Information Press, an imprint of The Haworth Press, Inc.) No. 94, 2006, pp. 33-51; and: *The Changing Face of Government Information: Providing Access in the Twenty-First Century* (ed: Suhasini L. Kumar) The Haworth Information Press, an imprint of The Haworth Press, Inc., 2006, pp. 33-51. Single or multiple copies of this article are available for a fee from The Haworth Document Delivery Service [1-800-HAWORTH, 9:00 a.m. - 5:00 p.m. (EST). E-mail address: docdelivery@haworthpress.com].

KEYWORDS. Technical reports, access to government information, government information policy, scientific and technical information (STI), National Technical Information Service, Department of Energy, Environmental Protection Agency, Science.gov

INTRODUCTION

For over 50 years, the federally funded technical report literature, the results from nationally supported research and development (R&D), has grown extensively. Unfortunately, this literature has been difficult to find for much of its history. On the whole, federally sponsored technical report literature has been less well distributed and identified than other federal government publications. The literature discussing federally funded technical reports suggests several stumbling blocks for the creation, dissemination, cataloging, discovery, and preservation of these publications including weak federal information policies, the need for a federal information policy specifically for science and technical information (STI), differences in missions and mandates in scientific government agencies, and a basic lack of awareness of the technical report literature.

While the federal government spends much money to perform federally sponsored R&D, the same government "spends virtually nothing on research for how to best manage, increase access to, and ensure high impact and use of its technical report literature."[1] In addition to federal agencies that are mandated to collect and disseminate technical report literature, most notably the National Technical Information Service (NTIS) and to a much lesser extent the Government Printing Office (GPO), many scientific agencies disseminate their technical reports directly. However, this dissemination is often "closely linked to the agency's perceived mission and their interpretation of how that mission fits within the larger Federal information policy system."[2] While the Office of Management and Budget requires that Executive Branch agencies manage their federal information resources through OMB Circular No. A-130, the policy is very general and "agencies that specialize in the management of scientific and technical information (STI) face circumstances not contemplated in A-130."[3] Although many have called for a separate federal information policy specifically for STI, a comprehensive policy still does not exist to "provide a payback for the taxpayer's investment in R&D and promote the attainment of broader national goals."[4]

Because of these issues and problems, technical report discovery has been difficult for information professionals and researchers leading to less than complete collections in many libraries and research centers nationwide. Often a barrier experienced by those searching for technical reports is insufficient knowledge of the agency responsible for the research. Sometimes the technical reports are available only from the scientific research agency, and being unaware of the research performed by government agencies can certainly hinder the information discovery process. The lack of bibliographic control is another problem that makes the identification process even more difficult. While historically there have been paper indexes to access most of these technical report collections, typically more than one index or finding aid needs to be used to identify the desired technical report. Furthermore, some technical reports have not been included in these indexes, making their discovery almost impossible. Online databases, such as the National Technical Information Service Database, became available to the public in the late 1980s, but generally did not include access to the entire technical report literature of government agencies and were often only available through paid services such as Dialog and STN. However, most of this technical report literature is not available in other widely used commercial databases with related journal literature. The problems with dissemination, accessibility, and bibliographic control have led, understandably, to the belief that the federally funded technical report literature is difficult, if not impossible, to identify and locate.

To examine the elusive qualities of federally sponsored technical reports this article will look at the roles of the National Technical Information Service. Since there is much activity at the scientific agency level, the Department of Energy and the Environmental Protection Agency will be discussed to illustrate the dissemination and accessibility issues from the perspective of a single agency. Finally, some 21st century endeavors that are greatly increasing the availability of federally sponsored technical report literature will be reviewed.

THE NATIONAL TECHNICAL INFORMATION SERVICE– ACCESS TO ALL FEDERAL TECHNICAL REPORTS?

The National Technical Information Service (NTIS), initially created to act as a clearinghouse for World War II research and development, is charged with the collection, indexing, dissemination, and preservation of federally funded scientific and technical information. However, its road to accomplishing this mission has been difficult–partly because some agencies had become more self-reliant regarding printing before the establishment of NTIS and due to the early decision to create NTIS as a self-sustaining agency with limited public funding. In fact, the agency has not received federal appropriations since FY 1987.[5]

One of the most important concepts in scientific publishing, including the publishing of technical reports, is the prompt publishing of time-sensitive scientific results to benefit the larger scientific community. As far back as the 1920s, long before NTIS was established, Congress was already failing to provide enough appropriations for the printing of agency research and development results. Without adequate federal help, agency scientists "embarked on a program of self-reliance"[6] and often sought the skills of society and commercial publishers. The federally sponsored technical report literature continues to lack adequate financing today. For instance, the issue of Congressional appropriations for the agency's "public good" aspect (the collecting, cataloging, dissemination, and preservation of STI) continues to be discussed in the 21st century. Debate about the NTIS self-sustaining mandate has continued throughout the agency's existence, especially during the privatization discussions of the 1980s and the 1990s business plan modernization discussions to "preserve NTIS' dual character–that of a public Agency and that of a self-supporting enterprise."[7] In spite of all of the debate and political maneuvering that has occurred around the National Technical Information Service since its inception, the agency has managed to collect and preserve a large collection (currently over 3 million) of federally sponsored scientific and technical information. The majority of this STI falls within the technical report literature.

While the agency offers a good collection of this literature, it is not complete by any measure. Before the passage of the 1991 American Technology Preeminence Act (APTA–Public Law 102-245) requiring all government agencies to "transfer in a timely manner to the National Technical Information Service unclassified scientific, technical, and engineering information which results from federally funded research and development activities for dissemination,"[8] it was estimated that NTIS acquired approximately one third of all federally funded reports produced by scientific government agencies.[9] Unfortunately for the overall NTIS collection, "a number of the Federal agencies that funded R&D failed to require contractors to provide a copy of the resultant reports to a national clearinghouse such as NTIS."[10] Because submission of the federally funded literature was voluntary, some agencies provided only irregular submissions to NTIS. Moreover, the agency scientists continued to distribute their results themselves to make the time-sensitive information available as soon as possible, often not understanding or acknowledging the role of NTIS.

To reinforce the agency's self-supporting mandate, the ATPA confirmed that the "operating costs associated with the acquisition, processing, storage, bibliographic control, and archiving of information and documents would be recovered primarily through the collection of fees (specifically no longer called 'appropriations')."[11] The law also directed the agency to consider the feasibility of using an online locator system for the NTIS collection. The eventual outcome of this examination was the NTIS FedWorld portal to help the agency market their products and assist government agencies and the general public in finding federal STI. However, due to its self-supporting mandate, NTIS did not use the FedWorld portal to provide no-fee access to their extensive NTIS bibliographic database, much less provide no-fee full-text access to the parts of its collection that were available electronically.

While ATPA certainly helped NTIS collect more of the agencies' technical report literature, some never made it into the NTIS collection. This trend of irregular submissions increased with the advent of the Internet and a federal agency's ability to "submit" to the public their technical reports on the agency's Web site. Understandably, federal agencies found Web-based dissemination preferable to other methods: dissemination could occur faster and cost the initiating agency less. However, because it is not in most federal agencies' missions to be responsible for continued access or preservation, this generated great concern immediately among NTIS personnel, information professionals, and others.

A recent examination of NTIS occurred in August of 1999, when the Department of Commerce announced that it was closing the agency because of the ability of the American public to receive technical reports on the Internet and stated that the "core function of NTIS, providing government information for a fee, was no longer needed in this day of advanced electronic technology."[12] The National Commission on Libraries and Information Science (NCLIS) was directed by the Congress to conduct a study on this proposal. This examination led to two reports: the *Preliminary Assessment of the Proposed Closure of the NTIS*, published in March 2000, and the *Comprehensive Assessment of Public Information Dissemination*, published in January 2001. As is evident from the titles of the two reports, the *Preliminary Assessment* focused on NTIS while the *Comprehensive Assessment* was much broader in scope. These extensive studies examined many aspects of NTIS and included participation from many "stakeholders" including those in government, academia, interest groups, and the private sector. The Commission concluded that the value of NTIS's "public good" aspect (the collection, organization, dissemination, and permanent public availability of federally funded scientific and technical information) has an enormous impact on the nation's economy and should be financed with appropriated funds. The suggested appropriations of $5 million per year are only a small fraction of the total annual budget for federal R&D. While NTIS had envisioned that its successor would keep the scientific and technical information available on the Internet for "long periods of time," the Commission indicated from past studies "that two thirds of all requests from NTIS users are for materials that are over ten years old."[13] In addition to recommending appropriations for NTIS, the Commission also recommended that NTIS remain, at least temporarily, within the Department of Commerce and conduct an examination of the NTIS business plan and implement improvements. Of great concern to the Commission was how the self-sufficiency requirement in the business plan was harming the agency, and the Commission recommended basic statutory changes to correct this flaw.

The completion of the Commission's studies coincided with the change in both the Presidential administration and Congress. The George W. Bush administration and the 108th Congress have not taken action on this report. At the end of 2003, the National Technical Information Service remains in the Department of Commerce, but the agency has received no regular appropriated funds since the completion of the study. However, there have been some marked improvements in the dissemination and accessibility of scientific and technical information, particularly since the completion of this report. Whether as a result of the NCLIS studies, increased abilities with information technology in the early 21st century, or a combination of the two, the access to federally sponsored technical reports is much greater today than it ever was in the past. According to the NTIS Director of the Office of Database Services, currently the agency is actively gathering federally funded scientific and technical publications available on agency Web sites and archiving them.[14] The agency is also providing bibliographic access to their collection (1990 to the present) from their Web site at no cost to the user. Other federal agencies are not only better able to manage their information, including technical reports, but also to provide increasingly better access to this literature. The use of Internet technologies is positively affecting the accessibility to current technical report literature, as well as greatly improving access to older technical report literature or legacy collections. The scientific agencies all use information technology to enhance their dissemination of their technical reports, although some are providing better access to their collections than others.

To illustrate this progress over time, two agencies will be looked at in more depth. The efforts of the Department of Energy and the Environmental Protection Agency will provide examples of different ways the agencies have approached technical report dissemination and accessibility.

ACCESS TO THE DEPARTMENT OF ENERGY'S TECHNICAL REPORT COLLECTION

Some government agencies have a long history of disseminating their information, including technical report literature. One of these agencies is the Department of Energy (DOE), established as the Atomic Energy Commission in 1946. Due to the importance of energy to the United States of America, DOE has had a large and relatively interested audience, both inside and outside of the federal government. The collection, dissemination, and preservation of energy-related scientific and technical information produced by DOE (and its predecessor agencies, the Atomic Energy Commission and the Energy Research and Development Administration) has been consistently required in the legislation passed creating the agencies.[15] DOE is one of three agencies producing the majority of federally sponsored technical report literature (the National Aeronautics and Space Administration (NASA) and the Department of Defense (DOD) being the other two). For decades, DOE has been disseminating their technical reports to the public. The agency has many laboratories and offices nationwide, but the agency determined that a separate office, initially the Technical Information Division, was needed to perform central dissemination functions. Currently the Office of Science and Technical Information (OSTI), under the Department of Science, performs that function. OSTI and its predecessors have been the primary point of collection and dissemination for the agency which makes access to historical and ongoing DOE technical reports more achievable than perhaps in other agencies. DOE has had a strong relationship with the Government Printing Office (GPO) and has been using the Federal Depository Library Program as one of its main dissemination methods. The agency has also been depositing its information with the National Technical Information Service for decades.

The relationship between DOE and GPO led to many libraries, particularly Federal Depository libraries, collecting significant numbers of DOE publications, including technical reports. Many of these DOE publications were not cataloged by the Government Printing Office or by depository librarians. This lack of cataloging is especially true when examining the DOE technical reports. Therefore, many libraries around the country that have energy-related collections and a substantial amount of the DOE technical report literature do not have significant portions of these collections cataloged in their library databases. Likewise, many of these reports are not found in large bibliographic utilities like OCLC. Print indexes (i.e., Nuclear Science Abstracts, the Energy Research Abstracts, and the Government Reports Announcement and Index (for the NTIS collection)) and subscription online databases (i.e., DOE Energy available from STN or DIALOG and the NTIS Bibliographic Database) are used to identify technical reports. While these indexes and databases are fairly well organized it adds several extra steps in locating and using technical reports which only adds to the widely held belief that technical reports are hard to find and use.

In the mid-1990s, the agency began to use technology to make their technical information more accessible to the public. OSTI has been involved in several projects to make their legacy collection and results from new research available to the general public. Although these efforts include energy publications that do not fall into the technical report literature, only those projects including technical reports will be highlighted. In the mid-1990s, OSTI provided the DOE Bibliographic Database on their Web site for no cost. This database contained bibliographic information for DOE technical reports from 1994 forward. Shortly following the release of the database, OSTI, in partnership with the Government Printing Office, developed the DOE Information Bridge (http://www.osti.gov/bridge/) offering full-text access to the agency's technical reports from 1995 forward. At the time of its unveiling, the Information Bridge provided access to more of full-text publications than were found on most other agency Web sites. At the end of 2003, the DOE Information Bridge contained over 77,000 full-text documents.[16] However, OSTI realized that there was still much technical report literature that was not freely or easily available to the general public, namely the DOE technical reports published prior to 1994 and the literature from its predecessor agencies. OSTI's development of a publicly accessible database, based on a combination of two indexes (Nuclear Science Abstracts and the Energy Research Abstracts) and the formerly mentioned DOE Bibliographic Database, led to the creation of the Energy Citations Database (http://www.osti.gov/energycitations/) which became available in late 2001. This database provides bibliographic information for agency information, DOE and its predecessors, from 1948 to the present at no cost and currently provides access to over 2 million bibliographic records.[17] Since many of the early technical reports are not well represented in library catalogs or on the Internet, this database filled a void and provided no-fee access to the agency's early technical report literature. This database was well received, particularly by information professionals and researchers. Both the Information Bridge and the Energy Citations databases offer basic and advanced searching and even though the content of the databases is very different, OSTI has kept a similarity to the look and feel of the search pages for each. This undoubtedly helps the users of the databases.

One of DOE's new projects to increase access to its technical reports is the DOE Alert Service Pilot Project with seven Federal Depository Library Program libraries. In this alert service project, the participating libraries can provide OSTI with a profile of search logic based on the advanced search capabilities found in the DOE Information Bridge and the Energy Citations Database. These profiles will be automatically searched on a continual basis against the two main agency databases, DOE Information Bridge and the Energy Citation Database. This project allows the agency to actively supply information directly to the user based on his or her specific area(s) of interest. With the technology being used in this alert service, the information users, whether they are researchers, academics, business people, or the general public, can be informed of new DOE information that meets their needs without having to continually search multiple databases.

OSTI has also discussed the possibility of using this alert service for libraries to identify bibliographic information that could then be imported into their online databases. As was already mentioned, most DOE technical reports are not found within traditional bibliographic utilities and therefore most libraries do not have records for this literature in their databases. If technical difficulties can be overcome regarding the importing of these records, this project could benefit not only those who participate in the profiling alert service described above, but also many others who use the libraries' online databases.

While alert services have been used for many years now, especially by commercial database publishers, the majority have not accessed technical report literature. This is another example of OSTI experimenting with new and inventive ways to increase the accessibility to the DOE technical report literature.

ACCESS TO THE ENVIRONMENTAL PROTECTION AGENCY'S TECHNICAL REPORTS

While some might think that it would be an easier job to manage the resources from a newer agency, that does not seem to be the case for the Environmental Protection Agency (EPA) created in 1970. In the early years of the agency, it was determined that EPA could not build and maintain a suitable information collection and dissemination office. This led to an interagency agreement with NTIS to serve in this role for EPA.[18] While the agency has the Office of Research and Development (ORD), the science arm of the agency, other EPA offices and programs nationwide also produce significant research. In the late 1980s, policies created the Center for Environmental Research Information (CERI) to manage all ORD publications through a warehouse and distribution facility. CERI provided additional access to ORD publications through its free limited dissemination of ORD reports, but the agency still depended on NTIS for its repository collection. Other EPA Programs and Offices continued creating technical reports and using NTIS as the primary tool for public dissemination.

In a response to a National Commission of Libraries and Information Science (NCLIS) Public Information Dissemination Policies and Programs survey in September 2000,[19] EPA responded to questions regarding strengthening the dissemination of and access to the agency's publicly available information. The agency indicated that they faced a significant challenge in the integration of the data and information from the various EPA programs.[20] In 1999, the Office of Environmental Information "was created to coordinate the Program Offices' activities in collecting quality environmental information and making it available to the public."[21]

There are many sources that can be used to find EPA technical reports. The best source for finding EPA publications, especially from the early decades of the agency, is the NTIS collection. While the agency does participate with the GPO's Federal Depository Library Program, more of its publications have been historically deposited with NTIS due to the interagency agreement signed early in the agency's history. Locating older EPA technical publications will likely require searches in many different places: the NTIS database, the 28 EPA libraries across the nation, and a Federal Depository Library.

The EPA Web site is one of the first places to look for currently produced agency technical reports. However, unlike the DOE, the EPA does not provide easily searchable databases that provide access to the majority of the EPA technical reports collection. At the Federal Depository Library Conference in October 2003, the manager for the EPA National Library Network indicated that the entire EPA Web site provides access to approximately one million publications, but only 70,000 have been cataloged by EPA[22] (i.e., found in the various databases created by EPA). This fact is evident when one tries to search for a current EPA technical report. The EPA Web site is wonderfully rich in the amount of information that it contains, but it is difficult for even a more advanced searcher to locate an EPA technical report.

There are several databases to choose from on the EPA Web site:

- The National Service Center for Environmental Publications (NSCEP–formerly the National Center for Environmental Publications and Information (NCPEI) (http://www.epa.gov/ncepihom/)) includes a publications inventory of 7,000 print and electronic reports for no-cost distribution. One can search by EPA publication number, exact title, or words in the title. The title searches allow Boolean operators, quotation marks, and wild cards (*). There is no evident search help on the Web page.
- NSCEP links to the EPA Search, or Advanced Search, to search all EPA Web pages (http://www.epa.gov/epahome/search.html). From this page, a Publications Search link leads to a separate search page providing searching by EPA publication number, exact title, or words in the title (words and phrases need to be separated by commas). The exact title will accept quotation marks, though they are not needed, and the Web page indicates that the words and phrases need to be separated by commas, but Boolean operators work as well. The words in the title search seem to support a wild card function (*). If the search is not successful, the searcher is referred to the EPA Search (searching the entire EPA Web site), the EPA Online Library System, NTIS Web site (1990+), and EPA clearinghouses, hotlines, or the public information centers. The following disclaimer can also be found on the page:

> **Note:** EPA Publications have not been handled consistently across EPA's large Web site. This page uses a variety of techniques to search within the many different publications sites within EPA's overall site. Unfortunately, these techniques will miss some documents.[23]

- The National Environmental Publications System (NEPIS) (http://www.epa.gov/nepis/index.htm) provides access to electronic EPA information for over 10,000 full-text online publications. The system provides simple searching, enhanced searching, and a complete title list (grouped by publication number). The enhanced search requires that one select one or more databases (i.e., EPA Programs) and then type in search words or phrases (using periods or semi-colons to separate concepts–Boolean operators, quotation marks, and wild cards do not work).
- EPA Online Library System (OLS) (http://www.epa.gov/natlibra/ols.htm) provides searching for the entire EPA National Catalog or special collections within EPA's OLS (e.g., Air Pollution Technical Information Center). As a library database, the functionalities are greater when compared to other EPA databases mentioned in this section. The advanced search offers limiting by year and by type of publication (i.e., books, documents, journals) and provides sorting by year, title, or relevance.
- Publications of the EPA site (http://www.epa.gov/epahome/publications2.htm) directs the user to publications pages from the various EPA Office and Program pages.
- Alphabetical Listing of Projects and Programs (http://www.epa.gov/epahome/abcpgram.htm) is more comprehensive than the previous Publications of the EPA site. Although it requires more patience as the links do not go directly to publication pages, but to general Program and Offices pages.
- In late November 2003, EPA's Office of Research and Development launched its EPA Science Inventory (http://cfpub.epa.gov/si/) for public access. The agency-wide database includes over 4,000 scientific and technical work products. A publications link (http://cfpub.epa.gov/si/si_pubs.cfm) is available from the main Inventory page and leads to a search page for research publications by subject or author name. While there appear to be many overlapping titles, the site seems to identify unique titles as well. However, a more formal comparison between this new system and the existing EPA databases is needed.

While all of these sites provide much more access to EPA publications, including technical reports, than ever before, they are frustrating for users. First of all, there are many sites that need to be checked to determine if a technical report is available. While there are some overlapping titles in the databases discussed above, there is also a high percentage of unique titles in each database. Also, each of these databases presents information differently and the searching techniques used differ drastically as well. Some of this is expected, as the information presented is available in many formats and from many different Programs and Offices within EPA. However, more consistency would make the discovery of EPA technical information easier.

The Environmental Protection Agency is aware of many of the problems in the discovery of material on its Web site. The agency's National Library Network, responsible for the entire EPA Web site, is looking to improve the navigability of the site. As mentioned above, the agency is aware that there are considerably more titles available on its Web site than have been cataloged or identified by the EPA's search engines. To alleviate this problem, the agency's National Library Network is working on a pilot program with the Government Printing Office to complete some Web harvesting.[24] The goal of this project is to initiate a Web crawl of the EPA Web site to bring back EPA titles that would be compared against the already known titles found in various library collections (i.e., EPA, GPO, OCLC, and NTIS). If an automated spider could be created to collect some, most, or all of these "missing" titles available on the EPA Web site, but not available in standard catalogs and databases, then the addition of these titles to standard databases could occur making the discovery of EPA technical reports much easier. This project is just starting and several difficulties need to be overcome to make the desired results a reality.

Current DOE and EPA projects are encouraging, especially to those who have long desired a better way to discover the agencies' technical report literature. Other scientific government agencies also have projects, in various stages of development, that are providing better access to their technical report literature as well.

NEW TECHNOLOGIES– BRINGING MULTI-AGENCY TECHNICAL REPORTS LITERATURE TOGETHER

With the emergence of new information technologies, scientific government agencies and others like the Government Printing Office and the National Technical Information Service have been providing greater access to government information, including the technical report literature. While an overall federal mandate or policy is needed, as was recently called for in the *Comprehensive Assessment of Public In-*

formation Dissemination NCLIS study, many government agencies took new information capabilities and started to push forward without it. The results in the past 2-3 years have been remarkable, especially when considering access to technical report literature in previous decades. While the agencies made great strides in accessibility during the 1990s with their own technical report literature, currently there is movement to try to bring this progress together in a one-stop shopping approach. Much of this progress emanated from two workshops: "Information Infrastructure for the Physical Sciences," in 2000, and "Strengthening the Public Information Infrastructure for Science," in 2001.

The 2000 "Information Infrastructure for the Physical Sciences" workshop, held at the National Academy of Sciences, was hosted by the Department of Energy and examined the methods by which to use the current technology to reach a comprehensive collection of scientific and technical information "that would facilitate scientific communication and increase the productivity of the scientific enterprise in the United States."[25] Many themes were examined but the three that most closely relate to the continued access to technical report literature were (1) the supposition that scientists need access to more gray literature and not just on the peer-reviewed journals and other commercially published materials, (2) the understanding of the critical need for archiving, preservation, and access to information, and (3) the fact that "the government has a responsibility to disseminate the results of federally sponsored research as broadly as possible as a public good."[26] One of the first successes from this workshop was the creation of the GrayLit Network (http://www.osti.gov/graylit/). The Network is a database of full-text technical report literature from DOE, NASA, EPA, and DTIC. It was made available in 2001 and currently links to approximately 130,000 technical reports.[27] An agreement was reached between several agencies, DOE, NASA, EPA, and DOD, to establish this network where OSTI created a distributed search tool that was placed on top of the already existing technical report databases from these agencies. The simple search page allows the user to select one or more of the agencies' databases and enter search terms. However, there is no advanced search available to allow for more complex searching. The differences in the agencies' databases probably prevents the option of a meaningful advanced search.

One of the most difficult and frustrating challenges that many face in the discovery of technical reports is knowing where to start (i.e., which agency was responsible for particular research). The advances in agency services to their technical information are indeed valuable, but if a person is trying to search for environmental information from various EPA databases and the research was actually performed by a researcher from the Department of Energy, he or she will not find the desired information and probably will end their search. However, if the user started the search in GrayLit, there is a good chance that they could have been successful because the search engine searches all of the agencies' database content simultaneously and therefore the searcher does not need to know the agency where the research originated. The GrayLit Network is only as good as the individual agency databases, so as the databases improve and new databases are added to the Network, this service will become an increasingly useful tool.

The 2001 workshop entitled "Strengthening of the Public Information Infrastructure for Science," held at the National Institute of Standards and Technology, grew out of the first workshop described above and examined the need to use new technologies to improve access to scientific information from federal agencies. The result of this was an interagency agreement on the science portal Science.gov to "provide a coherent government R&D presence on the Web and streamline the process of identifying and accessing government science information."[28] The idea of Science.gov was to appeal not only to the academic and research communities, but also to a much broader, science-attentive audience. The Science.gov Alliance (see appendix A) was created during this workshop and closely resembles the CENDI (Commerce; Energy; Environmental Protection Agency; National Aeronautics and Space Agency; National Libraries of Agriculture, Education, Medicine; Defense; and Interior) Information Managers Group. CENDI, and its predecessor the Committee on Scientific and Technical Information (COSTI), is an interagency group that has been working on the accessibility of the federal government's R&D results for decades. CENDI has been very involved in the creation of Science.gov and will provide support and coordination for the Alliance.[29] CENDI's expertise in STI issues will be extremely useful to the Alliance when they are working on enhancements to Science.gov.

Science.gov currently provides science information from over 1,700 government science resources including technical reports, journal citations, databases, and federal Web sites. OSTI developed a distributed deep Web search capability for Science.gov that allows users to enter a single search to search the content of the multiple scientific agencies. Deep Web searching greatly enhances the quality of results from Science.gov as the majority of the federal agencies' scientific literature, especially the technical report literature, is found within the deep or invisible Web containing "a vast repository of underlying content, such as documents in online databases."[30] Standard search engines, such as Google, search the surface Web and cannot duplicate the results found in Science.gov. Similar to the GrayLit Network, this single search concept of Science.gov does not require the searcher to know the authoring agency of the research. The sites and databases included in Science.gov are selected by each agency, but the "agencies collectively decide on the subject taxonomy used to browse the Science.gov subject guide."[31] The Science.gov service is not static as new sites are added frequently.

The search interface for Science.gov allows for easy searching and browsing by topic. While it is not difficult for people to search or browse the site, the content of the Web site is extensive and the results can be overwhelming. However, in addition to the basic search feature, the Alliance has provided other entries into the Science.gov content by offering a listing by subject (as opposed to an agency listing), narrower topics within the subjects, and alphabetical lists of databases and Web sites with short descriptions of the content available at those sites.

CONCLUSION

Federally sponsored technical reports have had a long and arduous history when it comes to dissemination and accessibility. Although this literature remains somewhat elusive, it is certainly much less so than in the past. Over the last decade, increased access to the federally funded technical report literature is encouraging. In the early- to mid-1990s the majority of progress occurred within scientific agencies and there were no substantial cross-agency efforts to increase the dissemination of and accessibility to the technical report literature. However, since the late 1990s accessibility has been dramatically increased, both at the agency level and among agencies.

There is still much to be accomplished. A slowdown in the current progress could greatly damage future accessibility in this digital age. Agencies need to keep their information policies and procedures updated and have a keen awareness of new technological changes that could be implemented to further improve accessibility. It is crucially important that agencies approach enhancements in accessibility with an open mind. While improvements in the deep Web searching technologies should be examined, so should an examination of standard surface

Web search engines (as some agencies are already doing). Those involved in these new endeavors, such as the Science.gov Alliance,[32] need to remain aware of other, related groups, such as the group working on the National Science Digital Library (NSDL). There currently are and will continue to be some overlaps between these two projects; both groups could learn from the others' successes and failures along the way.

As with most activities, there is a pressing need for the funding to continue these and other related projects. In support of that funding, scientific agencies producing R&D, information professionals, academics, business people, and the general public, especially the science-attentive public, must advocate for this definite need so that the literature remains accessible for future citizens.

NOTES

1. Charles R. McClure, "The Federal Technical Report Literature: Research Needs and Issues," *Government Information Quarterly* 5, no. 1 (1988): 41.

2. Ibid., 37.

3. J. Timothy Sprehe, "Does the Federal Government Need an A-130 for STI?" *Government Information Quarterly* 12, no. 2 (1995): 213.

4. Harold B. Shill, "NTIS: Potential Roles and Government Information Policy Frameworks," *Journal of Government Information* 23, no. 3 (1996): 295.

5. Subcommittee on Technology on the Committee on Science, *National Technical Information Service: A Review of the Department of Commerce's Plan to Close the Agency,* 106th Cong., 1st sess., 1999, 99.

6. John Spencer Walters and Richard Schockmel, "Applied Science Publishing in the U.S. Government: Failure of Congressional Policy," *Journal of Government Information* 25, no. 2 (1998): 97.

7. Subcommittee on Technology, Environment and Aviation of the Committee on Science, Space, and Technology, *H.R. 820–The National Competitiveness Act of 1993,* 103rd Cong., 1st sess., 1993, 352.

8. *American Technology Preeminence Act of 1991,* Public Law 102-245, *U.S. Statutes at Large* 106 (1992): 13.

9. Shill, 289.

10. McClure, 33.

11. Sarah T. Kadec, "Chronology/Bibliography of Events Relative to NTIS's Position in Commerce," (January 26, 2000). Prepared for the National Commission of Library and Information Science. *Preliminary Assessment of the Proposed Closure of the National Technical Information Service (NTIS): A Report to the President and the Congress.* (Washington, D.C.: National Commission of Library and Information Science, 2000), http://www.nclis.gov/govt/ntis/kadec.html (accessed December 3, 2003).

12. National Commission of Library and Information Science. *Preliminary Assessment of the Proposed Closure of the National Technical Information Service (NTIS): A Report to the President and the Congress.* (Washington, D.C.: National Commission of Library and Information Science, 2000), 13, http://www.nclis.gov/govt/ntis/presiden. pdf (accessed December 3, 2003).

13. Ibid., 7.

14. Jean Bowers, "Re: Physical Copy vs. Web." In GovDoc_L [online discussion board]. Cited 1 July 2003. Available GovDoc_L Archives (http://lists1.cac.psu.edu/cgi-bin/wa?A2=ind0307a&L=govdoc-l&F=&S=&P=194) (accessed January 11, 2003).

15. Office of Scientific and Technical Information. *Short History of OSTI.* [updated August 2001; cited 26 Nov. 2003]. http://www.osti.gov/ostihist.html (accessed October 27, 2003).

16. Karen Spence, "Department of Energy Update," in *Proceedings of the 12th Annual Federal Depository Library Conference October 19-22, 2003* (Washington, D.C.: Government Printing Office, http://www.access.gpo.gov/su_docs/fdlp/pubs/proceedings/03pro.html, forthcoming).

17. Ibid.

18. Richard M. Laska, "Feasibility of Instituting User Charges for EPA's Office of Research and Development Reports," *Government Information Quarterly* 7, no. 1 (1990): 26.

19. National Commission of Library and Information Science. *Comprehensive Assessment of Public Information Dissemination.*, vol. 3 (Washington, D.C.: National Commission of Library and Information Science, 2001), 3-158-184, http://www.nclis.gov/govt/assess/assess.vol3.pdf (accessed December 3, 2003).

20. Ibid., 3-181.

21. Ibid., 3-164.

22. Richard L. Huffine, "Environmental Protection Agency Update," in *Proceedings of the 12th Annual Federal Depository Library Conference October 19-22, 2003* (Washington, D.C.: Government Printing Office, http://www.access.gpo.gov/su_docs/fdlp/pubs/proceedings/03pro.html, forthcoming).

23. http://www.epa.gov/epahome/pubsearch.html (accessed December 3, 2003).

24. George Barnum, George (Electronic Collections Manager at GPO's Library Program Services), in telephone conversation with author, November 18, 2003.

25. Department of Energy. "Workshop Report on a Future Information Infrastructure for the Physical Sciences" (Washington, D.C.: National Academy of Sciences. May 30-31, 2000.): 7, http://www.osti.gov/physicalsciences/wkshprpt.pdf (accessed October 27, 2003).

26. Ibid., 16.

27. Spence.

28. Science.gov Alliance. "Report of the Workshop Strengthening the Public Information Infrastructure for Science" (Washington, D.C: National Institute of Standards and Technology. April 18-19, 2001): 1-2, http://www.science.gov/workshop/finalworkshopreport.pdf (accessed October 27, 2003).

29. Gail Hodge, "Science.gov: FirstGov for Science," in *Proceedings of the 11th Annual Federal Depository Library Conference October 20-23, 2002* (Washington, D.C.: Government Printing Office, 2002), http://www.access.gpo.gov/su_docs/fdlp/pubs/proceedings/02pro.html (accessed January 11, 2004).

30. Walter L. Warnick, "Searching the Deep Web," *D-Lib Magazine*, 7, no. 1 (January 2001), http://www.dlib.org/dlib/january01/warnick/01warnick.html (accessed December 11, 2003).

31. David Dorman, "Making a Federal Case Out of Access," *American Libraries* 34, no. 2 (February 2003): 60.

32. Science.gov Alliance. See Appendix A.

APPENDIX A

Science.gov Alliance

Department of Agriculture
   National Agriculture Library

Department of Commerce
   National Institute of Standards and Technology
   National Technical Information Service

Department of Defense
   Defense Technical Information Center
   National Air Intelligence Center

Department of Education
   National Library of Education

Department of Energy
   Energy Library
   Office of Science
   Office of Scientific and Technical Information

Department of Health and Human Services
   National Institutes of Health
   National Library of Medicine

Department of Interior
   United States Geological Survey
   National Biological Information Infrastructure

Environmental Protection Agency
   Office of Research and Development

National Aeronautics and Space Administration
   Scientific and Technical Information Program

National Science Foundation

Government Statistical Data:
Changes Impacting Access and Service

Jocelyn T. Tipton

SUMMARY. Access and services for government numeric data and statistical information has changed dramatically in recent years. By making it easier to identify, acquire, and use, patron demand for government data continues to grow. These changes have affected the role and responsibilities of all librarians. This article examines how access to government data has changed and what that means for librarians. It focuses on the role of the government documents librarian in responding to these changes. *[Article copies available for a fee from The Haworth Document Delivery Service: 1-800-HAWORTH. E-mail address: <docdelivery@haworthpress.com> Website: <http://www.HaworthPress.com> © 2006 by The Haworth Press, Inc. All rights reserved.]*

KEYWORDS. Government data, government statistics, data librarian, government documents librarianship

Jocelyn T. Tipton is Government Documents Librarian, Booth Library, Eastern Illinois University, 600 Lincoln Avenue, Charleston, IL 61920 (E-mail: cfjtt@eiu.edu).

[Haworth co-indexing entry note]: "Government Statistical Data: Changes Impacting Access and Service." Tipton, Jocelyn T. Co-published simultaneously in *The Reference Librarian* (The Haworth Information Press, an imprint of The Haworth Press, Inc.) No. 94, 2006, pp. 53-67; and: *The Changing Face of Government Information: Providing Access in the Twenty-First Century* (ed: Suhasini L. Kumar) The Haworth Information Press, an imprint of The Haworth Press, Inc., 2006, pp. 53-67. Single or multiple copies of this article are available for a fee from The Haworth Document Delivery Service [1-800-HAWORTH, 9:00 a.m. - 5:00 p.m. (EST). E-mail address: docdelivery@haworthpress.com].

Available online at http://www.haworthpress.com/web/REF
© 2006 by The Haworth Press, Inc. All rights reserved.
doi:10.1300/J120v45n94_05

INTRODUCTION

In the last several years providing access and services for government produced numeric data and statistical information has changed dramatically. Library users can access data more easily now than ever before. Statistics have become a part of everyday life and data are being included in research by users at varying skill levels. What was once available only in printed reports or expensive data tapes is now easily accessible directly from the user's desktop. The primary example of this is the 2000 Census, but data from the Departments of Education, Labor, Health and Human Services, Justice and many others are also available. These government statistical agencies are providing user-friendly interfaces to data collections, allowing it to be manipulated, queried, and analyzed. Furthermore, new technologies have changed the way people use data, and new distribution media have improved access. By making it easier to identify, acquire, and use, patron demand for data continues to grow. As these demands for data continue to grow librarians need to discover new ways to adapt to the changes that they bring.

These changes have greatly affected the role and responsibilities of government documents librarians. This article provides an overview of government data and discusses significant changes in dissemination that have had a direct impact on government documents librarians. It explains how increased access to government data directly influences the work of government documents librarians. Specifically, it addresses changes to acquisitions, collection development, reference services, and technological issues. By addressing these changes, government documents librarians are able to meet patron demand and improve the quality of numeric data services.

OVERVIEW OF DATA

What has occurred in the last decade is the increased availability of data, resulting in less use of aggregate statistics. For the purpose of this article there are distinctions that need to be made between data and statistics. Data are the building blocks of statistics; they are the information gathered at the point of collection. Data are what are gathered by statistical agencies through surveys, censuses, and direct observation. In this form, data can be queried, manipulated, and analyzed. This manipulation and analysis generates statistics. Statistics, on the other hand, are data that have been summarized and are presented in a way that shows relationships and draws conclusions about the data. Statistics frequently appear as pre-formatted tables or are included within text documents.

Librarians are used to working with descriptive statistics, the information that is typically found in tables in standard reference sources, such as the Statistical Abstract of the United States, and Health United States. In this format, the numbers have already been analyzed and combined to describe something of interest. They also work with inferential statistics, where statistical procedures were used for estimating the characteristics of populations from data on samples. The most prominent example of this is the population projections from the Census Bureau.

Users need to remember that most government data is collected for primary purposes determined by the collecting agency then made available to the public for secondary research. Since the administrative data were collected for purposes other than what library patrons will be using them for, it raises potential difficulties because the information may be incomplete for their purposes or may be organized in a way that makes it difficult to use. It may also be inappropriate to combine data from different agencies together, because of differences in the methodologies used in the data collection. Another concern with using administrative data for secondary research is the issues surrounding confidentiality.

GOVERNMENT DATA

The United States government is the largest producer of data in the world.[1] As a result of this preponderance of data on a wide range of topics, seventy-five percent of all statistics-related questions rely on government data for the answers. In Fiscal Year 2004 the federal budget included requests for an estimated $4,719 million for statistical work.[2] This provides funding for ten agencies that have statistical activities as their primary mission as well as seventy other federal government agencies with direct funding for statistical activities of more than $500,000. It includes the following statistical work:

1. planning of statistical surveys and studies, including project design, sample design and selection, and design of questionnaires, forms, or other techniques of observation and data collection;
2. training of statisticians, interviewers, or processing personnel;

3. collection, processing, or tabulation of statistical data for publication, dissemination, research, analysis, or program management and evaluation;
4. publication or dissemination of statistical data and studies;
5. methodological testing or statistical research;
6. data analysis;
7. forecasts or projections that are published or otherwise made available for government-wide or public use;
8. statistical tabulation, dissemination, or publication of data collected by others;
9. construction of secondary data series or development of models that are an integral part of generating statistical series or forecasts;
10. management or coordination of statistical operations;
11. statistical consulting or training.[3]

The amount requested each year continues to rise by more than $100-$400 million dollars a year.[4] In the letter accompanying the budget report to Congress, Joshua B. Bolter, Director of the Office of Management and Budget, highlights the importance of government data when he says the "ability of our government, our citizens, and our businesses to make appropriate decisions about work, investments, taxes, and a host of other important decisions depends in part on the relevance, accuracy and timeliness of Federal statistics."[5]

Ida Gal provides an overview of government statistical agencies and offers reminders of the primary purpose of government data. He describes three types of statistical agencies:

- National/Central Agencies–These entities conduct censuses and collect national social and economic data.
- Thematic Agencies–These are organizations that focus on a specific area of research.
- International Agencies–These consist of groups of nations combined to report and collect data across geographic boundaries.[6]

Together these statistical agencies produce indicators, press releases, executive summaries, reports, aggregate data, technical documentation, and data files.

Historically, librarians have accessed these products in print and more recently in electronic formats, although much of the numeric information contained in these text documents remained pre-formatted in tables of graphs and did not permit any user interaction.

Government statistical agencies have, more recently, made available the ability for the user to query aggregate level statistics to create their own spreadsheets or tables. This allows the users to customize the output and to determine the variables of interest. Fedstats lists over thirty data access tools provided by at least ten government agencies.

Cathryn Dippo explains the various ways government agencies are making statistics and numeric data available via their Web sites. This includes text-based materials, articles prepared by staff, and internal memoranda. Most of these works include a substantial amount of graphs and tables. Also included on the Web site are aggregate level statistics accessible as spreadsheets or through relational databases.

A more recent event is the availability of access to raw microdata, where the user has access to individual responses to question in order to create specific summary tables. This level of access was not previously available because of confidentiality concerns.[7]

HISTORY OF DATA ACCESS AND DISSEMINATION

Judith Rowe, the former data librarian at Princeton University, said in 1996, "The same technology that has changed the way that researchers and students can search bibliographic data is now changing the way they search for text and numeric data. Direct or indirect access to such data is provided by many libraries for reference purposes. And today in academic institutions, data for secondary analysis by researchers are more likely to be supported by data reference librarians with the help of methodological and discipline specialists than by other campus units."[8] While her basic premise remains true, government documents librarians in all types of libraries are now being called upon to support the use of data, and new technology has increased the amount of data available as well as the demand. It is this author's contention that librarians are more familiar with bibliographic data files than with statistical resources, particularly those providing access to microdata that can be manipulated, queried, and analyzed. One reason for this may be that most bibliographic data files were created or at least distributed by commercial vendors, whereas files containing basic numeric data were more likely to be produced and/or distributed by academic data archives, by government agencies, research centers, or in some cases, by individual scholars. These have often been hard to identify and are less publicized.

However, in the case of government produced information, changes in the way we identify, acquire, and use data over the last five to ten years have greatly impacted its incorporation into traditional library services. The number of tools available to help identify data is continually growing. General descriptions of data files are appearing in traditional library resources, such as catalogs and indexes. New tools in print and online, such as Statistical Masterfile and Fedstats, can be used within the existing library environment for identifying government data files even at the question level.

One of the major barriers to providing access in the past was the cost of acquiring data sets. Most printed government statistics were available for free but microdata and the ability to manipulate the data was costly. In some instances commercial companies would pay to obtain access to government data then repackage it with a search interface and sell it to the public. While there are still rather large costs in acquiring some data, many others are available at lower costs or for free. More data is available for free on the Internet than ever before and this will continue to grow. Although some government data still has fees associated with its use, more and more agencies are making their data available electronically and bypassing the need for an intermediary. Products from the U.S. Census Bureau, Bureau of Labor Statistics, and the National Center for Health Statistics are only a few examples of data that would have cost libraries in the past. While not all free data will be able to answer all of the researcher's needs it does meet many of the needs. Even agencies that charge fees for data access (i.e., NTDB and USA-Trade) often provide it for free to depository libraries.

In addition to the reduced cost of acquiring data the cost of the computer technology required to access them has also been reduced. Electronic data for research had for several decades been exchanged on portable magnetic media such as round reels, or more recently, tape cartridges. In the 1990s, research data became available on the Internet typically via FTP or on CD-ROM for use directly on the researcher's desktop. It is this change in technology that has encouraged libraries to begin to assume responsibility for providing their patrons with access to numeric data. Also, the tools used in data analysis and manipulation have become easier to use. Statistical analysis packages and Web extractors now have easier-to-use interfaces and require little or no programming knowledge and are usable on a personal computer rather than a mainframe system. This makes it easier for even the novice users to begin to work with data. Desktop access, site licenses, and academic pricing for software have also helped to bring the cost down.

These changes to data access have changed the way libraries are working with data. Data, when only available on magnetic tape, did not get much use in libraries. The technology was expensive and the time and skill necessary to access and manipulate the data made it prohibitive for the general researcher. A few libraries, like the Yale Social Science Data Archive or the University of California Los Angeles, began to include data services by providing tools for identifying data sources and housing the data documentation. In the late 1980s, when CD-ROM technology was introduced as a way to distribute large amounts of information, electronic access to statistics and numeric data files became more widespread. According to Rieger, the Government Printing Office distributed thirty-four numeric CD-ROMs through the Federal Depository Library Program from 1989-1993.[9] This enabled libraries to use microcomputers to provide access to numeric files. It also integrated documentation and access software. By distributing these data through depository libraries it became available to people outside the academic arena.

Prior to the 1990 Census the only access to microdata files was through tape files. For most libraries without the ability to read these tapes they were not able to provide the data to their patrons. The Census Bureau did offer the option to run special reports off of their tapes for people but that was often more costly than the research was willing to pay. In 1999 the Census Bureau introduced the American Fact Finder, providing users the ability to manipulate the data themselves and create usable tables based on queries through the Internet. A major concern with this was that it required the user to be familiar with census terminology and how to develop a query. New releases and improved training has helped alleviate this concern. Ferret, Federal Electronic Research, Review, and Extraction Tool also was developed during this time period. This service allows the user to search nineteen different surveys and questionnaires for terms to identify surveys relevant to their needs. It provides access to data from multiple agencies, including the U.S. Census Bureau, Bureau of Labor Statistics, and the National Center for Health Statistics.

One of the reasons that government data use was restricted was the need to ensure the confidentiality of the respondents. There are new ways to protect confidentiality and still provide access to microdata. Cathy Dippo explains that with the development of Web-based software tools that allow remote users to create a special tabulation from the data, then have it screened to insure the confidentiality protection rules are met, more surveys can be made available.[10]

HOW THINGS ARE CHANGING

In the last decade the Internet has become the primary vehicle for accessing government data. A 2002 Pew Study found that 68 million American adults have used government agency Web sites. John Shuler explains that through legislative mandates, budget decisions and programmatic choices, government agencies now consider the Web and the provision of electronic government services as a logical way to reduce costs.[11] The proliferation of the data provided by agency Web sites has served to increase the amount of use that this data is getting. Prudence Adler reported that in 1994 the Census Bureau sold 40,000 printed reports, but in 1995 experienced 60,000 hits per day on its Internet site.[12]

More attention has also been spent in organizing the data in a way that users can correctly identify what they need. According to Tupek and Dippo, without metadata a number has no meaning.[13] With more people using government data the need for a common way to describe its contents has emerged. Two examples of this are the Global Information Locator Service (GILS) and the Data Documentation Initiative (DDI). GILS provides standard ways to find information by its description, whether a specific document, a collection of information, or an entire organization.[14] The DDI's focus is on data documentation. It establishes an XML-based standard for the content, presentation, transport, and preservation of documentation for empirical data.[15]

FedStats, launched in 1997 as a portal to statistical information from more than seventy-nine different government agencies, has helped identify and locate government data. Tupek and Dippo reported that in the first six months of its release, FedStats had over 44,000 visits from 240,000 unique sites.[16] The long-range goals of FedStats is to encourage the appropriate use of federal statistics and ultimately to help to improve the quantitative literacy of the general public. Every federal agency site varies in the way they are organized, the data formats provided, the method for data retrieval, and the amount and type of available metadata. Tupek and Dippo caution that putting statistical data in the hands of those who do not know how to use it appropriately could lead to the misuse of information.[17] The need for quantitative literacy skills and what it means for librarians will be discussed later in this article.

With the availability of microdata it has become easier to incorporate into other areas of research. Shuler and Obermeyer explain that there are expanded possibilities for including spatial analysis as a tool for working with data in all disciplines.[18] Many of the government agencies (i.e., Census, BLS, NCEC, HHS) are providing datasets through the Web that are geocoded to allow for this type of analysis. It has also become easier to get similar data from multiple geographic areas. The launch of MapStats in February 2004 has made it easier to find government statistical information about cities, counties, states, and the nation.

IMPACT ON GOVERNMENT DOCUMENTS LIBRARIANSHIP

By making it easier to identify, acquire, and use, the demand for data continues to grow. Libraries need to continuously evaluate how they are meeting this demand and determine the best way to improve services. In some libraries there is a data librarian who is responsible for all data related services in the library but more often this responsibility is falling on the shoulders of the government documents librarians. A review of many of the job postings on the govdoc-l listserv over the last few years indicates at least some responsibility for data services. Whatever the case, as more people are using data and the number of available resources continues to increase it is becoming evident that librarians need to reevaluate their roles and to shift some of the data responsibilities to more staff in the library. Government documents librarians need to explore ways to expand the number of people who can answer basic data related questions and at the same time maintain the quality of service that we strive for. For some, this transition will be fairly easy, for others, including data into their current responsibilities will be a challenge. Rieger says that an essential component of providing numeric file services is the availability of qualified library personnel who can advise and assist patrons in the use of data sets.[19] Kuhlman and Lee further explain that the interpretation and manipulation of numeric data require different knowledge and skills than traditional library training has offered.[20] Rieger describes four categories of challenges for numeric CD-ROMs that also relate to the distribution of numeric data via the Internet. These challenges include: hardware, access software, staff skills, and organizing services, which all have a direct impact on a number of library jobs.[21]

To facilitate this transition to providing data services a first step should be to create a service plan. Jim Jacobs has outlined different levels of service and some considerations for implementing the various levels that may help libraries as they tackle the impact of data availability in their libraries.[22] His suggestions cover four areas: general data service, computing services, library data services, and reference data services. Libraries can use these to identify what is currently being done and to set the framework for services that they can provide. This plan can outline the kinds of services and tools your library will provide. Knowing this will make it easier for others involved to know what their role in the process will be.

The remainder of this article focuses on how different types of library jobs are being impacted by the incorporation of data services. In some instances these responsibilities may be spread out among several employees, but in other cases the government documents librarian may be the sole person trying to implement these suggestions. In practice, not everything being suggested in this article is appropriate for every library, and it is ultimately the decision of the library on how to handle data. What follows demonstrates how great an impact increased access to government data can have on all aspects of librarianship.

COLLECTION MANAGEMENT/SELECTION

Government documents librarians are traditionally responsible for selecting what documents to receive as part of the depository library program. As government information is transitioning to a more electronic environment, selecting materials has shifted from deciding between paper or microfiche, to determining the benefits of selecting a document that is only available electronically. Numeric data products are an important consideration; however, as Aimee Quinn has pointed out, there are often misconceptions that electronic formats imitate print counterparts.[23] Various electronic formats of the same product will also have differences. While making selections it will be important to know these distinctions and which will best serve the needs of your users.

In selecting products it helps to be familiar with new data being released and the secondary publishing being done using the data. Your knowledge of the content of data files and how they are being used will help you communicate with researchers and maintain your role as central to the information delivery process. You also have the knowledge of how the data you are selecting fits with other items in the collection. Remember when selecting data that it is only as useful as the documentation that comes with it. Make sure that you are getting everything you need or your selection will not be usable. As a selector for acquiring government data your decision then impacts how others in the library will need to respond.

ACQUISITIONS AND CATALOGING SERVICES

A key to the accessibility of numeric data is identifying what is available and how to locate it. This is where the technical services staff plays a crucial role. The technical services staff can be incorporating numeric data products into their responsibilities. They need to develop procedures to keep track of acquisitions acquired through non-standard routes. Seventy percent of all depository items are now in electronic format. Data often come into libraries through electronic means and bypass the acquisitions department entirely. The acquisitions librarian should have some mechanism for tracking or recording the fact that libraries have access to these products.

As with other electronic government information, cataloging librarians also have a role in providing data services. They should be incorporating data holdings into the library catalog or some other database of holdings in order for users to know what is available. These catalogs and databases need to be the primary tool for finding data and their related documentation.

As decisions are made regarding electronic titles, data products should also be included. Catalogers will need to work with selectors to answer the question of what data to include in the catalog. With more data resources available on the Internet there need to be criteria developed that will help to determine what should be cataloged and what shouldn't be. The catalogers can also be using their knowledge of controlled vocabulary and indexing to develop better tools for resource discovery. There may also include a role in implementing metadata standards for data such as the Data Documentation Initiative. Catalogers are often tied to rules created prior to the insurgence of machine readable data files. By understanding how library catalogs are used to find data and the types of information users are looking for, the cataloger can be better positioned to advocate changes to these rules.

REFERENCE SERVICES

The responsibility of the reference librarian has changed from providing information about data to providing the data themselves. Reference staff needs to have a basic knowledge of statistical data in order to advise users of the existence of and content of files, the means by which they are accessed, and to make appropriate referrals to data collections. Numeric reference questions can take two forms. One is the desire of the user to obtain a numeric fact. Such a user is unlikely to be willing to cope with a complex interface or complex software. In this case a numeric reference source may be the easiest answer. The second type of question involves finding some numbers to analyze requiring the use of a data set then selecting a subset for analysis. It is important for the public service staff to be able to distinguish between these types of questions. In the later case reference staff will need a deeper knowledge of statistical concepts. Rieger explains that the data users from the second example often need help interpreting technical documentation to find definitions and understand the structure of the data files.[24] Librarians who are familiar with this can help the user select the most efficient way to create subsets.

The reference librarian will also be the one who can offer cautions about using the data correctly. Reference staff should be aware of basic data vocabulary such as variables, unit of analysis, level of observation (micro vs. aggregate data), time (time series, longitudinal, one time survey), and geography. Librarians should be aware of limitations of data and know the kinds of questions to ask when conducting a reference interview for data. It may be useful to have a standard set of questions to ask. Being familiar with these concepts will help to conduct a reference interview that will lead to a better understanding of what the user is looking for. Familiarity of all types of resources will allow users to be steered from one source to another depending on need. From a service standpoint, the user should be able to ask for information about a topic and be directed to all appropriate resources, whether print, electronic, or numeric.

Because the reference librarian is often the point of contact for the data user it is also important to be sure that the user has the statistical literacy skills necessary to use the data correctly. Katherine Wallman, Chief of Statistical Policy of the Office of Management and Budget, defines statistical literacy as "the ability to understand and critically evaluate statistical results that permeate our daily lives–coupled with the ability to appreciate the contributions that statistical thinking can make in public and private, professional and personal decisions."[25]

TECHNOLOGY REQUIREMENTS

The minimum technical requirements put out by the Government Printing Office each year reflect the impact that data availability is having on libraries. Agencies that offer large amounts of data, such as the Census Bureau, are moving from distributing products on CD-ROM to distributing them on DVD, therefore requiring DVD drives be available in depository libraries. These requirements now include the need for software or viewers that can read spreadsheets. There are also separate requirements that help users to incorporate data into geographic information systems. Data is still available in multiple formats, CD-ROM, DVD, Internet, and from different sources. The librarian will need to know what all this means for access, including the differences between formats, so that he/she can make decisions about access, what to load locally and what to access remotely, and the impact that these decisions have on selection and use.

NEW SERVICES AND RESPONSIBILITIES

Librarians need to continue to encourage the integration of content knowledge and statistical data files and ensure that high quality data are being collected. We can train other librarians in how to select, budget for, and understand the service implications of data acquisition and service provision. We can work together to examine the data needs of our users, assess how the library can provide the best coverage of data, work out a service strategy to support and publicize these products, and investigate ways to develop partnerships outside of the library in using and supporting data.

Since the technology and access tools are continuously developing, it is important for documents librarians to stay abreast of these changes by attending training sessions offered by agencies and working with user groups to determine the best way to meet their needs. Training sessions for new data products are frequently conducted in conjunction with national and state depository library conferences, often with no charge to attend.

Paris sums up the impact on librarians nicely when she says that librarians should learn how to exploit new technology to the benefit of their users' information needs. Furthermore, they have a responsibility to have the knowledge and skills necessary to use and teach the most efficient information techniques the current technology makes possible. The end-user accessibility of information is one of the primary issues of concern in satisfying information needs. No matter how organized the information, it will not realize its value until it is made known and put to effective use. She goes on to stress the importance of librarians continuing to be active in influencing the newly emerging national and international standards for electronic information.[26] One area where this is particularly important is in archiving and preserving government data. Since most of this is now being distributed only in electronic format, working to ensure permanent public access is critical.

CONCLUSION

Government documents librarians have moved from working only with statistical tables to having access directly to the data. This change provides both challenges and opportunities, not only for government document librarianship, but all other areas of the library as well. Despite the increased availability of data on the Internet, librarians continue to play an important role in facilitating access. Judith Rowe, although focusing on academic libraries, describes these new roles when she said

> "clearly the role of academic libraries and academic librarians in providing data services is growing. It is essential that libraries assume increasing responsibility for organizing and maintaining research data collections and that they support, either in the library or in cooperation with other University staff, the use of these data. It is essential that librarians or their colleagues become familiar with the full range of data resources, with the files themselves and with the sources of the files; and that the same or other individuals become familiar with appropriate analytic software and with all available computing platforms. Patrons can best be served in a collegial environment."[27]

With the advances in technology and the increased availability of data her comments are now applicable to all documents librarians. Data use will continue to increase and new technologies will continue to develop that will change the way data is accessible. As long as the government continues to produce this data, the government documents librarian will always find ways to adapt.

REFERENCES

1. Nancy K. Herther, "The new information age for the federal government–CP interviews SIGCAT's Jerry McFaul," *CD-ROM Professional* 5, no. 5 (1992): 17.

2. Executive Office of the President. Office of Management and Budget, Statistical programs of the United States government, fiscal year 2004. http://www.whitehouse. gov/omb/inforeg/04statprog.pdf, p. 13.

3. Ibid., 9.

4. Ibid., 7.

5. Ibid., 3.

6. Iddo Gal, "Teaching for statistical literacy and services for statistics agencies," *American Statistician* 57, no. 2 (2003): 81.

7. Cathryn Dippo, "FedStats promotes statistical literacy," *Communications of the ACM* 41, no. 4 (1998): 58.

8. Judith Rowe, "Electronic research data for scholars and students," *Serial Review* 22 no. 2 (1996): 5.

9. Oya A. Rieger, "Introducing numeric CD-ROMs in your library: Challenges and issues," *Microcomputers for Information Management* 10, no. 2 (1993): 93.

10. Dippo, "FedStats promotes statistical literacy," 59.

11. John A. Shuler, "Beyond the depository library concept," *Journal of Academic Librarianship* 27, no. 4 (2001): 299.

12. Prudence S. Adler, "Federal information dissemination policies and practices: One perspective on managing the transition," *Journal of Government Information* 23 (1996): 435.

13. Alan R. Tupek and Cathryn S. Dippo, "Qualitative literacy: New Website for federal statistics provides research opportunities," *D-Lib Magazine* December (1997), http://www.dlib/org/dlib/december 97/stats/12tupek.html.

14. Gils. http://www.gils.net/about.html.

15. DDI-About Specifications. http://www.icpsr.umich.edu/DDI/codebook/index. html.

16. Tupek and Dippo, "Qualitative literacy."

17. Tupek and Dippo, "Qualitative literacy."

18. John A. Shuler and Nancy J. Obermeyer, "Spatial data and data centers," *Journal of Academic Librarianship* 27, no. 5 (2001): 391-393.

19. Rieger, "Introducing numeric CD-ROMs," 105.

20. James R. Kuhlman and Everett S. Lee, "Data power to the people," *American Libraries* 17, no. 10 (1986): 757-760.

21. Rieger, "Introducing numeric CD-ROMs," 94.

22. Jim Jacobs, "Providing data services for machine readable information in an academic library: Some levels of service," *Public Access Computer Systems Review* 2, no. 1 (1991): 144-160.

23. Aimee Quinn, "Collection development in the electronic library: The future isn't what it used to be," *DTTP* 29, no. 3 (2001): 11.

24. Rieger, "Introducing numeric CD-ROMs," 110.

25. Katherine K. Wallman, "Enhancing statistical literacy: Enriching our society," *Journal of the American Statistical Association* 88, no. 421 (1993): 1.

26. Julia Dawn Paris, "The need to train librarians in data and related issues," *IASSIST Quarterly* Summer (1996): 7.

27. Rowe, "Electronic research data," 9.

The Way We Work Now:
A Survey of Reference Service Arrangement in Federal Depository Libraries

Joseph A. Salem, Jr.

SUMMARY. As the Government Printing Office completes its transition to an electronic distribution system for government information, reference services within the Federal Depository Library Program (FDLP) are changing as well. In addition to meeting new user needs and using new resources to do so, many government information librarians find themselves working in new environments within their libraries. Throughout the 1990s, many FDLP institutions reorganized reference services in order to provide government information assistance at the library's main reference service point. This article reports the results of a survey of FDLP institutions identifying the factors contributing to the reorganization of services, the process and success of reorganizing within these libraries, and the pros and cons of these service arrangements. *[Article copies available for a fee from The Haworth Document Delivery Service: 1-800-HAWORTH. E-mail address: <docdelivery@haworthpress.com> Website: <http://www.HaworthPress.com> © 2006 by The Haworth Press, Inc. All rights reserved.]*

Joseph A. Salem, Jr. is Coordinator of Government Documents and Head of the Map Library, Libraries and Media Services, Kent State University, 1 Eastway Drive, Kent, OH 44242 (E-mail: jsalem@lms.kent.edu).

[Haworth co-indexing entry note]: "The Way We Work Now: A Survey of Reference Service Arrangement in Federal Depository Libraries." Salem, Jr., Joseph A. Co-published simultaneously in *The Reference Librarian* (The Haworth Information Press, an imprint of The Haworth Press, Inc.) No. 94, 2006, pp. 69-94; and: *The Changing Face of Government Information: Providing Access in the Twenty-First Century* (ed: Suhasini L. Kumar) The Haworth Information Press, an imprint of The Haworth Press, Inc., 2006, pp. 69-94. Single or multiple copies of this article are available for a fee from The Haworth Document Delivery Service [1-800-HAWORTH, 9:00 a.m. - 5:00 p.m. (EST). E-mail address: docdelivery@haworthpress.com].

KEYWORDS. Government information, reference services, Federal Depository Library Program

INTRODUCTION

It is an understatement to assert that the environment for government information access has changed over the recent past. In the early 1990s, the emergence of the World Wide Web as a viable resource for sharing information prompted a shift in the dissemination of government information to the public from the century-old Federal Depository Library Program (FDLP) to an electronic distribution system. Congress began the migration to the electronic environment by mandating that the Government Printing Office (GPO)–which provides printing services for federal agencies as well as overseeing the more traditional depository system–provide electronic access to key publications of the federal government with the Government Printing Office Electronic Information Access Enhancement Act of 1993 (107 Stat. 112). This legislation not only launched a new dissemination tool for government information, *GPO Access*, it also launched the full-scale migration from paper distribution of government information to the Web-based system with which government information librarians now work.

In fiscal year 1993, GPO distributed 56% of its titles in microfiche format, 43% in paper, and less than 1% in electronic formats.[1] A decade after this migration began, the impact of the Web on government information access is obvious. In fiscal year 2002, GPO distributed 59% of its titles online through *GPO Access* and other agency Web sites, 24% in print, 16% in microfiche, and 1% in tangible electronic formats such as optical discs and floppy diskettes.[2] With Bruce James, the Public Printer of the United States, estimating that within five years 95% of the titles distributed by GPO will be available on the Web only,[3] it is safe to assume that electronic distribution of government information is firmly in place and that the migration that began in 1993 is nearly complete.

In addition to having an impact on the way users interact with government information, this electronic distribution system also challenges the way that assistance is provided to users. Since its formal inception in 1895, the FDLP provided expert assistance to citizens using government information through a system of depository libraries located throughout the nation. Although Web-based government information does increase access beyond the FDLP, finding, evaluating, and using government information on the Web still require expert assistance. With its increased profile due to the Web, assistance with government information is needed more than ever before. A November 2001 survey commissioned by The Council for Excellence in Government found that 76% of Americans with Internet access and 51% of all Americans already visited a government Web site.[4] While government information use is increasing as a result of the Web, this very trend toward electronic distribution for government information is challenging the role and vitality of the FDLP. With the increase in freely available titles on the Web and the inherent decrease in tangible documents, libraries are leaving the program.[5] In fiscal year 1993, the FDLP boasted 1,404 member institutions.[6] By the end of fiscal year 2002, membership declined by 9.25% to 1,300 institutions[7] with the decline in participation apparently continuing. As of November 2003 The *Federal Depository Library Directory* on the *GPO Access* site listed 1,280 member institutions.[8] So much has happened to influence the work of the FDLP that the very future of the program is under consideration. As part of a planning process for the future of the FDLP, Bruce James and Superintendent of Documents Judith Russell invited the Depository Library Council to begin a discussion of the role of the program in an increasingly networked and connected environment at the Spring 2003 Council Meeting.[9]

It is against this backdrop that government information librarians work to maintain existing reference services and create new opportunities to assist both their direct user population and their communities at large as part of the program's mission to provide open access to government information to each member institution's constituents. At the local level, the provision of reference services within many FDLP institutions changed over this dynamic last decade and continues to do so. Those libraries remaining in the FDLP must adjust to providing reference services with materials over which they assert little bibliographic control, within the context of other shifts in the library profession. The mandate to do more with less as a result of shrinking budgets and resources, increased levels of cataloging for tangible government documents, and this migration to an electronic FDLP contributed to the decision by many libraries to reorganize their government information services and departments. At least one long-term question in the FDLP seems to have been settled over the last decade–whether to integrate government information reference services into the general reference service point of the library. For decades, the best way to provide services to government documents collections was the topic of some dispute within the profession and its literature; however, the results of the

2001 *Biennial Survey of Depository Libraries* indicate that this debate is somewhat settled with 78% of member libraries indicating that reference services for government documents are provided at the library's main reference service point.[10] Although the trend toward consolidated service points within the FDLP is apparent, this trend warrants further examination as it has an impact on users, librarians, and support staff at each FDLP library, as well as on government information access in general.

This study serves as a follow-up examination of the integration of reference services identified in the 2001 *Biennial Survey* data. Unfortunately, GPO did not tabulate the results of the 1991 or 1993 *Biennial Survey*,[11] so this study first attempts to determine whether this trend toward integration is rooted in the changes in the FDLP and government information access over the last decade. The survey first identifies trends in the arrangement of government information reference services, including the reorganization of services over the last decade. The survey also asks institutions that did reorganize services over the 10-year period from 1993-2003 to rate the importance of key factors commonly cited in the literature regarding the decision to reorganize reference services. Data were also collected on the efficacy of the reorganization process for those institutions. Finally, the survey asked all respondents, regardless of whether they reorganized services within the last decade, to indicate the user and staff satisfaction with the current arrangement of services as well as to comment on the strengths and weaknesses of their service arrangement. This study, therefore, is intended not only as an examination of this trend toward reference service integration, but also as a guide to the 22% of FDLP libraries now maintaining a separate government information service point that may be considering a reorganization of services.

LITERATURE REVIEW

The issue examined in this study, the provision of government information services in general, and whether to integrate those services into other reference services in particular, is not new to the field. It is rooted in a disconnect between theory and practice based in necessity with regard to the organization of government publication collections and the reference services provided to assist patrons in their use. In theory, government publications should be treated like any other resource and integrated into the collection by subject; however, economic necessity often required segregating government documents collections and reference services due to the high volume of publications distributed through the FDLP throughout the twentieth century. This split between theory and practice necessitated the discussion of whether to integrate documents collections and services in the professional literature over the decades of the twentieth century.

The literature on government information reference services can be divided into two main categories: those studies giving an overview of the issue and how reference services have been provided in the past or are being provided at the time of the study, and articles offering recommendations on how to reorganize government information reference services by taking a case study approach to report on the process at one or more FDLP institutions. The current study attempts to synthesize these two approaches to the issue; however, a brief review of the literature is necessary to contextualize this approach.

Overviews of Government Documents Collections and Reference Services

Any research into whether to integrate government documents collections and services should begin with Michael Waldo's historical study of the issue. Waldo examined the debate over services and collections in the professional literature beginning at the turn of the twentieth century. His study offers a good articulation of both the separatist approach to collections and services as well as the integrationist approach. Simply stated, Waldo found that throughout the decades of the debate, the integrationist argument was rooted in a preference for treating documents collection and services like any other publication or information resource in order to insure use, and separatists tended to base their position in economic necessity. With FDLP institutions receiving more documents, cataloging each was prohibitively expensive, therefore separatists argued for organizing government documents collections by the SUDOCS number so that the *Monthly Catalog of United States Government Publications* could be used as an index to these largely uncataloged collections. In addition to laying out the arguments of each side in the debate, Waldo's study offers a historical survey of studies conducted to identify the ways in which collections and services were organized throughout the first half of the twentieth century.[12]

Naomi Kerze's study updated Waldo's work through the late 1980s. As Kerze observed, Waldo's study is particularly fitting as it runs through 1975. The single greatest factor in the debate, affordable bibliographic access for government publications, received its biggest boon with the 1976 decision by GPO to update its cataloging procedures to include full AACR cataloging, the addition of MARC records for FDLP publications in OCLC, and an improved *Monthly Catalog* with better indexing and additional access points. At the time of Kerze's study, not all FDLP institutions had taken advantage of these new cataloging opportunities; however, she did conclude that the increase in easy and affordable bibliographic access made the debate over how to arrange FDLP collections and services moot.[13]

More recently, literature dealing with the issues surrounding the arrangement of government documents reference services is often treated among the many issues facing FDLP institutions. Most overviews resemble an article from Suzanne Taylor and Fred Schmidt in which the availability of bibliographic access for government documents in the library's catalog, the increase of information on the Web, and the treatment of historical documents collections are examined as creating the environment in which reference services are provided. Although these issues have an impact on the arrangement of services, most of the current literature focuses on the issues themselves with little emphasis on whether that impact is greater in an integrated or segregated government information service point.[14]

Recommendations and Case Studies on Integrating Services

Perhaps Kerze's assertion that the debate is settled is accurate as much of the more recent literature focuses on the ways in which libraries can effectively integrate their services or collections. Although much has been published throughout the last decade on the topic, common themes emerge from this case study literature. Many case studies point to the need for post-merger assessment of service efficacy and use. For example, Philip Van de Voorde's case study of the merger between the Government Publications and Reference department at Iowa State University Library gathered data on patron use levels of government publications and perceived service quality before their merger and just afterward. Van de Voorde found declines in both government information usage and the perceived quality of service after the merger.[15] At the very least, Van de Voorde's study points to the need to assess the impact of a merger on users. Even if results are negative, as in the case at Iowa State, any effort to improve service in this merged environment will require the use of patron feedback.

Much of this case study literature also stresses the role of training on the success of any integration project. For example, Atifa Rawan and Jennifer Cox offer a good case study of the integration process at the University of Arizona Library. In addition to outlining their training methods, the case study reports the results of focus group testing to identify training needs and methodologies.[16] In addition to the emergence of training as a key element in a successful reorganization project, it has also emerged as the topic for professional trade literature. Maggie Farrell's article in *DTTP* is a good example of the way in which training is treated in the professional literature. Farrell outlines the environment in which these integration projects take place, offers tips for the integration of technical service responsibilities for government documents, and lists training methods and resources for the integration of reference responsibilities.[17]

Finally, good communication and the involvement of both the government documents staff and the reference staff in the reorganization process also emerge as key elements to success. Perhaps the best case study to consult regarding staff involvement and communication is that of the team-based approach used by Old Dominion University Library by Stuart Frazer et al. Old Dominion used teams of staff to provide training, write documentation, create new signage, and provide user hand-outs and guides.[18] Although this team-based approach may not be selected by other reorganizing institutions, the stress on communication and staff involvement advocated in this study echo similar needs expressed elsewhere in the case study literature.

METHODOLOGY

In an effort to integrate a case study approach as well as the descriptive overview of the topic of providing reference services for government information, this study surveyed FDLP institutions over the summer of 2003. In July, the questionnaire was posted online using Flashlight, a Web-based survey program provided by Washington State University. The questionnaire can be found in the Appendix to this paper. The survey was announced through an e-mail notice sent to 1,276 FDLP institutions on July 16, 2003. Although the FDLP directory listed 1,280 members in July 2003, the database file listed an e-mail address for each library's FDLP coordinator for only 1,276 members. A second e-mail notice was sent on August 7, 2003 thanking participants and encouraging further response before the end of the survey on September

15, 2003. Although each e-mail notice was sent to 1,276 libraries, 44 messages were returned each time due to inactive or incorrect e-mail addresses; therefore, a total of 1,232 libraries received these notices and were thus invited to participate. Throughout the three months that the survey ran–July 16 through September 15, 2003–FDLP coordinators from 275 member libraries responded, representing 21.5% of all 1,280 FDLP institutions and 22.3% of the 1,232 libraries receiving an e-mail invitation to participate.

Although this 22.3% response rate seems low, it is slightly higher than the 20% response rate commonly anticipated for unsolicited surveys and is well above the 10% rate that some online surveys receive.[19] Perhaps more important than the size of the sample is the level to which it represents the total population. The sample reached in this study is representative of the entire FDLP based on three criteria: depository type, library type, and library size. In order to accurately gauge these criteria, as well as to provide additional demographic information for each library included in the survey, the questionnaire asked each respondent to include the depository number for his or her institution. This was then used to link the data set gathered through the survey with the database file from the *Federal Depository Directory* online. Once linked, the depository type, library type, and library size as defined by GPO was included in the survey data set and the depository numbers were removed from the data to ensure institutional privacy throughout the data analysis process. Using the GPO definitions of these three criteria for the responding institutions ensured consistency not only when determining the level to which the survey sample represents the FDLP as a whole based on these criteria, it also ensures consistency when using these variables in data analysis.

Based on all three criteria, the survey sample is indeed representative of the FDLP. Regarding depository library type, 53 of the 1,280 institutions are designated as regional depositories, making up 4.1% of the program. Seventeen regional depositories responded to the survey representing 6.8% of the survey sample. The differences between the survey sample and the FDLP as a whole are even lower when considering the library types of each. For example, the majority of the FDLP and the survey sample are considered academic libraries. Of the 1,280 institutions in the FDLP, 880 or 68.7% are community college libraries, general academic libraries, and academic law libraries. Of the 275 survey respondents, 193 or 70.3% are found in these types of institutions. See Table 1 for a distribution of FDLP libraries and survey respondents by library type.

TABLE 1. Distribution of FDLP and Survey Sample by Library Type

Library Type	FDLP Frequency	FDLP Percent	Survey Sample Frequency	Survey Sample Percent
Community college	65	5.1%	15	5.5%
Academic general	661	51.6%	158	57.4%
Academic law	154	12.0%	20	7.3%
Federal agency	44	3.4%	6	2.2%
Federal court	13	1.0%	1	0.4%
Public library	242	19.0%	52	18.9%
Service academy	4	0.3%	0	0.0%
State court	37	2.9%	8	2.9%
State library	43	3.4%	13	4.7%
Special library	17	1.3%	2	0.7%
Total	1280	100.0%	275	100.0%

The survey sample is also representative of the FDLP as a whole based on the size of the library as defined by GPO. Of the 1,280 libraries in the FDLP, 380 (30%) are considered large, 537 (42%) are considered medium size, and 359 (28%) are considered small libraries. The size of libraries in the survey sample breaks down similarly with 99 of the 275 responding libraries (36%) considered large, 108 (39%) considered medium size, and 68 (25%) considered to be small in library size.

Finally, and most significantly for the purposes of this study, the survey sample is extremely representative of the FDLP based on the arrangement of reference services for government information. As previously mentioned, 78% of all FDLP libraries indicated that they offer government information reference services at the library's general reference service point when responding to the 2001 *Biennial Survey of Depository Libraries*. Of the 275 libraries making up the current survey sample all but three answered the question regarding their library's government information service points. Of those 272 respondents, 204 (75%) indicated that reference services are provided at their library's general reference service point. Based on these criteria, it is appropriate to treat this survey sample as representative of the FDLP.

SURVEY DATA ANALYSIS

The questionnaire included 28 questions divided into three sections. The first nine questions focused on general FDLP member information including depository library number, selection rate, organization of government documents collection and services, as well as any changes over the last ten years in document selection, use, and organization. All respondents were asked to answer the questions in this first section. Those indicating that their library reorganized reference services over the last decade were asked to complete the second section of the questionnaire, questions 10 through 23, which focused on the process of reorganizing reference services. This section asked respondents to rate the importance of factors commonly cited as part of the decision to reorganize, the success of the reorganization process, and the quality of selected aspects of the reorganization process. Respondents completing this section were also given an opportunity to comment on their library's experience of reorganizing services. Finally, all respondents were asked to complete the third section of the questionnaire, which focused on the library's current organization of reference services, regardless of any changes therein. The last five questions asked respondents to rate their staff and user satisfaction with the library's reference service arrangement, comment on the overall strengths and weaknesses of that arrangement, and provide any additional comments for which no opportunity was provided elsewhere in the questionnaire.

Library Information

As previously indicated, the questionnaire did ask respondents to include their depository library number so that the survey data set could be linked with GPO's *Federal Depository Library Directory* database file to provide additional and consistent information for each responding library including the depository library type, library type, and the size of the library as defined by GPO. For discussion of these library demographics, see the preceding Methodology section.

Respondents were also asked to list their current FDLP selection rate, which ranged from 1% to 100% with a mean selection rate of 37.9%. This mean selection rate will be used in data analysis regarding the arrangement of government documents collections and reference services, as well as the reorganization of those services. In addition to asking for the current selection rate, the questionnaire asked whether that rate reflected any significant change (10% or more) from the library's FDLP selection rate a decade ago. Although the majority of respondents, 165 of the 272 libraries responding to this question (60.7%), indicated that their current rate did not reflect any significant change over the last decade, there was a significant change in selection rate for many libraries over the last decade. Sixty-one respondents (22.4%) indicated that their FDLP selection rate increased by 10% or more over the last decade, and 46 libraries (16.9%) indicated a decrease of 10% or more in their selection rate over that same period. The survey sought this change in selection rate both as a descriptive variable for understanding reorganization decisions and projects as well as to create a better understanding of the environment in which reference services are provided within the FDLP. Although the amount of tangible depository material continues to decline, these increases in selection rate reflect increased levels of specificity in GPO profiles as well as continued interest in receiving depository library material and indicating subject strengths for Web-based government information by member institutions.

Similar to questions found on many of the *Biennial Survey of Depository Libraries* questionnaires, respondents were also asked to indicate first whether government documents were integrated into their library's main collection and then whether they were reflected in their library's catalog. The majority of respondents maintain a separate government documents collection. With three respondents declined to answer this question, 22 of the 272 libraries (8.1%) indicated that all federal documents are integrated into the library's general collection, 28 (10.3%) indicated that most documents are integrated, 171 (62.9%) indicated that some federal documents are integrated, and 51 (18.8%) integrate none of their federal documents into the general collection. The majority of respondents also indicated that federal documents are reflected in their library's catalog. Fifty-seven of the 273 libraries responding to this question (20.9%) indicate that all federal documents can be found in their library's catalog, 134 (49.1%) indicated that most federal documents are included in the catalog, 81 libraries (29.7%) include some federal documents into their collection, and 1 respondent (0.4%) indicated that no federal documents are found in the library's catalog. Although federal documents are physically segregated in the majority of the FDLP members in the survey sample, bibliographic access to them is integrated into the more general search strategies of the library and as a result of being included in the general catalog.

The questionnaire also sought to identify changes in the level of government information reference service use over the last decade as well as any changes in staffing levels for government information reference services over that same period. Despite expectations that use may have decreased over the last decade due to the emergence of Web-based government information on the Web, the majority of respondents indicated either an increase in reference service use or no change at all. Of the 266 libraries answering this question, 96 (36.1%) noted an increase in reference service use, 95 (35.7%) indicated no change, and 75 (28.2%) noted a decrease in reference service use over the last decade.

While reference service use tended to remain constant or increase despite the migration to an electronic distribution system for government information and publication, staffing levels remained constant for a majority of respondents as well. Of the 272 libraries responding to the question regarding staffing, 165 (60.7%) indicated no change in staffing levels for government information reference services since 1993. When staffing levels did change over this 10-year period, they tended to decrease. While 79 libraries (29%) indicated a decrease in staffing levels, 28 responding institutions (10.3%) saw an increase in staffing levels over this 10-year period.

The questionnaire then asked participants to select the response that best described their library's arrangement of reference services for government information. As discussed in the preceding Methodology section, 204 of the 272 libraries (75%) responding to the question described their government reference service as integrated into the library's general reference service point. Of the remainder of the sample, 53 libraries (19.5%) provide assistance with government information at a separate service point and 15 libraries (15.5%) provide those services at a combined subject-specific reference service point. The tendency to integrate reference services remains constant regardless of library type with 73.8% of academic libraries, 76.9% of public libraries, and 79.3% of other library types providing services at the library's general reference desk. Slight differences do emerge between library types regarding whether services are provided at a separate service point or at another subject-specific desk. For example, while 23% of the academic libraries not integrating services provide government information reference at a separate service point, 9.6% of the public libraries provide their services at a separate service point. See Table 2 for a breakdown of the arrangement of government information reference service points by library type.

Within this sample, the level of collection integration does have an impact on the organization of reference services. Although the differences are slight, responding institutions with a higher level of collection integration tend to provide services at an integrated service point. For example, of the 22 libraries integrating all of their FDLP documents into the library's general collection only one (4.5%) provides services at the general service point or at another subject-specific service point. Of the 51 libraries maintaining a completely segregated collection of FDLP

TABLE 2. Government Information Service Points by Library Type

Library Type		Government Information Service Points			Total
		Separate Reference Service Point	General Reference Service Point	Combined Subject-Specific Service Point	
Academic library[a]	Count	44	141	6	191
	Percent	23.0%	73.8%	3.2%	100.0%
Public library	Count	5	40	7	52
	Percent	9.6%	76.9%	13.5%	100.0%
Other library[b]	Count	4	23	2	29
	Percent	13.8%	79.3%	6.9%	100.0%
Total	Count	53	204	15	272
	Percent	19.5%	75.0%	5.5%	100.0%

[a] Includes academic general, academic law, and community college libraries.
[b] Includes federal agency, federal and state court, state, and special libraries.

documents, 17 (33.3%) provide services at a separate service point. Despite these differences, government information reference services are provided at an integrated service point for the majority of respondents regardless of collection arrangement. See Table 3 for a breakdown of government information reference service points by level of collection integration.

A similar relationship emerges regarding the level of cataloging provided for FDLP collections. For example, whereas 86% of those libraries adding all federal documents to their catalog provide government information reference at a general reference desk, 77% of libraries cataloging most of their documents, and 62.5% of libraries cataloging some documents provide services at general reference desks. Although a higher frequency of cataloging seems to be related to a higher frequency of reference service integration among the survey sample, a majority of respondents provide government information reference services at their library's general reference desk regardless of the amount of material cataloged.

The most significant element influencing the organization of reference services within FDLP institutions is their selection rate. Within the survey sample, libraries with lower selection rates tend to integrate their services more often than those with higher rates. Of the 168 libraries with a selection rate below the survey sample's mean selection rate of

TABLE 3. Government Information Service Points by Level of Collection Integration

Documents Integrated into Library Collections		Government Information Service Points			Total
		Separate Reference Service Point	General Reference Service Point	Combined Subject-Specific Service Point	
All	Count	1	19	2	22
	Percent	4.5%	86.4%	9.1%	100.0%
Most	Count	0	26	1	27
	Percent	0.0%	96.3%	3.7%	100.0%
Some	Count	35	126	10	171
	Percent	20.5%	73.7%	5.8%	100.0%
None	Count	17	32	2	51
	Percent	33.3%	62.8%	3.9%	100.0%
Total	Count	53	203	15	271
	Percent	19.6%	74.9%	5.5%	100.0%

37.9%, 14 (8.3%) provide services at a separate government information desk, 148 (88.1%) provide assistance at the general service desk, and 6 (3.6%) assist users with government information at a subject-specific reference service point. Of the remaining 104 respondents who answered the question regarding their library's service arrangement, 39 (37.5%) provide assistance at a government information desk, 56 (53.8%) provide government information reference at the library's general service desk, and 9 (8.7%) assist users at a subject-specific reference desk.

The final question of the first section asked all respondents to indicate whether the current arrangement of reference services reflects a change over the last decade. Of the 271 libraries responding to this question, 213 (78.6%) indicated that no change occurred over the last decade in their reference services; however, when a change had occurred over that 10-year period, the trend was overwhelmingly toward reference service integration. Fifty-one of the 58 libraries that indicated a change in the arrangement of reference services over the last decade (87.9%) merged government information reference with general reference. Four (6.9%) merged with a subject-specific service point, and three (5.2%) moved from an integrated service to a government-specific reference desk.

Changes in selection rates over the same 10-year period did not have an impact on reorganization. For example, 20% of the libraries increasing their selection rate over the last decade merged services, 19.6% of those decreasing their selection rate merged services, and 18.3% of those libraries that saw no significant change in selection rate merged services. Although selection rate did not seem to make a difference on whether services were reorganized, decreased staffing levels did coincide with integration projects. Of the 51 libraries that merged services, 12 (23.5%) increased their staff for government information reference, 25 (49%) decreased their staff, and 14 (27.5%) made no change in staffing. Although the majority of the libraries that merged services also decreased staffing, the structure of the questionnaire does not make it possible to determine whether the decreased staffing was due to the merger or vice versa.

Reorganizing Reference Services

Participants who indicated that their library's current arrangement of reference services reflects a change over the last decade were asked to complete the second section of the survey, which focused on the process of reorganizing services. Any responses to the questions in this section from institutions that indicated that no reorganization of services had occurred when answering question nine were removed from the data set in order to limit the analysis of data collected in this section of the survey to those institutions that reorganized reference services over the last decade.

The first set of questions in this section asked respondents to rate the importance of factors commonly cited as having an impact on the decision to reorganize services: the increase of government information available on the Web, the appearance of government documents in the library's catalog, the level of use of government information reference services, changes in staffing levels, budgetary concerns, and changes in physical facilities. Of the 58 institutions that reorganized reference services since 1993, 29 (50%) rated the proliferation of Web-based government information as a very important or important element in the decision to reorganize; however, a surprising number, 15 (25.9%) rated the migration of government information to the Web information as not important on the decision to reorganize. The presence of cataloged documents rated higher as a factor in the decision to reorganize services. The majority of respondents (63.8%) rated the appearance of government documents in the library's catalog as a very important or important element in the decision.

Use of government information reference services had slightly less of an impact on the decision to reorganize. Ten respondents (17.2%) rated service use as very important, 17 (29.3%) rated use as important, 16 (27.6%) rated use as somewhat important, and 15 (25.9%) rated use as not important. Whether service use increased, decreased, or remained constant had some impact on the rating of this element on the decision to reorganize. While 37.9% of the 29 libraries that saw an increase in reference service use since 1993 rated use as very important or important when deciding to reorganize, 56.3% of those that saw use decrease over the same period rated use as very important or important. See Table 4 for a breakdown of the rating of service use as an element in deciding to reorganize by the level of use over the last decade.

Changes in staffing levels had a higher impact on the decision to reorganize services. The majority of libraries responding to this question (63.2%) rated their staffing level for government information as very important or important when the decision was made to reorganize services. There was no significant difference between the rating of staffing level among those libraries that changed staffing level regardless of whether staff increased or decreased. While the majority of those libraries that increased their government information staffing (75.0%) rated staffing as very important or important, a similar majority (73.1%) of those libraries that decreased staffing rated it as very important or important when deciding to reorganize. It should come as no surprise that

TABLE 4. Rating of Service Use on Decision to Reorganize by Level of Use

Use Level for Government Information Services since 1993		Rating of Use of Government Information Services on Decision to Reorganize				
		Very Important	Important	Somewhat Important	Not Important	Total
Increased	Count	5	6	8	10	29
	Percent	17.2%	20.7%	27.6%	34.5%	100.0%
Decreased	Count	4	5	5	2	16
	Percent	25.0%	31.25%	31.25%	12.5%	100.0%
No change	Count	1	6	3	3	13
	Percent	7.7%	46.1%	23.1%	23.1%	100.0%
Total	Count	10	17	16	15	58
	Percent	17.2%	29.3%	27.6%	25.9%	100.0%

those libraries that did not change government information staffing rated it as less important when deciding to reorganize. Only 42.1% of the libraries in which staffing remained constant rated staffing level as very important or important and another 42.1% rated staffing as not important on the decision to reorganize services. See Table 5 below for a breakdown of the rating of staffing level as an element in deciding to reorganize by changes in staffing over the last decade.

Respondents indicated that budgetary concerns had a significant impact when deciding to reorganize services. The vast majority (68.4%) rated budgetary concerns as a very important or important element in reorganizing, and only 14% indicated that their library's budget was not important when the decision to reorganize was made. Although the budget did have an impact on the decision, changes in physical facilities seemed to have little impact. While 32.75% of the libraries responding to this question rated facility changes as a very important element in the decision making process, another 32.75% rated their facility as not important. See Table 6 for respondent ratings of all the deciding factors addressed in questions 10 through 15 of the questionnaire.

After rating selected elements of the decision to reorganize services, respondents were asked to rate the success of the reorganization process. No respondent rated his or her library's reorganization as unsuccessful. Of the 57 libraries responding to this question, 12 (21.1%) rated their reorganization as very successful, 24 (42.1%) rated it as successful, and 21 (36.8%) indicated that their library's government informa-

TABLE 5. Rating of Staffing Level on Decision to Reorganize by Change in Staffing

Staffing Level for Government Documents since 1993		Rating of Use of Staffing Level on Decision to Reorganize				Total
		Very Important	Important	Somewhat Important	Not Important	
Increased	Count	6	3	2	1	12
	Percent	50.0%	25.0%	16.7%	8.3%	100.0%
Decreased	Count	11	8	6	1	26
	Percent	42.3%	30.8%	23.1%	3.8%	100.0%
No change	Count	3	5	3	8	19
	Percent	15.8%	26.3%	15.8%	42.1%	100.0%
Total	Count	20	16	11	10	57
	Percent	35.1%	28.1%	19.3%	17.5%	100.0%

TABLE 6. Rating of Factors Cited in Decision to Reorganize

Factors in Decision to Reorganize		Very Important	Important	Somewhat Important	Not Important	Total
Government info	Count	19	10	14	15	58
on the Web	Percent	32.8%	17.2%	24.1%	25.9%	100.0%
Cataloged	Count	20	17	11	10	58
documents	Percent	34.5%	29.3%	19.0%	17.2%	100.0%
Use of reference	Count	10	17	16	15	58
services	Percent	17.2%	29.3%	27.6%	25.9%	100.0%
Changes in	Count	20	16	11	10	57
staffing levels	Percent	35.1%	28.1%	19.3%	17.5%	100.0%
Budgetary	Count	26	13	10	8	57
concerns	Percent	45.6%	22.8%	17.6%	14.0%	100.0%
Changes in	Count	19	9	11	19	58
facilities	Percent	32.75%	15.5%	19.0%	32.75%	100.0%

tion reference service reorganization was somewhat successful. This success rating was originally intended as a variable for analyzing respondent ratings of commonly cited elements in successful reorganization; however, the positive responses to this question allow the analysis of the data gathered from questions 17 through 22 to assume at least a somewhat successful reorganization project.

The next six questions asked respondents to rate elements that are commonly cited within the professional literature as crucial to a successful reorganization project: planning, communication, leadership, staff involvement, training, and overall enthusiasm of the staff and administration. Considering the positive success rates of the reorganization projects as indicated by responses to question 16, it is not surprising that the majority of participants rated each of these six elements as excellent or good. Only staff and administrative enthusiasm stood out as having a lower rating even among these successful reorganization projects. Although still a majority, just 50.9% of the libraries responding to this question rated the overall enthusiasm of staff and administration as excellent or good. See Table 7 for a complete breakdown of respondent ratings of these selected elements commonly cited as essential to successful reorganization projects.

Finally, this second section of the questionnaire provided participants an opportunity to offer comments on the process of reorganizing government information reference services. The role of the government

TABLE 7. Rating of Elements Cited in Successful Reorganization

Elements of Reorganization		Excellent	Good	Adequate	Poor	Total
Planning	Count	7	32	15	2	56
	Percent	12.5%	57.1%	26.8%	3.6%	100.0%
Communication	Count	8	32	13	4	58
	Percent	34.5%	29.3%	19.0%	17.2%	100.0%
Leadership	Count	12	28	14	4	58
	Percent	20.7%	48.3%	24.1%	6.9%	100.0%
Staff involvement	Count	13	28	11	6	58
	Percent	22.4%	48.3%	19.0%	10.3%	100.0%
Training	Count	6	32	15	5	58
	Percent	10.3%	55.2%	25.9%	8.6%	100.0%
Enthusiasm of	Count	7	22	25	3	57
staff/admin.	Percent	12.3%	38.6%	43.8%	5.3%	100.0%

information specialist during the reorganization process and in the newly reorganized service was stressed throughout the comments. According to these comments, the familiarity with FDLP regulations and procedures as well as with government information resources makes the government information specialist invaluable to the process. A few commented on the challenges of integrating services, including training general reference staff on the use of government information as well as preparing government documents staff to provide general reference services. Finally, a few respondents also indicated that the decision to reorganize services was made with little participation of the government information services staff as a result of changes not only within the FDLP, but also within a general library environment in which budgets and resources are tight and services need to be designed to meet user needs and expectations.

Overall Evaluation of Service Arrangement

All respondents were asked to complete the third section of the questionnaire in which the overall reference service arrangement was evaluated. In this section, the questionnaire first asked respondents to rate the overall level of user satisfaction with the arrangement of reference services at their library. Of the 272 responses to this question, 267 (98.2%) indicated overall user satisfaction with the library's arrangement. Participants also rated staff satisfaction similarly. The majority of the 271 responses to this question (93.4%) indicated that members of their staff were satisfied with the library's reference service arrangement. Originally, this question was to be evaluated by breaking down responses by the different ways in which services are provided; however, these overwhelmingly positive responses make such an evaluation unnecessary.

The last three questions of the questionnaire offered participants an opportunity to provide comments on the positive aspects of their library's reference service arrangement, the negative aspects of that arrangement, and any additional comments. Positive aspects of an integrated reference service included a higher profile for government publications, extended service hours for government information, and increased staff awareness of government resources and proficiency in their identification and use. As one respondent described this last point, "Everybody now has to know some of the basics of federal government information service. They can't just point out the government documents department and send people there, and forget the question." These integrated reference service points were also cited along with catalog access and Web-based information as making government information easier to use and more convenient for patrons. Respondents also cited efficient use of staff and resources as another positive aspect of integrated reference services. The availability of expert government information assistance was the most commonly cited positive aspect of those respondents working in FDLP libraries maintaining a separate government information reference service point.

Commonly cited negative aspects of integrated services include the reluctance of some staff to work with government information, a lack of expertise to handle more demanding questions leading to heavy referrals to the library's FDLP coordinator, and time spent by the government information librarian on non-FDLP work. Some respondents also cited lack of cataloging, particularly for historical collections, as a problem when working in an integrated service point. Being physically removed from the federal documents collection also posed a problem for some respondents working in integrated services. Respondents working in a library maintaining a separate government information service desk cited a lack of prominence as a library collection and service, low staffing levels, and shorter service hours as negative aspects of this service arrangement.

The questionnaire also provided an opportunity for respondents to include any additional comments, which loosely fell into three categories: government information reference services, general issues related to working in the FDLP, and the questionnaire itself. Comments pertaining to reference services included more stress on the need for training and good communication, the continued need for expert assistance despite electronic distribution of government information, and the importance of cataloging documents to ensure use and effective reference assistance. A few respondents also indicated that although their library currently maintains a separate government information service point, reorganization projects are being discussed and may be implemented in the near future. Comments on working in the FDLP included the continued need for collection development despite electronic distribution, funding constraints, and the need for reconsidering some of the demands placed on member institutions considering decreasing resources and increasing responsibilities. Respondents also offered feedback on the questionnaire itself. A few noted that the options provided for the question on the organization of reference services were too narrow and did not fully reflect their library's arrangement and a few others also remarked on the difficulty of accurately gauging staff and user satisfaction when answering questions 24 and 25. It was also observed that the questionnaire focused solely on reference services, which is often only half of the equation when reorganizing within an FDLP institution since responsibilities for technical services are often merged as well.

CONCLUSION

The survey reinforces the findings of the 2001 *Biennial Survey of Depository Libraries*, which indicated that the majority of FDLP institutions now provide government information reference assistance as part of an integrated service point. It also confirms that the prevalence of integrated services within the FDLP is the result of a relatively recent trend. Within the survey sample, 21.4% of the responding libraries indicated that their current arrangement of reference services reflect a reorganization project over the last ten years. For those institutions that did reorganize, survey data indicate that although information technology (i.e., Web-based government information and increased cataloging of existing documents) did have an impact on the decision to reorganize services, budgetary concerns had a significant role to play in reorganization as well. The role of economics in service arrangement and staffing was also emphasized in the survey's open-ended comments.

For those institutions that did reorganize over the last decade, their input reinforces the recommendations offered in much of the professional literature on successful reference service reorganizations. The vast majority of these libraries ranked their project as successful and also ranked the most commonly cited essential elements of these projects as either excellent or good. The survey data also indicate that staff resistance to the project can be overcome, as the ratings of staff and administrative enthusiasm were noticeably lower than the other essential elements for which data were gathered. Overall, the survey results indicate that for many within the FDLP, the way in which they assist users can be viewed as one of the many changes in their professional environment since the federal government began its migration to electronic information distribution in the early 1990s.

Of course, the provision reference assistance is not the only aspect of working within a depository library that is affected by a merger. Future research should focus on the impact of service and unit reorganization on the provision of technical services and the maintenance of bibliographic control of government information in the electronic distribution environment in order to get a more complete sense of the professional environment within depository libraries not only over the recent past, but as the program moves forward into an ever-changing and somewhat uncertain future.

NOTES AND REFERENCES

1. U.S. Government Printing Office. *Annual Report, 1993*. Washington: Government Printing Office [1994]: p. 23.

2. U.S. Government Printing Office. *Library Programs Service FY 2002 Annual Report* [Online]. Available: http://www.access.gpo.gov/su_docs/fdlp/pubs/annrprt/02lpsar.html [2004, January 4].

3. Peter Brand. "Public Printer James Steers GPO into the Digital Future." *The Hill*, 25 June 2003.

4. Hart-Teeter. *E-Government: To Connect, Protect, and Serve* [Online]. Available: http://www.excelgov.org/displayContent.asp?Keyword=ppp022602 [2004, November 4].

5. See Lorraine Kram. "Why Continue to Be a Depository Library if It Is All on the Internet Anyway?" *Government Information Quarterly* 15, no. 1 (1998): 57-71.

6. U.S. Government Printing Office. *Annual Report, 1993*. Washington: Government Printing Office [1994]: p. 22.

7. U.S. Government Printing Office. *Library Programs Service FY 2002 Annual Report* [Online]. Available: http://www.access.gpo.gov/su_docs/fdlp/pubs/annrprt/02lpsar.html [2004, January 4].

8. U.S. Government Printing Office. *Federal Depository Library Directory* [Online]. Available: http://www.access.gpo.gov/su_docs/fdlp/tools/ldirect.html [2004, January 4].

9. See U.S. Depository Library Council to the Public Printer. *Envisioning the Future of Federal Government Information: Summary of the Spring 2003 Meeting* [Online]. Available: http://www.access.gpo.gov/su_docs/fdlp/council/EnvisioningtheFuture.html [2004, January 4].

10. U.S. Government Printing Office. *Biennial Survey of Depository Libraries: 2001 Results* [Online]. Available: http://www.access.gpo.gov/su_docs/fdlp/bisurvey/01survey.pdf [2004, January 4]: p. 13.

11. E-mail communication with GPO Program Analyst Joseph Paskoski dated 12/3/2003.

12. Michael Waldo. "An Historical Look at the Debate over How to Organize Federal Government Documents in Depository Libraries." *Government Publications Review* 4, no. 4 (1977): 319-329.

13. Naomi V. Kerze. "Separate vs. Integrated: The Disappearing Debate over the Organization of United States Government Publications in Depository Libraries." *Government Publications Review* 16 (1989): 439-334.

14. Suzanne N. Taylor and Fred C. Schmidt. "Reference Services and Federal Documents: Current Status and Issues." *Colorado Libraries* 27, no. 2 (2001): 21-24.

15. Philip E. Van De Voorde. "Should Reference Service for U.S. Government Publications and General Reference Be Merged?" *Government Publications Review* 16 (1989): 247-257.

16. Atifa R. Rawan and Jennifer Cox. "Government Publications Integration and Training." *Journal of Government Information* 22, no. 3 (1995): 253-266.

17. Maggie Farrell. "Training for Documents Reference in a Merged Reference Center." *DTTP* 28, no. 4 (2000): 11-16.

18. Stuart L. Frazer, Kathryn W. Boone, Vernon A. McCart, Teresa L. Prince, and Anne D. Rees. "Merging Government Information and the Reference Department: A Team-Based Approach." *Journal of Government Information* 24, no. 2 (1997): 93-102.

19. Diane F. Witmer, Robert W. Colman, and Sandra Lee Katzman. "From Paper-and-Pencil to Screen-and-Keyboard," in Steve Jones, ed. *Doing Internet Research* (London: Sage Publications, 1999), 145-161.

APPENDIX. Reference Services Within FDLP Libraries Questionnaire

1. Depository Library Number:

2. What is your current depository selection rate?

3. Does your library's current depository selection rate reflect any significant change (ten percent or more) over the last ten years?
   - ○ Rate has increased over the last ten years
   - ○ Rate has decreased over the last ten years
   - ○ Rate has not significantly changed over the last ten years

4. Are Federal depository documents integrated into the library's main collection?
   - ○ All
   - ○ Most
   - ○ Some
   - ○ None

5. Are Federal depository documents represented in the library's catalog?
   - ○ All
   - ○ Most
   - ○ Some
   - ○ None

6. Have there been any changes in the level of use of government information reference services at your library over the last ten years?
   - ○ Increased
   - ○ Decreased
   - ○ No change

7. Have there been any changes in the level of staffing for government information reference services over the last ten years?
   - ○ Increased
   - ○ Decreased
   - ○ No change

8. Are reference services for the depository collection provided at a separate service point or are services provided at a combined reference service point?
   - ○ Separate government information service point
   - ○ Reference services for government information are provided at the library's main reference service point
   - ○ Reference services for government information are provided at a combined subject-specific reference service point

9. Please select the statement that most accurately describes any changes made to reference services for government information resources over the last ten years.
   - ◯ Reference services for government information were merged with the library's main reference service point
   - ◯ Reference services for government information were merged with another subject-specific reference service point
   - ◯ Reference services for government information were separated from another reference service point and are now provided at a separate service point
   - ◯ There have been none of the above changes in the arrangement of reference services for government information at my library

If you answered "none of the above changes" to question #9, proceed to question #24.

Please rate the importance of the following items on the decision to reorganize reference services for government information at your library.

	Very Important	Important	Somewhat Important	Not Important
10. Increase in the amount of government information available on the Web	◯	◯	◯	◯
11. The appearance of government documents in the library's catalog	◯	◯	◯	◯
12. Level of use of the government information reference services	◯	◯	◯	◯
13. Changes in staffing levels	◯	◯	◯	◯
14. Budgetary concerns	◯	◯	◯	◯
15. Changes in physical facilities	◯	◯	◯	◯

16. Please rate the process of reorganizing government information reference services at your library.
    - ◯ Very successful
    - ◯ Successful
    - ◯ Somewhat successful
    - ◯ Unsuccessful

The following items are often cited as essential to the success of any new service implementation or the reorganization of existing services. Please rate the quality of the following items with regard to the process of reorganizing reference services for government information at your library.

	Excellent	Good	Adequate	Poor
17. Planning	◯	◯	◯	◯
18. Communication	◯	◯	◯	◯
19. Leadership	◯	◯	◯	◯
20. Staff involvement	◯	◯	◯	◯
21. Training	◯	◯	◯	◯
22. Overall level of enthusiasm of staff and administration	◯	◯	◯	◯

APPENDIX (continued)

23. Please provide any comments that you may have regarding your library's experience of reorganizing reference services for government information.

24. Overall, are staff members satisfied with the current arrangement of government information reference services at your library?
    - ○ Satisfied
    - ○ Not satisfied

25. Overall, are users satisfied with the current arrangement of government information reference services at your library?
    - ○ Satisfied
    - ○ Not satisfied

26. What are the positive aspects of the current arrangement of reference services for government information at your library?

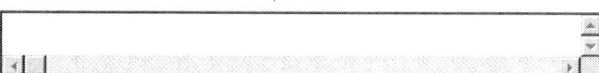

27. What are the negative aspects of the current arrangement of reference services for government information at your library?

28. Any additional comments?

Mapping New Horizons
in Government Documents Reference Service:
A Unique Collaboration

Andrew Nicholson
Tom Stave
Kaiping Zhang

SUMMARY. Throughout the 1990s, many academic libraries undertook major restructuring initiatives. In many cases, this involved merging a Government Documents Department with a General Reference Department. At the University of Oregon Libraries, a different approach was taken. Between 1998 and 2000, the Business Reference service and Map Collection was successfully integrated into the Government Documents Collection. With these three collections now available through one service point, many new opportunities have been created for enhanced reference services, library instruction, collection development, and outreach across campus and into the community. *[Article copies available for a fee from The Haworth Document Delivery Service:*

Andrew Nicholson is GIS/Data Librarian, University of Toronto at Mississauga Library, Ontario, Canada (E-mail: anichols@utm.utoronto.ca).

Tom Stave is Head, Document Center (E-mail: tstave@uoregon.edu); and Kaiping Zhang is Business Librarian, Document Center (E-mail: kzhang@uoregon. edu), University of Oregon Library, University of Oregon, Eugene, OR 97403-1299.

[Haworth co-indexing entry note]: "Mapping New Horizons in Government Documents Reference Service: A Unique Collaboration." Nicholson, Andrew, Tom Stave, and Kaiping Zhang. Co-published simultaneously in *The Reference Librarian* (The Haworth Information Press, an imprint of The Haworth Press, Inc.) No. 94, 2006, pp. 95-108; and: *The Changing Face of Government Information: Providing Access in the Twenty-First Century* (ed: Suhasini L. Kumar) The Haworth Information Press, an imprint of The Haworth Press, Inc., 2006, pp. 95-108. Single or multiple copies of this article are available for a fee from The Haworth Document Delivery Service [1-800-HAWORTH, 9:00 a.m. - 5:00 p.m. (EST). E-mail address: docdelivery@haworthpress.com].

KEYWORDS. Government documents, business information, maps, GIS, reference, library instruction, collection development

INTRODUCTION

Over the past ten years, academic libraries have witnessed a growing consolidation of reference services across subject areas and type of material formats. The combination of Government Information materials with Map and Geospatial data collections is among the most common. Some libraries have combined their Business Information Services with Government Documents. Few libraries have tried to combine Government Information, Maps, and Business Information Services. Between 1998 and 2000, the University of Oregon Libraries successfully integrated its Business Reference service and Map Collection into its Government Documents collection. The convergence of three distinct collections has provided unique opportunities for enhanced reference services and Library Instruction, as well as new approaches to collection development. The growing role of geographic information systems in the department has only served to bring these distinct, but inter-related collections even closer together. By linking business data to geographic information produced by government agencies and others, the University of Oregon Libraries has provided an in-depth reference experience that can be an example for other libraries.

LITERATURE REVIEW

Over the past several years, academic libraries have been continually monitoring and reconfiguring their reference services and resources to best meet the needs of their patrons. Typically, a restructuring of reference services has involved a merger of library departments and service points, with government document services often included. As outlined in much of the literature, the "urge to merge" stems from many different factors affecting a library. These include budget constraints, an increase in number of patrons, and a desire to best maximize available physical space.[1] Government Documents collections and services are frequently involved in such restructuring plans for a variety of reasons including a desire to broaden experience among library staff in Government Information Resources, a necessity to support a growing public awareness of government documents, or just a need to add more staff to a General Reference Department. Despite such objectives, however, the integration of Government Documents with General Reference has often not been successful. In Van de Voorde (1989), the author finds that the quality of service and even the use of government documents declined after the Government Documents service point merged with General Reference at Iowa State.[2] A merger of Government Documents with Social Science Reference was found to be a "mistake" at BYU.[3] Other studies noted that the amount of cross training needed among staff should not be underestimated for such an integration to be successful. Even in cases where training did occur, staff continued to be anxious about dealing with Government Documents and a "dumbing down" of Document Reference became the norm.

Although a plethora of literature exists detailing the experiences of library restructuring and the integration of collections and general reference points, very few authors have specifically mentioned Business or Map reference services in their studies. As each area is so specialized and almost always involves in-depth reference help, what literature that does exist tends to focus on recommending the best reference resources for these areas. For example, one of the best articles written for the Business Librarian is Priscilla Cheng Geahigan's 1991 article on "Government Sources for Business Reference Inquiries." Geahigan highlights how many standard business reference sources reprint much of the same information found in government depository collections. With a thorough knowledge of a government documents collection, a business librarian does not need to rely on costly business resource books and databases to answer patron questions. The answers can in fact be found in many government documents, perhaps months or even years before they appear in Business reference sources.[4]

For Map reference questions, the literature often focuses on the best atlases or Web sites as ready reference resources. As map collections are often combined with government documents collections, one might think that there would be a substantive body of literature outlining the pros and cons of this arrangement. In fact, almost no literature exists on the topic of combined map/government document reference. Despite long established depository programs in both the United States and

Canada, the roles of Government Information and Cartographic material are still regarded by some librarians as two mutually exclusive parts. In a Canada-wide survey of Depository Libraries, service quality at Government Information Desks suffered when it came to looking up cartographic information.[5] When asked to find information about obtaining aerial photography, many of the Government Document reference staff became perplexed, with some responding that aerial photos were not government documents.[6]

While this perception of separateness between government documents and maps may be longstanding, a number of new trends indicate that this may be rapidly changing. Recent developments with information technologies and a set of new freer policies for information dissemination have lead to a rethinking of how to manage geographic information especially in the context of government information. Certainly, the role of Geographic Information Systems (GIS) has not escaped the notice of Government Document Librarians. In fact, the collecting of digital geospatial data (much of it produced by government agencies) and the offering of geographic information services has only brought Maps and Government Documents closer together. In their excellent 1999 article, Lippencott and Cheverie see the thickening "blur" in government information dissemination as an opportunity to integrate product and service including the use of geographic information systems (GIS) and purpose built mapping tools or "pathfinders" for online, networked information.[7]

For many university libraries, the challenge has been in how best to integrate the data and technology into an existing government document reference service. By 2000, some GIS capability/expertise in a Government Documents Department had come to be expected as a given at many large university libraries. At the 1999 ALA conference, Karen Wihoit noted that training and familiarity in GIS resources has now become essential for any kind of Government Documents work, including both Reference and Technical Services staff.[8]

DOCUMENTS AT THE UO LIBRARIES: A HISTORY

The University of Oregon Libraries' Document Center had been a federal depository library since 1883, and also managed depository and non-depository collections from the State of Oregon, the Canadian federal government, the European Union, and other inter-governmental organizations. Its collections included both paper and microform documents, which were organized by standard non-LC classification schemes, such as SuDoc. During all of its recent history it has maintained a separate service point from the general reference desk, due to its large collection size, its special organization, and the need for specialized reference and collections expertise. When the library building was expanded in 1993, the unit moved from a location on the second floor down to the same floor as the general reference desk. The Reference Department served clients in the humanities and social sciences, as well as the College of Education and the Business School. Business School clients made frequent use of both reference desks.

Closer proximity led to more active collaboration between the two units, including the cross-training of business librarians in the reference use of government information. The sharing of experience revealed several interesting commonalities between government and business reference. First, in the judgment of the librarians involved, both types of transactions typically took more time to complete than did other reference questions. Successful encounters in each area often required librarians to teach complex finding tools and esoteric information structures, explain unfamiliar programs for the creation and collection of data, and work closely with the clients through multi-step information-seeking strategies. Second, there was a sizable overlap in the information sources required. Both groups of clients were heavy consumers of government laws and regulations, patents, census and other demographic data, economic and trade figures, and financial information. It was no surprise that the activities and information of the regulating agencies, and of the regulated entities, were found to be two sides of the same coin. To deal with one category of information effectively meant understanding the other as well.

In 1996, the Libraries decided to combine government and business reference into the same service point. Upon the appointment of a new business librarian, that position was transferred to the Document Center, along with the business reference sources (LC classes HB through HJ, and selected other titles). The librarians spent several months cross-training each other on the unfamiliar areas of their specialties: for example, teaching investment sources to some, and legislative documents to others. In the common areas, however, librarians were astonished to discover how much the others' resources reinforced and enriched their own.

The successful integration of Business Information service with Government Documents served as a model for the integration of the Map Collection in 2000. Established as a separate branch collection in 1967, the Map Collection had outgrown its available space in rooms near the Geography Department. With well over 700,000 cartographic items, new space for the map library was needed and found in the Document Center. As the Map Collection is a depository for several U.S. and state mapping programs, a combination of maps and government documents seemed a happy union. The Libraries also believed that locating the map collection in the Document Center would improve service by broadening the potential base of users, providing more staffing flexibility, and extending hours of opening.

COMBINATIONS OF GOVERNMENT DOCUMENTS REFERENCE SERVICE: A SURVEY

The Question

When the authors began thinking about this paper, they started with the assumption that the University of Oregon Libraries was unique in that it offered reference service dealing with Government Documents, Maps, and Business Information from one department and service point. To informally test this assumption, the authors sent an identical message to five e-mail lists, which were available to the library community. The message asked readers to indicate if their institution offered

> any specified library reference structures that combine government documents, maps, or business reference in any of the following combinations listed below, but not in a general reference setting.

The combinations listed were:

1. ____ Government and business reference
2. ____ Government and maps
3. ____ Business and maps
4. ____ Government, business and maps

The message was sent to Govinfo, GIS4LIB, Maps-L, Carta, and Libref-L in late May and early June 2003.

The Results

In a matter of hours of distributing the question via the listservs, responses began to be received. In total, the authors received thirty-nine responses from academic libraries across the United States. The responses were then broken down into the following categories:

1. ____Government and business reference **(6/39 responses)**

2. ____ Government and maps   **(22/39 responses)**

3. ____ Business and maps   **(0/39 responses)**

() ____ Not Applicable   **(7/39 responses)**

4. ____ Government, business and maps **(3/39 responses)**

As expected, the results confirmed our belief that we had a unique combination of Reference resources and service.

1. ____ Government and business reference **(6/39 responses)**

From a total of 39 responses, 6 institutions indicated that they offered Government and Business information services from one service point, but not maps.

2. ____ Government and maps   **(22/39 responses)**

The combination of Government Documents and Maps was, as expected, the most common among respondents with 22 of 39 institutions reporting this combination.

3. ____ Business and maps   **(0/39 responses)**

As expected, no institution reported that they were offering Business Information services and Map Reference exclusively.

() ____ Not Applicable   **(7/39 responses)**

Several respondents fell outside our criteria of Government Documents, Maps, and Business and were placed into a "Not Applicable" category. These included some responses, which indicated that Government Publications and Map Reference Service were being offered as part of a General Reference service. Another response highlighted an interesting combination of Government Documents, Maps, and Law materials. One other respondent indicated that they would be shortly merging Government Documents and Business Information services, while another institution indicated that they were moving in the opposite direction by separating their collections and service points.

4. ____ Government, business and maps **(3/39 responses)**

In total, only three of the thirty-nine institutions who responded indicated that they had a combination of Government Documents, Business Information, and Maps. Nevertheless, upon further research it was found that the three institutions were doing something that was in fact quite different from the Oregon experience. One library in the Midwest indicated that they were creating a new Data Services Librarian position, which would assist in each of the Government Documents, Maps, and Business subject areas. Nevertheless, reference for each area would continue from the General Reference Desk.

A California library also noted that they provided Government Information and Business Information from the same General Reference Desk. Maps and GIS service are provided from a separate reference desk. The third respondent based in the southeast did not return a follow-up message, but their Web site indicated that all three collections were all served from a General Reference Desk with a Data Librarian helping with GIS questions.

Based on these service descriptions provided by these libraries, it seems apparent that they offer something quite different from the Documents experience at the University of Oregon. In other words, the authors are correct in their initial assumption: the combination of Government Documents, Business Information, and Maps/GIS service at the University of Oregon Libraries is something unique among academic libraries.

WORKING TOGETHER:
A NEW KIND OF SERVICE MODEL FOR GOVERNMENT
DOCUMENTS, BUSINESS INFORMATION, AND MAPS

Since 2001, the University of Oregon Libraries Document Center has provided specialized reference service for Government Documents, Maps, and Business Information. The Document Center librarians encounter specific questions for these areas on a daily basis. The expertise and knowledge of the subject specialists are important factors in providing reference services. A collaborative and cooperative approach from each of the librarians has only increased the quality level of our services.

In examining the success of merging these distinct subject areas, one cannot overemphasize both the role of training and the importance of clear communication. In many libraries, questions involving Government Documents, Business, or Maps are often seen as troublesome and difficult to answer effectively. Bringing the three services together has made the necessity of training particularly acute. All librarians in the Document Center were trained to provide reference services at a strong basic level in each of the three areas. The initial objective with any inquiry is to at least get the patrons started in their research. When reference inquiries become complex and subject specific, they are referred as promptly as possible to the subject specialist in that area. We brief each other on the sources used to answer that particular question. When useful resources are found on the Web, they are linked to the Document Center Web site.

Additional training also occurs through the academic year. Usually once per year, often before the beginning of fall term, a lengthy training session is conducted in which each librarian will bring others up to date on new or updated print and electronic resources for their subject areas. Refresher sessions in using the best resources are also done periodically through the year so that staff can achieve and maintain a high comfort level in these particular areas. For example, the Map Librarian will learn more about changes to Congressional Universe, while Government Documents Librarians will then find out more about additions to the Sanborn Map Database and the Business Librarian will instruct Document Center staff on the latest Business database.

While the Subject Specialists in the Document Center each have their particular areas, the range of questions, electronic resources, and technology have provided all staff with many excellent opportunities for collaboration in reference, collection development, and instruction sessions. The benefits of such cooperation have benefited not only individual staff, but also the patrons who bring their questions to the desk or attend a Library instruction session. Students and members of the community are often exposed to additional resources and technologies that they may not have encountered before. The Business Librarian, for example, has exposed Business students to GIS by bringing traditional business data found in spreadsheets and reports and mapping them for the first time. The Map/GIS Librarian, in turn, has provided GIS presentations to Business classes, demonstrating the power of technology and data and how it can help ambitious entrepreneurs. Reaction to such presentations has always been overwhelmingly positive. Following the presentations, students always linger with questions and often come back to the library to engage the technology for their research. Such presentations have allowed non-geography students, perhaps for the first time, to re-conceptualize their projects in geospatial terms.

Collaboration has occurred not only between the Business and Map Librarians. It has also worked well between the Business and Government Documents specialists. Questions involving international trade and taxation are frequent, especially from business students. With both the Business and Government Documents Librarians together in one department and with the collections close at hand, students could access both expertise and the necessary materials. For example, a student project on the importation of T-shirts from Thailand to the United States needed to consult both Industry Reports on the Apparel industry in the United States, but also documents and data (tariffs and tax rates) released from the United States International Trade Commission.

In some cases, Maps, Business, and Government Documents come together to answer questions. Often student projects relating to statistics are involved. For example, a student working on a project involving single-parent families in the United States needed comparative international data. Documents and Web sites were found which contained reliable international statistics on families. The data could in fact be downloaded and placed in a GIS, where the students could make their own maps for the project.

Keys for Collaboration: Useful Reference Resources That Can Be Used for Documents, Maps, and Business Information Questions	
Business and Documents	**Examples:**
Regulation of businesses	Documents from U.S. Securities and Exchange Commission; Congressional Documents.
International trade statistics	Yearbooks produced by agencies such as the United Nations and the World Trade Organization.
Domestic labor, commerce, industry statistics	Documents from the Federal and State Labor agencies. U.S. Census Statistics
Patents	U.S. Patent and Trademark Annual publications; USPTO database currently available online.
Census data (both economic and population censuses)	U.S. Census Data available in print and online.
Documents and Maps	**Examples:**
Depository programs (map sources)	USGS Topographic base mapping available in both print and digital format
Environmental studies	Environmental Assessments conducted by local agencies using historic, current and projected mapping information.

Documents and Maps	Examples:
Climate and weather data	National Weather Reports available in print and online for researchers.
Maps included in government reports	Maps illustrating new government initiatives such as mineral exploration forest management initiatives.
U.S. Serial Set maps	Maps produced for Congressional reports; many historic maps of the United States and its development can be found in any Serial Set collection.
Attribute data for GIS applications	Statistical data produced by government agencies. Census data, forest fire data, etc.
Maps and Business	**Examples:**
Business-related attribute data for GIS applications	Business data such as address information, # of employees, revenue, parking spaces. All can be analyzed and compared with competitors.
GIS support of business decisions such as retail or plant location	Location decisions based on demographic information of the target market (age, income) and location of competitors.
Land use history for land development decisions	Using aerial photos, historic and current maps as well as GIS, developers can trace the history of a chosen site for a project and make the appropriate decisions regarding clean up, suitability, etc.

The presence of Government Documents, Business Information, and Maps/GIS in one department has also allowed for greater flexibility and even creativity in collection development. Like many institutions, the University of Oregon Libraries has had to balance shrinking acquisition budgets with the rising costs of monographs, serials, and electronic resources. Making the situation particularly challenging is the growing inter-disciplinary aspect of many subject areas. Despite such complexity, however, the multifaceted approach taken by the Document Center staff in answering patron questions has also now been applied to collection development. For example, resources pertaining to United States Census data, including geospatial data, are often joint purchases from Maps, Government Documents, and Business funds. Serial cancellation decisions have also benefited from closer consultations about cross-disciplinary use of business and geography journals.

Perhaps the most interesting and potentially rich area for collaboration has come from Library Instruction opportunities. Along with bringing GIS to Business students, the GIS Librarian has also worked with the Government Documents Librarian in a number of credit courses. The University of Oregon Libraries offers a credit class in "Government Information" taught by the Government Documents Librarians. As Maps, GIS, and other geographic information materials were available as a service from the Document Center desk, it only seemed natural that a "map" component be added to the Government Information course. To this end, the Map/GIS Librarian presented a class on geographic information materials produced by government agencies. This included printed maps available through the depository program, and also digital data and aerial photographs available from federal, state, and local governmental bodies. While only one class was used for this purpose, it was clear from the reaction of the students and the breadth of geographic information resources that additional classes could be added to examine this dynamic aspect of Government Information.

The opportunities for collaboration in instruction are also available in areas that are not natural fits for either Government Documents or Maps. In 2003, the University of Oregon History Department began offering a course on the "European Union as History." As the Document Center had been a depository for European Union documents for several years, the instructor for the course approached the Government Documents Librarians for assistance in identifying useful materials for the course. At the instigation of the Document Center Librarians, a course Web site was soon established with both research resources and weekly readings available. The course also became a model for the Libraries' Information Literacy program and sought to instruct the students on the core competencies on information literacy. As the Web site developed, a mapping component was added and the GIS Librarian developed maps using existing geographic data to create maps of Europe highlighting specific course themes such as the History of the European Union from its infancy in the 1950s to the present, and countries that have adopted the Euro currency. Over the next several years, the mapping component can be developed into an interactive Web mapping tool using existing datasets made available by Document Center staff.

CONCLUSION

Many libraries have undertaken restructuring in recent years. In many cases, such a reorganization of services has involved an integration of Government Documents Reference Service with General Reference service. In several cases, reorganization has been limited to combining Government Documents and Maps Reference Service. Very few libraries have integrated Government Documents, Maps, and Business Information into one service point. In fact, based on an informal poll, the University of Oregon Libraries may in fact be the only library that has such a unique service point.

Despite offering such a diverse collection of resources and reference expertise, the Document Center librarians have found that the combination of resources has opened new and exciting collaborative opportunities. With the help of annual training sessions and periodic refreshers, the quality of reference service continues to be enhanced. This collaboration has also been extended to collection development strategies and library instruction programming.

With fast developing technologies such as the Internet and GIS, the potential for Document Center librarians at the University of Oregon to undertake exciting new initiatives is almost limitless. While training is certainly a key component when integrating collections into one service point, the University of Oregon experience indicates that it is also very important to foster a collaborative spirit. Moreover, it is especially crucial that staff involved in such a merger continue to build on the advantages and opportunities that are created. These include offering new and enhanced reference services; collaborative approaches to collection development and library instruction; and perhaps, most importantly, developing new outreach strategies for reaching new users across campus and in the local community.

NOTES

1. Nicole Urquhart. The Effects on Government Documents Reference Service as a Result of a Merger between the Government Documents Department and the Reference Department in an Academic Library. Master's Thesis. University of North Carolina, 2002.

2. Philip E. Van de Voorde. "Should reference service for U.S. government publications and general reference be merged? A case study." Government Publications Review. Vol. 16, pp. 247-257, 1989.

3. Ben Amata. "Shotgun weddings and amicable divorces: Integration vs. separation of government documents and reference services. Papers presented at a GODORT program at the 1994 ALA Conference." Documents to the People. Vol. 24 (March 1996) pp. 54-57.

4. One of the best is Priscilla Cheng Geahigan. "Government sources for business reference inquiries." Reference Librarian. Vol. 32 (1991) pp. 85-138.

5. Juris Dilevko. "'My Mother can't quite understand why I decided to go to library school': What patrons say about library staff when asking government documents reference questions at depository libraries." Journal of Government Information. Vol. 27 (2000), pp. 299-323.

6. Ibid. p. 307. The aerial photo question was one of fifteen questions asked at Depository libraries throughout Canada through late 1997 and early 1998. The aerial photo question was as follows:

My mother's birthday is coming soon, and I want to order a color enlargement of an aerial photograph of the lake where my parents have their summer cottage as her present. Could I have a price list for the enlargements, and information about what I need to order such a photograph?

7. Joan K. Lippincott and Joan F. Cheverie. "The 'blur' of federal information and services: Implications for university libraries." Journal of Government Information. Vol. 26, No. 1 (1999) pp. 25-31.

8. For the Technical Services perspective, please see: Karen H. Wilhoit. "To merge or not to merge–What are the questions? Integrating documents into reference or technical services: Highlights of the GODORT program at the 1999 ALA Conference." Library Collections, Acquisitions, and Technical Services. Vol. 24, No. 2 (Summer 2000) pp. 310-11.

Libraries in the Aftermath of 9/11

Georgina Martorella

SUMMARY. Libraries are a symbol of a free, democratic society. Open access to information and patron privacy allow intellectual inquiry and the creation of new knowledge. Librarians have a long tradition of protecting these liberties. In the wake of the terrorist attacks of September 11, concerns have been raised that the passage of the USA Patriot Act and other anti-terrorism measures threaten these liberties. Librarians need to educate staff, users, and their communities as to the impact these measures have on libraries and access to information. Policies, procedures, and guidelines need to be developed that balance the traditions of intellectual freedom and issues of national security. This article examines access to government information issues and threats to

Georgina Martorella is Assistant Professor and Government Documents Librarian, 123 Hofstra University, 210A Axinn Library, Hempstead, NY 11549 (E-mail: libdcgdm@hofstra.edu).

[Haworth co-indexing entry note]: "Libraries in the Aftermath of 9/11." Martorella, Georgina. Co-published simultaneously in *The Reference Librarian* (The Haworth Information Press, an imprint of The Haworth Press, Inc.) No. 94, 2006, pp. 109-137; and: *The Changing Face of Government Information: Providing Access in the Twenty-First Century* (ed: Suhasini L. Kumar) The Haworth Information Press, an imprint of The Haworth Press, Inc., 2006, pp. 109-137. Single or multiple copies of this article are available for a fee from The Haworth Document Delivery Service [1-800-HAWORTH, 9:00 a.m. - 5:00 p.m. (EST). E-mail address: docdelivery@haworthpress.com].

patron privacy and confidentiality of patron records resulting from the passage of the USA Patriot Act. *[Article copies available for a fee from The Haworth Document Delivery Service: 1-800-HAWORTH. E-mail address: <docdelivery@haworthpress.com> Website: <http://www.HaworthPress.com> © 2006 by The Haworth Press, Inc. All rights reserved.]*

KEYWORDS. Patriot Act, intellectual freedom, Freedom of Information Act, homeland security, libraries, Presidential Records Act, critical infrastructure, Foreign Intelligence Surveillance Act

INTRODUCTION

Libraries are a symbol of a free, democratic society. Open access to information and patron privacy allow intellectual inquiry, participation in a democratic society, and the creation of new knowledge for the advancement of society. Librarians have a long tradition of protecting these liberties. Intellectual freedom, a core value of libraries in this country, is defined by the American Library Association (ALA) as the right to express one's ideas and the rights of others to hear them. Intellectual freedom is guaranteed by the freedoms of speech and press in the Constitution and forms the basis for a democratic society because it is an essential part of government by the people–the right to vote is not enough–citizens need to take part in the formation of public opinion by debating on controversial matters.[1] Every person has the right to seek and obtain the information required, without fear, so that ideas can be examined from all sides in order to form his or her own opinion. ALA vigorously upholds the principles of intellectual freedom by opposing censorship and supporting free access to library materials and the privacy and confidentiality of patron records. The concept of privacy, or the right to open inquiry free from examination by others, is crucial to intellectual inquiry. People must have the ability to freely express opinions without fear of intimidation, reprisal, or punishment. It is only when that freedom exists–that they can examine, explore, conduct research, draw conclusions and make judgements–that new knowledge is created. "The privacy of library users is and must be inviolable."[2]

Judith Krug, the director of the ALA Office for Intellectual Freedom, states that "[democracy] assumes that the best guarantee of effective and continuing self-government is a thoroughly informed electorate capable of making real choices. Denying the opportunity of choice for fear it may be used unwisely destroys freedom itself."[3] If people are expected to participate in the democratic process and make these choices, they must be well informed. Libraries play a vital role in this democratic process by providing unrestricted access to the information required by people to be better informed. According to Robin Rice, "Intellectual freedom, expressed not only as the freedom of expression and opinion, but particularly as the freedom to read and be informed, is a creed built into the very profession of librarianship, taught alongside the rules of cataloging and the art of conducting a reference interview."[4] Rice also points out that librarians traditionally have been strong defenders of the First Amendment to the Constitution, which protects individuals' freedom of speech and citizens' right to assemble as well as freedom of the press. Library policies support this tradition by allowing public groups to use meeting rooms in library buildings, opposing censorship, and protecting patron confidentiality.[5] In response to concerns that the passage of the USA Patriot Act and other anti-terrorism measures taken in the aftermath of September 11 threaten these liberties, ALA issued a resolution "Reaffirming the Principles of Intellectual Freedom in the Aftermath of the Terrorist Attacks." The resolution, passed in January, 2002 stated, "ALA believes that freedom of expression is an inalienable human right necessary to self-government, vital to the resistance of oppression, and crucial to the cause of justice, and further, that the principles of freedom of expression should be applied by libraries and librarians throughout the world."[6]

This article will examine changes to public information policy resulting from the terrorist attacks and subsequent passage of the USA Patriot Act that affect access to government information as well as threats to patron privacy and confidentiality. The federal government undertook other actions that many feel seriously threaten civil liberties but are beyond the scope of this article. These actions affect access to information on terrorist and immigration proceedings, restrictions placed on biochemicals and toxic agents research, restrictions placed on foreign students and scholars, restrictions placed on journalists covering the wars in Afghanistan and Iraq, and the use of military tribunals. This article will not cover information-gathering programs such as the Total Information Awareness Program, the Terrorist Threat Integration Center, and Operation Tips.

ACCESS TO GOVERNMENT INFORMATION
AFTER SEPTEMBER 11

The very nature and success of a democratic system of government relies on a citizenry that has the information to make informed decisions necessary to participate in a government by the people. Information produced by the government at public expense also needs to be accessible so that the government may be held accountable for its actions. Free and open access to government information safeguards the public's "right to know." Congress established the Federal Depository Library Program (FDLP) in 1813 to provide the public with access to this information. It serves as a guardian of public information, and in that role, collects, organizes, and provides access to government information in all formats. Federal Depository librarians support an information policy that assures fairness, accountability, privacy, security, reliability, and efficiency as well as the preservation of the public record.[7] Many statutes have been enacted in support of these ideals, especially the Freedom of Information Act (FOIA) and its amendments. Government information policy during the 1990s supported proactive dissemination of information to ensure free public access and support the concept of open government. Since September 11, the public's right to know has been threatened. This section will examine government information policy concerning the implementation of FOIA, the Department of Homeland Security, the Presidential Records Act, and the removal of government information from agency Web sites.

Freedom of Information and Electronic Government

Freedom of information supports the principles of open government by providing public access to information regarding government activities, allocation of public resources, results of publicly funded research, the enforcement of laws and regulations, and encourages participation in these processes. Thomas Susman points out that an open government will perform better; the quality of government decisions will benefit from public input and those affected by decisions, regulations, orders, or laws will understand them better and be more apt to obey them if they are part of the process.[8] Government information that is created with public monies belongs to the public, and unless the public would suffer harm from disclosure, access should remain open. According to Laura Gordon-Murnane, the "Bush administration has had to deal with a threat unseen by previous administrations. One of the greatest challenges this administration will face is how to safeguard the American public from future terrorist attacks, while at the same time providing accountable government, open government, and access to information which lies at the core of American beliefs and values."[9]

The Freedom of Information Act (FOIA),[10] enacted in 1966, recognized the rights of Americans to access government agency documents and records. The purpose of FOIA was to create government transparency, thereby holding the government accountable to the public. It created procedures by which ordinary citizens could obtain agency records. The strength of FOIA lies in the presumption that all government records are open to the public except those excluded by law, it is not necessary to show need of the information, and all citizens have equal rights under FOIA. FOIA applies only to executive branch agencies and cabinet level departments. The types of information available under FOIA include agency records describing their actions, how they comply with various laws, how they spend money allocated by Congress, and reports on topics covered by that agency. Agency records on individual citizens allow those citizens access to records that relate to themselves and allow them to change, correct, or amend information that is outdated or no longer accurate. Government officials are allowed to deny requesters information based on the following nine exemptions:

- National security
- Internal Agency Rules (personnel procedures and practices)
- Information governed by other statutes
- Business information such as trade secrets
- Internal government agency memos
- Private files and materials such as personnel and medical information
- Law enforcement investigations
- Reports from regulated financial institutions
- Oil and gas drilling information[11]

Journalists use FOIA to do a better job of keeping their readers informed and educated by obtaining unclassified government records that officials might not otherwise release. Historians, scientists, and scholars use FOIA to show abuse, fraud, waste, and other government wrongdoing, and to gain access to research undertaken by the federal government. FOIA is also used to understand the workings and decision-making processes of government agencies. According to Thomas Blanton, Director of the National Security Archive at George Washington University,

FOIA "ranks as the most heavily invoked access law in the world. In 2000, the U.S. federal government received more than 2 million FOIA requests."[12]

Three major developments in information policy that increased open access to government occurred during the Clinton administration. These developments were Attorney General Janet Reno's FOIA policy, the Paperwork Reduction Act of 1995, and the Electronic Freedom of Information Act. In 1993, then Attorney General Janet Reno renewed government support of FOIA by rescinding a 1981 rule that "encouraged federal agencies to withhold information whenever there was a substantial legal basis for doing so."[13] The new policy, as outlined in Reno's memo, strongly recommended disclosure whenever possible and encouraged agencies to increase the amount of information released to the public. From 1996 to 2000, the Clinton administration declassified and released 795 million pages of government information under this new FOIA standard.[14]

The administration saw in the growth of the Internet another opportunity to increase open government. Electronic dissemination of government information would make the government more accountable and responsive to the needs of the public. Federal agencies, executive departments, and congressional committees began to disseminate information electronically. Legislation was enacted that moved the government away from a paper-based information policy to an electronic one, now known as "e-government." According to Gordon-Murnane, the Paperwork Reduction Act of 1995[15] was the impetus for e-government because it used technology as a way to make the government more responsive to the needs of the public. The goal was to simplify the process of doing business with the federal government. In effect, it changed policy by making government information more accessible, timely, and efficient. The federal government developed a set of guidelines, the National Information Infrastructure (NII) that allowed agencies to replace paper and microfiche distribution with electronic dissemination. It reduced paper and printing costs and widened dissemination.[16]

The Electronic Freedom of Information Act (E-FOIA)[17] was signed into law by President Clinton on October 2, 1998. It expanded the definition of a record to include electronic records and documents, databases, word-processed documents, and e-mail. E-FOIA effectively broadened the scope of FOIA and allowed the public access to a wider selection of government information. The law required the development of agency e-reading rooms, the creation of electronic FOIA reference guides, and publication of an annual FOIA report.

The Paperwork Reduction Act and E-FOIA, along with GPO Access (the official Web site of the Government Printing Office and government information portal),[18] has created a system of e-government that helps agencies carry out their missions more efficiently and brings convenience of government services to the public. However, the most important benefits of e-government are that government can be held accountable to the public because of increased access to government information.

In contrast to the actions of the Clinton administration, after the terrorist attacks of 9/11, the Bush administration began to take steps to shift information policy from one of openness to one of secrecy. Two memos to government agency heads effectively changed FOIA policy: a directive from Attorney General John Ashcroft and a memo from White House Chief of Staff, Andrew Card. On October 12, 2001, Ashcroft released a memo that changed government information policy with respect to FOIA. The memo stated, "Any discretionary decision by your agency to disclose information protected under FOIA should be made only after full and deliberate consideration of the institutional, commercial, and personal privacy interests that could be implicated. . . . Access to information must be balanced with other issues, including national security. . . ."[19] The Ashcroft memo also states that agencies that legally withhold information will have the full backing of the Justice Department. This is a shift from Reno's policy that advised officials to release records unless disclosure would result in foreseeable harm. Reno's policy promoted disclosure where possible while Ashcroft's policy promotes withholding information where possible. The new policy creates an atmosphere of secrecy hiding behind privacy issues. Ashcroft not only states the issue as one of national security but also directs officials to keep in mind institutional and individual privacy issues. This is unnecessary given that FOIA already provides privacy exemptions. According to Martin E. Halstuk, the purpose of the privacy exemption is to protect individuals; it is not meant to shield the activities of the government. Halstuk proposes that "rather than cast a cloak of confidentiality over all government records that may raise privacy issues, a better solution is for agencies to use a balancing test that weighs–case by case–the social and public benefits of disclosure against the individual value of privacy."[20] The intent of FOIA is to provide the public with the information it needs; the Ashcroft policy places a barrier between the public and such information. Martin D. Snyder surmises that the Ashcroft memo "seems to be part of a strategy to enhance federal secrecy. Both conservative and liberal public interest groups have complained that the administration's penchant for with-holding information has become routine."[21]

On January 13, 2002, William Broad of the *New York Times* pub-lished an article that described how anyone could order bioweapons "cookbooks" from the government; documents that had been declassi-fied years earlier.[22] In response, White House Chief of Staff Andrew Card, in March 2002, issued a memo to agency heads ordering them to review procedures for protecting information pertaining to weapons of mass destruction and report their results to the Office of Homeland Se-curity. He cautioned officials to carefully consider the need to protect "sensitive but unclassified" information from disclosure, thereby creat-ing a new category of information. The memo also directs agencies to keep classified information classified if it "would reveal information that would assist in the development or use of weapons of mass destruc-tion" even if it is older than ten years. Under the current classification order, Executive Order 12958, 1995, documents are usually declassi-fied after ten years–this can be extended up to twenty-five years if there is a need to keep the information classified. The memo instructs agen-cies to protect weapons information older than twenty-five years wher-ever possible. The Card order states that FOIA requests should be processed in accordance with the Ashcroft directive "by giving full and careful consideration to all applicable FOIA exemptions."[23] The intent of the previous classification order was to avoid too much classification of government materials and required that where there is doubt about whether information should be classified then it should not be classified. Card's memo is in opposition to this policy. The memo leaves the term "sensitive but unclassified" undefined and subject to broad interpreta-tion.

Withholding information from terrorists also withholds the informa-tion from the public. Documents such as bioweapons "cookbooks" clearly should be withheld; they should be reevaluated and reclassified. But it is the less obvious type of information that causes consternation among information professionals. The Card memo, by creating a new category of "sensitive but unclassified" information, leaves open the possibility that other types of information that should be available to the public will be withheld (e.g., information describing chemical or other toxic threats to the environment, risk assessment management, and emergency preparedness plans). FOIA entitles the public to learn about the weaknesses of government and allows the public to lobby for change. Sensitive information in the wrong hands can be disastrously harmful but an uninformed public does not have the tools needed to promote change. It is not yet clear how these policy changes will affect implementation of FOIA. In addition to changes to FOIA policy, access to government information was also affected by the creation of the Department of Homeland Security and the removal of government information from agency Web sites.

The Department of Homeland Security and Critical Infrastructure Information

After the events of September 11, it became imperative for the government to look at ways of protecting the nation's critical infrastructure. The Homeland Security Act of 2002[24] was signed into law on November 25, 2002. Title II of the Act states that information voluntarily submitted to the Department of Homeland Security (DHS) that deals with critical infrastructure is exempted from disclosure under FOIA. Critical infrastructure information deals with national power, transportation, health, and telecommunications systems. Once this information is disclosed to the DHS, it cannot be used in litigation against the company. Also, if officials do disclose critical infrastructure information, they could be subject to up to a year of imprisonment, fines, and dismissal. However, the bill makes no distinction between information that could be withheld based on protecting the infrastructure and information that should be disclosed in order to protect the public. A company could release information to the DHS regarding a system weakness vulnerable to terrorists or an environmental report that exposes a danger to the public. DHS would have the obligation to keep this information secret, even from state and local officials. As Rebecca Daugherty, director of the FOI Service Center at the Reporters Committee for Freedom of the Press stated, "Exempting critical infrastructure information from disclosure could hide potentially serious flaws. One of the best ways to solve a problem is to put a lot of eyes on it. But if the problem only belongs to industry, or industry and government–and other people aren't allowed to see it, then you diminish the number of people who could help you solve that problem."[25] Critics of the new legislation argue that critical infrastructure information is already adequately protected by FOIA exemptions.

Presidential Records Act

The records of former Presidents make up a critical part of our nation's history. Under the Presidential Records Act of 1978, presidential records become public property after twelve years, subject to FOIA exemptions. This act also creates a release schedule to be followed. Reagan later issued Executive Order 12667 that requires the archivist at the National Archives (who monitors the disclosure and holds the records before release) to notify the sitting president about pending disclosure. On November 1, 2001 President George W. Bush, through an executive order (EO 13233), changed the way these records are released; however, it should be noted that the administration had begun looking at this process in January 2001, before the terrorists attacked. Bush's order could effectively seal the records for an undetermined amount of time and allows both a former president and incumbent to stop the release of records even after twelve years. The records that President Bush did not want to release were those of former President Ronald Reagan; 68,000 pages were due for release on January 20, 2001. Lawsuits were filed by historians and journalists and, as a result, some, but not all of the Reagan records have been released. Until the case is settled, the NARA archivist is abiding by the Bush order. If the order stands, public access to presidential history will be seriously compromised.

Agency Response to Government Information Policy

After September 11, government agencies began to rethink what information should be made available in light of the terrorist attacks and feared that information posted on the Web for the American public could easily get into the hands of international terrorists. A number of agencies made changes to their Web sites. For example, the Nuclear Regulatory Commission, one of the first agencies to offer a public reading room, shut down its site in response to a request from the Department of Defense. The site is now back up and selected information is available. Other agencies removed information from their sites. The Federal Aviation Administration removed information on enforcement actions as well as a database that is used to identify security breaches at airports. The Department of Transportation discontinued access to the National Pipeline Mapping System; however, access was provided to government officials and pipeline operators. The Environmental Protection Agency removed risk management plans required by the Clean Air Act and other "worst case scenario" information. The Agency for Toxic Substances and Disease Registry removed a report that rated security at chemical plants, and the National Imagery and Mapping Agency stopped selling large-scale digital maps through the Web. Other agencies that removed information include the Department of Energy, the

Geological Survey, the National Archives and Records Administration, the Internal Revenue Service, and the NASA Glenn Research Center. Agencies shifted from releasing information on a "right to know" basis to a "need to know" basis. In some cases, notices were posted on the Web that the information had been removed due to the terrorist threat.[26]

On October 12, 2001, the Government Printing Office (GPO), at the request of the U.S. Geological Survey, asked Federal Depository libraries to destroy CD-ROMs containing details of surface water supplies in the U.S. Although the GPO had recalled information from depositories in the past when it was incorrect or outdated, it had never before recalled information because of a policy decision to withhold it. The resulting order caused concern in the library community, especially since FBI agents visited several Arkansas depositories to make sure they were complying with the order and to ask questions about who had previously used the CDs. The CDs were destroyed but the information is stored on databases and still available from the U.S.G.S.

When agency officials assess online public access to information, they need to determine the importance of having the information publicly available as well as what the dangers are if it is not. Before removing entire Web sites, agencies' officials can determine if there are ways to remove only that information that may have national security implications. If information is to be removed, it is important to maintain bibliographic records of the information for future access and keep account of what is being removed. It is necessary to preserve the information elsewhere and make it accessible and retrievable.

Librarians, as well as other information professionals, are working within their professional organizations to develop federal information principles to help guide current and future administrations in developing clear information dissemination policies. These principles are based on the concept that the public has a right to freely and openly access government information and the government has an obligation to provide this access, guarantee its integrity, and safeguard the privacy and confidentiality of users of public information. It is also a responsibility of the government to preserve this information, as it is an important part of the historical record, and keep this information in the public domain.[27]

The terrorist attacks of 9/11 made us vulnerable and open access to government information suffered. Issues of national security are very real; however, these issues must be weighed against the public's right to be informed.

PATRON PRIVACY AND CONFIDENTIALITY

Many in the library community are concerned with the potential impact on patron privacy and the confidentiality of library records stemming from the enactment of the Uniting and Strengthening America by Providing Appropriate Tools Required to Intercept and Obstruct Terrorism, commonly known as the Patriot Act.[28] The legislation is intended to provide the government with stronger tools to fight terrorism by strengthening existing federal surveillance and law enforcement powers. It also removes communication barriers that previously existed between law enforcement agencies and intelligence agencies. As the Electronic Privacy Information Center (EPIC) points out, it does not provide for the traditional checks and balances that protect civil liberties[29] and many question the impact of the legislation on intellectual freedom.

The Patriot Act consists of ten titles that amend fifteen existing federal statutes and deals with activities ranging from foreign surveillance, money laundering, and providing relief and support to victims. The Act also creates new federal crimes, increases the penalties for existing crimes, and modifies immigration laws. Many of the provisions are problematic to those who are dedicated to library patron privacy and confidentiality. These areas include the enhanced ability of the government to conduct electronic surveillance and access personal records, secrecy clauses, and the lack of information provided by the government needed to assess the efficacy of these measures. Some of these provisions were being considered before 9/11.

According to Senator Russell Feingold, many provisions relating to electronic surveillance had been previously proposed but seriously questioned as to their impact on civil liberties. Members of Congress were concerned that expanded surveillance powers could open the door to abuse by law enforcement and intelligence agencies.[30] In the aftershock of September 11, with little opportunity for Congress to examine or debate, those provisions were rushed through. Signed into law by President Bush merely six weeks after the attacks on the World Trade Center and the Pentagon, the Patriot Act was passed rapidly and with little debate.

Although many of the provisions of the Patriot Act are needed to protect against future acts of terrorism, many in the library community are greatly concerned that those provisions that expand law enforcement surveillance powers and access to records do not achieve an acceptable balance between national security concerns and civil liberties. The laws governing surveillance, as they existed prior to the Patriot Act, will be discussed to establish a framework for the ensuing discussion of those provisions affecting patron privacy and confidentiality of library records.

Surveillance Powers of the Federal Government: Pre-Patriot Act

Government interception of communications in criminal cases historically has been treated differently than in foreign intelligence cases. In criminal investigations, interception of communications is governed by a system consisting of three statutes that reflect the level of content of communications sought. The higher the level of content, the more stringent the requirements are to obtain the appropriate legal authority. Title III (the Wiretap Statute) of the Omnibus Crime Control and Safe Streets Act of 1968,[31] the most stringent of the statutes, governs the interception of real time content of voice and electronic communications. A Title III order, or wiretap order, requires a showing of probable cause that the target of the investigation is in the process of committing, has committed, or is about to commit one of several specifically listed serious crimes. Less stringent is the Electronic Communications Privacy Act (ECPA)[32] that governs law enforcement access to communications stored on electronic networks, such as electronic mail (e-mail). Law enforcement can obtain a warrant, court order, or a subpoena to access these records in connection with any criminal investigation. Again, the type of authority required is based on the level of content sought. Least stringent is the Pen Register Statute[33] that governs federal law enforcement's use of trap and trace devices and pen registers (devices that track the source and destinations of telephone calls made to and from a particular telephone). An order for a pen register/trap and trace installation does not require probable cause. The government agency applying for the order need only certify that the "information likely to be obtained is relevant to an ongoing criminal investigation"; there is no judicial discretion, and the court must authorize the surveillance.

The Foreign Intelligence Surveillance Act (FISA)[34] governs surveillance activities that are connected to foreign intelligence gathering or counterintelligence activities. FISA was a reaction to government abuse of wiretapping and other forms of electronic means used to spy on United States citizens in the name of national security during the 1960s and 1970s. It was intended to erect a wall between criminal investigations and foreign intelligence investigations. The purpose of the wall was to provide Fourth Amendment protections in criminal cases but allow the government more extensive powers for foreign intelligence gathering. According to Paul Jaeger, John Carlo Bertot, and Charles McClure,

> FISA created a clear distinction between investigative conduct in domestic criminal investigations and in foreign intelligence investigations. By creating this distinction, FISA served to protect the Fourth Amendment rights of U.S. citizens in criminal investigations, requiring probable cause before a search warrant is issued and preserving freedom from unreasonable search and seizure. Under FISA, these Fourth Amendment protections did not apply in full force in foreign intelligence investigations, allowing law enforcement agencies to get court orders for wiretaps and searches with a much lower standard of proof than required in a criminal investigation. Rather than needing to demonstrate probable cause of criminal activity, a FISA order could be issued by demonstrating that the purpose of the investigation was to gather foreign intelligence information.[35]

The FISA Court (FISC) is a "secret court" that, along with the attorney general, approves or denies the use of electronic surveillance by federal law enforcement for intelligence purposes. The Department of Justice submits an application for a warrant; all evidence, records of the proceedings, and files are sealed and the target is not informed of the investigation. The FBI is required to certify that the purpose of the investigation is the collection of foreign intelligence information. Jaeger, Bertot, and McClure also state that "under FISA, a surveillance warrant generally required the approval of the Attorney General and of a Foreign Intelligence Surveillance Court (FISC). If the subject under surveillance was a U.S. citizen, the warrant was required to include a minimization plan to ensure that reasonable steps were taken to only intercept information related to the investigation. Any information gathered about a U.S. citizen under FISA was of extremely limited use in any other law enforcement investigation and could only be used with the permission of the Attorney General."[36]

Although the FISC was established to provide judicial oversight and guard against abuses of FISA, in actuality, few if any applications are denied. Between 1979 and 1999, the court approved over 11,000 FISA applications and rejected none.[37] The attorney general is required to report semi-annually to House and Senate intelligence committees the total number of applications received, the number granted, modified, or denied for the six month period. Section 208 of the Patriot Act increases the number of FISC judges from seven to eleven and requires that three of these judges reside within twenty miles of Washington, DC. As Tracy Mitrano notes, this may be because the FBI expects the numbers of FISA applications to increase and judges may have to get to Washington on short notice.[38]

A FISA order can be directed against any person, including United States citizens. The legal requirement for obtaining a FISA order is "belief that the target is a foreign power or an agent of a foreign power" and that "the purpose of the surveillance is intelligence gathering." FISA governs the investigation of criminal acts that are suspected of having been backed by a hostile foreign power and fall outside the scope of Fourth Amendment protections from unreasonable searches and seizures.

The Patriot Act modifies statutes governing surveillance in a number of ways. The modifications to FISA, in particular, are extensive but it is not clear what impact these changes will have. According to Jaeger, Bertot, and McClure, the Patriot Act has "created a large volume of legal scholarship devoted to trying to discern the meanings of the changes to FISA."[39] Furthermore, as the Reporters Committee for Freedom of the Press states, "Congress is kept in the dark about how the FISC is interpreting the provisions of the Patriot Act. The court is not required to reveal its legal opinions, thereby establishing a secret body of case law unprecedented in American jurisprudence."[40]

Surveillance Powers of the Federal Government: Post-Patriot Act

The provisions that provide the government with increased access to business records and expand pen register/trap and trace authority have the greatest potential to impact patron privacy and confidentiality of library records. Those provisions, Section 215, Section 214, and Section 216 of the Patriot Act, are discussed.

Prior to the Patriot Act, under FISA, a court order could be granted to FBI officials seeking access to certain records in connection with foreign intelligence investigations and were limited to the records of common carriers, storage facilities, car rental agencies, and public accommodations (hotel and motel records). Section 215 of the Patriot Act expands the definition of records obtainable under a FISA order to include "any tangible thing" (e.g., books, records, papers, documents, and other items) which could include library circulation records as well as Internet use records. Officials need only certify that the items sought are related to an investigation to "obtain foreign intelligence information not concerning a United States person or to protect against international terrorism or clandestine intelligence activities." This means that the FBI can access any kind of record in any type of format that is "sought for" an authorized investigation even when the owner of such records may not be a suspected terrorist. The section also includes a gag order. Persons presented with a court order to produce records cannot disclose to anyone other than persons necessary to secure the records that the FBI has requested these records and cannot be held liable for the production of the records in any other proceeding. The American Association of University Professors state in their report that this secrecy requirement "makes it impossible to determine what records the government has sought, how searches are conducted and whether the records obtained have helped to protect the nation's security."[41] Section 215 makes an exception to prohibit an investigation of a U.S. person based solely on activities protected by the First Amendment. Although intended to protect U.S. persons, this provision could have serious consequences for innocent non-U.S. persons such as visiting students and scholars who do not meet the criteria for this First Amendment exception. It should be noted that the government always had the ability to access library records if probable cause of criminal activity could be shown. Section 215 now allows the government to access these records without such a showing of probable cause.

Pen registers are devices that are used to identify telephone numbers dialed from a particular telephone. Trap and trace devices are used to identify the source of incoming telephone calls. Before the Patriot Act, these orders only applied to the telephone industry; under the Pen Register Statute, court orders for these devices did not have the same Fourth Amendment protections as wiretap orders. The Supreme Court had not recognized any threats to privacy since no content was revealed.[42] Therefore, it was relatively easy to obtain these orders. Probable cause did not have to be shown, and as long as the government attorney certified that the information sought was likely to be relevant to an ongoing criminal investigation, the order was obtained.

Section 216 of the Act redefines pen registers/trap and trace devices to include Internet communications and allows for the capture of dialing, routing, signaling, and addressing information (e.g., e-mail addresses, IP addresses, and URLs of Web pages visited). Although the provision prohibits the capture of content, more can be learned about an individual by monitoring Web URLs than could previously be learned by mere phone numbers dialed or received. According to Mary Minow, "Critics contend that e-mail addresses and URLs sometimes reveal content and tools intended to 'surgically' separate content from transactional information are imperfect."[43] This provision also paves the way for the authorization of the use of the FBI's controversial electronic monitoring system, Carnivore, a system of hardware and software that captures communications over an Internet Service Provider (ISP). Although intended only to capture communications that are lawfully authorized, an examination of the Carnivore system, performed by the ITT Research Institute (an independent research organization) showed that although Carnivore can perform fine-tuned surgical searches, if incorrectly configured, it can record any traffic it monitors,[44] potentially monitoring the communications of thousands of innocent Americans connected to the ISP. The provision requires law enforcement to report the details of these installations and uses to the issuing court within thirty days of termination of the order, which may provide some judicial review of this expanded authority. The section also allows for a single pen register/trap and trace order to apply to multiple jurisdictions. A gag clause applies to this provision; the person owning or leasing the line to which the device has been attached, or a person ordered to assist in the installation of the device, cannot disclose the existence of the device or the existence of the investigation unless otherwise ordered by the court. Libraries that provide Internet access could easily become the target of such an investigation, and, in some cases, may not be aware of the surveillance.

Prior to the Patriot Act, FISA limited pen register/trap and trace orders to facilities that were used by foreign agents or those engaged in international terrorism or clandestine foreign intelligence activities. Section 214 modifies that requirement to allow the government to obtain pen register/trap and trace orders in those investigations that are likely to reveal information relevant to a foreign intelligence investigation; the target need not be suspected of terrorism or any crime. A gag clause is attached to this section also. As EPIC states in their report, Section 214 "significantly eviscerates the constitutional rationale for the relatively lax requirements that apply to foreign intelligence surveillance. That laxity is premised on the assumption that the Executive Branch, in pursuit of its national security responsibilities to monitor the activities of foreign powers and their agents, should not be unduly restrained by Congress and the courts. The removal of the foreign power predicate for pen register/trap and trace surveillance upsets that delicate balance."[45] Under this section, the definition of pen registers and trap and trace devices also applies to electronic communications. If the FBI gets permission to track a target's Internet use, they are allowed to install hardware and/or software on library computers or to seize those computers used by the target. Again, Section 214 makes an exception to prohibit the use of FISA pen register/trap and trace orders against a United States person solely on the basis of activities protected by the First Amendment.

Other sections of the Patriot Act do not directly impact libraries; however, librarians should be aware of the civil liberties implications of these provisions. These provisions follow:

- *Expanded FISA Authority.* Previously, FISA authority applied to situations where foreign intelligence gathering was "the purpose" of an investigation. Section 218 of the Patriot Act expands this authority to situations where foreign intelligence gathering is a "significant" purpose of an investigation. The term "significant" is not defined by the Act and could be interpreted to mean one of several purposes. This means the lower FISA standards of probable cause can be applied to any investigation that might have some peripheral relationship to foreign intelligence.
- *Voice Mail.* To strengthen privacy protections, voice mail communications stored with third party providers were governed under wiretap statutes. Under section 204, voice mail communications, like e-mail, can now be obtained with a search warrant rather than a wiretap order. In foreign intelligence investigations, the lower standard FISA warrants will provide authorization for obtaining stored voice mail rather than the more stringent wiretap order. Messages stored on home answering machine tapes are not covered under this provision.
- *Sneak and Peek Searches.* Section 213 provides for "sneak and peek" searches to be conducted by law enforcement agencies. As defined by Charles Doyle, a "sneak and peek" search is "one that authorizes officers to secretly enter (physically or electronically), conduct a search, observe, take measurements, conduct exams, take pictures, copy documents, download or transmit, and depart without taking any tangible evidence or leaving notice of their presence."[46] Prior to the Act, a target of a search was provided with contemporaneous notification of the search. Delayed notification was only permitted in a limited amount of circumstances. The provision requires that delayed notice be given within a "reasonable [undefined] period of its execution, which period may thereafter be extended by the court for good cause shown." This provision is not limited to terrorist investigations and threatens Fourth Amend-

ment protections against unlawful searches and seizures. Critics find this provision particularly objectionable. As EPIC states, "The expansion of this extraordinary authority to all searches constitutes a radical departure from Fourth Amendment standards and could result in routine surreptitious entries by law enforcement agents."[47]

- *Roving Wiretap Authority.* Prior to the Patriot Act, investigators needed to identify the specific service (ISP) or telephone company being monitored and secure a new warrant anytime a suspect changed location and/or service. Terrorist suspects and foreign agents are often trained to impede intelligence investigations by changing locations often, causing the investigating officers to take the time to secure new warrants from a FISA court. That is no longer necessary. Section 206 of the Patriot Act amends FISA to allow the court to issue a "roving wiretap" order that can be presented to new common carriers, landlords, or custodians to assure that surveillance takes place as soon as possible. The target of the investigation must still be identified. As analyzed by EPIC, such "generic orders could have a significant impact on the privacy rights of large numbers of innocent users, particularly those who access the Internet through public facilities such as libraries, university computer labs, and cybercafes. Upon the suspicion that an intelligence target might use such a facility, the FBI can now monitor all communications transmitted at the facility."[48]

Section 224 provides a clause that will terminate several of the amendments that give the government increased electronic surveillance powers unless expressly renewed by Congress. Some of the provisions discussed above that are subject to sunset on December 31, 2005 include sections 204, 214, 215, 218, and 206. This will give Congress the opportunity to review the application of these provisions as well as their efficacy. Due to gag clauses and the secrecy of the FISC, it is questionable how much information Congress will have to make this assessment.

Libraries and the Patriot Act

Because of the gag clauses attached to Section 215 and other provisions of the Patriot Act, it is difficult to determine how, or even if, the Act is being used in libraries. In October, 2002, Leigh Estabrook, the Director of the Library Research Center at the University of Illinois at

Urbana-Champaign, reported that federal and local law enforcement officials visited at least 545 (10.7%) of the 5,094 U.S. public libraries serving populations greater than 5,000 in the year following September 11. Of these, 178 (3.3%) received visits from the FBI. It is not known if these requests used Patriot Act authority. It is interesting to note that the number of visits reported was lower than the previous year (703). This may be attributable to the secrecy provisions contained in the Patriot Act. Estabrook also notes that not all of these requests relate to suspect terrorist activities.[49]

Attempts have been made to compel the Justice Department to disclose how often and to what extent the Patriot Act has been used. In June 2002, the House Judiciary Committee asked the Justice Department to supply some statistical information about the FBI's use of new surveillance powers. Ashcroft refused to answer many of the questions, claiming that much of the information was classified.[50] In August 2002, the American Civil Liberties Union (ACLU), the Electronic Privacy Information Center, the American Booksellers Foundation for Free Expression, and the Freedom to Read Foundation filed a Freedom of Information Act request for statistical aggregate data about how the FBI is using its new powers and a letter asking for expedited processing. Although it was conceded that the groups were entitled to expedited processing of the request, the Justice Department did not release the information and a lawsuit was filed. Before the case was dismissed the government released 341 pages of records that had large portions blacked out. Despite the blackouts, the ACLU was able to learn that the FBI is frequently using National Security Letters (NSLs) to obtain information. The FBI use NSLs, which require no judicial oversight, to compel certain customer records. The ACLU also learned that the FBI is relying heavily on FISA authority to conduct surveillance in criminal investigations. Statistics on the use of Section 215 were not disclosed, nor were statistics describing the use of pen registers/trap and trace devices made available.[51]

Librarians are among the most vocal critics of the Patriot Act provisions that threaten privacy and civil liberties. Reaction was swift because librarians have been subjected to FBI visits before. In 1987, it was disclosed that FBI agents had been visiting libraries and requesting circulation records and reference requests of "suspicious looking foreigners" as part of its Library Information Awareness Program. The program was intended to identify Soviet spies trying to access information in research libraries.[52] Despite attempts by ALA to have the program discontinued, Judith Krug states that "the FBI has never publicly abandoned the Library Awareness Program and may still be conducting it."[53]

The American Library Association, during its 2003 Midwinter Meeting, presented a "Resolution on the USA Patriot Act and Related Measures that Infringe on the Rights of Library Users." The resolution supports the traditional library values of "promoting the free flow and unimpeded distribution of knowledge and information" and patron privacy and resolves that the ALA "considers sections of the USA Patriot Act a present danger to the constitutional rights and privacy rights of library users." The resolution urges librarians and administrators to educate staff and users about compliance with the Act and also the dangers to privacy that the Act poses. ALA also urges Congress to provide oversight on the implementation of the Act, hold hearings as to how the Act is being used in libraries, and to amend or change those provisions that threaten "the rights of inquiry and free expression."[54]

In the summer of 2003, Attorney General John Ashcroft embarked on a cross-country tour to garner support for the Patriot Act. According to news reports, he accused critics of the Patriot Act, including librarians, of "baseless hysteria." He mocked the American Library Association for "believing the FBI is not fighting terror. Instead, agents are checking how far you have gotten in the latest Tom Clancy novel." The reports state that subsequently, Ashcroft released a memo that said that FBI agents had not requested any business records [which would include library records] under Section 215 of the Patriot Act. Ashcroft said he decided to release the memo to "counter the troubling amount of public distortion and misinformation in connection with Section 215."[55] Regardless of the Attorney General's statements, Section 215 is law and can be used at any time. And, again, because of the gag clause, it is likely the public may never know how, or to what extent, the Patriot Act is being used.

What Librarians Can Do

The provisions of the Patriot Act increase the FBI's ability to get permission in the form of search warrants, subpoenas, and wiretap orders to legally obtain any kind of records in any format and enhance the ability of law enforcement to conduct surveillance of individuals. It is crucial that libraries have policies in place before the FBI or other law enforcement agencies visit and request patron records. The American Library Association (ALA) provides information on how to formulate such policies and procedures that comply with the law and supplies library staff with guidelines to follow when approached by law enforcement agencies. ALA suggests that these guidelines be formulated in consultation with legal counsel and be shared with staff, administration, and the library community.[56] Library personnel also need to understand the different types of legal processes (court orders, subpoenas, warrants, NSLs) that are available to law enforcement seeking access to patron records.[57]

A particular aspect of library policy that merits careful consideration is records management and retention. Libraries, especially public and academic, maintain records that contain information about library collections and patrons such as holdings records, online catalog transactions, interlibrary loan requests, circulation records, and online database transaction records. The Patriot Act does not mandate revising existing policies and as Jaeger, Bertot, and McClure point out, "there is no evidence to suggest that law enforcement agencies are requesting that [government] agencies revise their privacy statements or records management practices, nor is there any evidence that shows that law enforcement agencies are visiting systematically various organizations and/or agencies to request that they maintain Weblog files, provide those files to select agencies, track specific users through particular systems, or insert various tracking capable cookies on user client computers."[58] In light of this, institutions must have adequate policies to ensure that records are kept only for as long as they are needed for operational, legal, or historical purposes. ALA encourages librarians to keep informed, educate their communities, communicate with local, state, and federal representatives, join coalitions, and require accountability from government.

Legislation Before Congress

As of this writing, there is a great deal of pending legislation. Some of these bills attempt to scale back provisions that enhance government authority and threaten privacy while others seek to even further expand it. Some of this legislation calls for exempting libraries and booksellers from Section 215 and requiring a showing of probable cause to secure library and bookstore records, repealing governments' authority to use "sneak and peek" searches in both criminal and terrorism investigations, restoring the "primary purpose" requirement to FISA investigations, repealing the access to records provision (Section 215), and the pen register/trap and trace provision (Section 216).[59]

The "Domestic Security Enhancement Act of 2003" (also known as Patriot II) has also been proposed. The measure would provide law enforcement with even greater powers to gather foreign intelligence and further limits access to information on the use of these expanded powers. Patriot II allows investigators to obtain "administrative subpoenas" under FISA without any evidence that the target is an agent of a foreign power and with no judicial review. One of the provisions would allow investigators to conduct intelligence surveillance without a court order fifteen days after an attack on the United States or a formal declaration of war. Another provision expands the definition of terrorists that could be interpreted to include political protestors. Under Patriot II, the disclosure of information on detainees being held and investigated by the government on suspected terrorist activities is prohibited. The disclosure of "worst case scenario" reports submitted to the EPA by private companies that use dangerous controlled substances is also prohibited.[60]

Patriot Act and Government Accountability

Librarians have a long tradition of promoting and protecting intellectual freedom. Freedom of speech implies freedom to inquire. If the government is collecting information about these constitutionally protected freedoms, the public has a right to demand an accounting. Because of the secrecy provisions of the Patriot Act, there is no accounting on the part of the government. The American Association of University Professors (AAUP) cites a report that states the Department of Justice "is confident that the Patriot Act has helped to prevent other catastrophic attacks against the United States by 'substantially' enhancing the government's 'ability to prevent, investigate and prosecute acts of terror.'"[61] Because of the lack of information provided to the public, the assertion by the Justice Department that information regarding FBI visits is classified, and the secrecy of the FISA court, it is hard for the public to assess how successful the Patriot Act has been in preventing terrorist attacks. The threat of terrorism is a grave danger, but it is disputed as to what measures are necessary to protect national security. The Patriot Act enables a system of surveillance and control that may be beyond the bounds of national security concerns. It is still to be determined what the costs of the Patriot Act will be to civil liberties, privacy, and freedom.

Jaeger, Bertot, and McClure believe that "the most important issue at hand is determining how to balance defense against terrorism and protection of individual civil liberties. The government must take adequate steps to protect its citizens from the threat of terrorist attacks and it must be able to obtain information about potential terrorist activities to help minimize or stop such attacks. At the same time, the government must also protect individuals from excessive intrusion on their privacy and basic civil liberties as guaranteed in the Constitution and the Bill of Rights."[62]

CONCLUSION

It has never been demonstrated that restricting intellectual inquiry makes us safer. Many believe that the way to combat terrorism is through greater access to knowledge, not less. Testimony provided at congressional hearings into the attacks of 9/11 suggests that excessive secrecy on the part of intelligence and law enforcement agencies contributed to intelligence failures that led to the lack of detection or reporting of the terrorist conspiracy of September 11.[63] Knowledge creation that results from intellectual freedom, especially in the fields of science and technology, can be used to identify the means for detecting terrorist threats and preventing terrorist acts.

Librarians and administrators are well aware that some patron records may contain information relevant to a criminal investigation. There has always been a legal process in place under which law enforcement could obtain these records. Librarians and administrators are also aware that certain information, if disclosed to those intending to do harm, could threaten national security. The classification system and exemptions to FOIA, however, protect this information. When the government goes beyond these laws and policies and further restricts access to such information or otherwise monitors a person's reading habits, it makes the assumption that what one reads or researches influences how he or she acts. The principles of intellectual freedom become seriously threatened.

Intellectual freedom will only flourish when privacy and confidentiality are protected. Librarians are entrusted with this responsibility and must be ready to defend the principles of intellectual freedom and confidentiality. As mentioned earlier, libraries should have well-formed policies, procedures, and guidelines in place. These should be communicated and made familiar to administration and staff prior to a challenge arising.

The Reporters Committee for Freedom of the Press states that "we live in a nation built on the concept of balance. When the government, with the best of intentions, goes too far in its efforts to shield information from the public, it is up to the public and the media to push back. Through a vibrant, information based democratic process in our legislature, and through an independent judiciary, we as a society will come to a balance that hopefully will protect our liberties for generations to come."[64] Blanton, however, challenges this concept of balance and argues that government openness should be central to national security policy:

> Openness empowers citizens, weeds out the worst policy proposals, ensures the most efficient flow of information to all levels of law enforcement, makes a little more honest the despots who are our temporary allies against terrorism . . . But we need to drop the idea of balancing this fundamental value against national security. To admit the notion of balance is to lose the debate over where to balance . . . so our task is to reframe the debate and leave behind the balancing act. We need to place openness where it belongs, not only at the center of our values, but also at the center of our strategy for security.[65]

It is clear that there are many more questions than answers. Librarians, as well as other information professionals, are feeling the impact of government information policy changes in terms of both information access and patron privacy and confidentiality. Civil liberties groups, library associations, and other professional organizations are challenging government policies that threaten civil liberties that are so important to intellectual freedom. It is crucial that librarians keep updated on current legislative efforts and continue to work within their own organizations as well as with professional groups to promote and protect the concept of intellectual freedom.

REFERENCES

1. American Library Association, Office of Intellectual Freedom, *Intellectual Freedom Manual* 6th ed. Chicago: American Library Association, 2002, xiii.

2. American Library Association, Office of Intellectual Freedom, "Intellectual Freedom Principles for Academic Libraries: An Interpretation of the Library Bill of Rights," in *Intellectual Freedom Manual* 6th ed., 163. Chicago: American Library Association, 2002.

3. Judith F. Krug, "ALA and Intellectual Freedom: A Historical Overview," in *Intellectual Freedom Manual* 6th ed., 3-32, 4. Chicago: American Library Association, 2002.

4. Robin Rice, "The USA PATRIOT Act and American Libraries," *Information for Social Change* 16 (2002) [online] [cited 1 December 2003]; available from World Wide Web @ http://libr.org/ISC/articles/16-Rice.html.

5. Ibid.

6. American Library Association, "Resolution Reaffirming the Principles of Intellectual Freedom in the Aftermath of Terrorist Attacks" Adopted by the ALA Council, January 23, 2002. [online] [cited 23 December 2003]; available from World Wide Web @ http://www.ala.org/Template.cfm?Section=IF_Resolutions&Template=/ContentManagement/ContentDisplay.cfm&ContentID=32463.

7. University of California at Berkeley, "GODORT's Principles on Government Information." (As published in *Documents to the People.* 19:1 (March 1991): 12, 14. [online] [cited 11 August 2003]; available from World Wide Web @ http://sunsite.berkeley.edu/GODORT/prin_GODORT.html; and University of California at Berkeley, "NCLIS Principles of Public Information." (As published in Federal Register: June 9, 199560:111 (9 June 1995): 30609 [online] [cited 11 August 2003]; available from World Wide Web @ http://sunsite.berkeley.edu/GODORT/prin_nclis.html.

8. Thomas M. Susman, "The Good, the Bad, and the Ugly: E-Government and the People's Right to Know," *Vital Speeches of the Day* 68 no. 2 (2001): 38-43, 39.

9. Laura Gordon-Murnane, "Access to Government Information in a Post 9/11 World," *Searcher* 10 No. 6 (June 2002). [online] [cited 30 November 2003] html available on Academic Search Premier database.

10. Freedom of Information Act (5 USC Sec. 552 as amended by PL 104-231, 110 STAT 3048).

11. United States Department of Justice, *Freedom of Information Act Guide* (May 2002) [online] [cited 6 December 2002] available on World Wide Web @ http://www.usdoj.gov/oip/foi-act.htm.

12. Thomas Blanton, "The World's Right to Know," *Foreign Policy* 131 (2002): 50-58, 50.

13. Gordon-Murnane, "Access to Government Information in a Post 9/11 World."

14. National Archives and Records Administration, Information Security Oversight Office, *ISOO 2000 Report to the President.* (September 17, 2001). [online] [cited 1 December 2003]; available on World Wide Web @ http://www.fas.org/sgp/isoo/2000rpt.html.

15. Paperwork Reduction Act of 1995 (PL 104-13, 109 STAT. 163, 44 USC 3501-3520).

16. Gordon-Murnane, "Access to Government Information in a Post 9/11 World."

17. Electronic Freedom of Information Act (5 USC 552 as amended by PL 104-231, 110 STAT. 2422).

18. GPO Access [online]; available on World Wide Web @ http://www.gpoaccess.gov.

19. United States Department of Justice, Office of Information and Privacy, *FOIA Post: New Attorney General FOIA Memorandum Issued.* [online] [cited 1 December 2003]; available on World Wide Web @ http://www.usdoj.gov/oip/foiapost/2001foiapost19.html.

20. Martin E. Halstuk, "In Review: The Threat to Freedom of Information." *Columbia Journalism Review.* 40 No. 5 (2002): 8.

21. Martin D. Snyder, "Academic Research and Access to Information." *Academe.* 88 No. 3 (May/June 2002): 79. [online] [cited 30 November 2003] html available on Academic Search Premier database.

22. William Broad, "A Nation Challenged: The Biological Threat; U.S. Is Still Selling Reports on Making Biological Weapons," *New York Times* 13 January 2002, 1.

23. Federation of American Scientists, *Memorandum for the Heads of Executive Departments and Agencies from Andrew H. Card, Jr. Assistant to the President and Chief of Staff.* March 19, 2002. [online] [cited 1 December 2003]; available on World Wide Web @ http://www.fas.org/sgp/bush/wh031902.html.

24. Homeland Security Act of 2002 (PL 107-296, 116 STAT. 2135).

25. As quoted in Mike Sherry, "Protecting Critical Infrastructure: Which is Safer–Openness or Secrecy?" *Quill Magazine.* 90 No. 7 (2002): 14-16, 15.

26. See OMB Watch for a list of agencies that have removed information from their Websites. [online]; available on World Wide Web @ http://www.ombwatch.org/article/articleview/213/1/104/#agency.

27. University of California at Berkeley, "GODORT's Principles on Government Information"; and University of California at Berkeley, "NCLIS Principles of Public Information."

28. Uniting and Strengthening America by Providing Appropriate Tools Required to Intercept and Obstruct Terrorism (USA PATRIOT Act). (PL 107-56, 115 STAT. 272).

29. Electronic Privacy Information Center, *The USA PATRIOT Act.* Updated October 20, 2003. [online] [cited 18 November 2003]; available on World Wide Web @ http://www.epic.org/privacy/terrorism/usapatriot/.

30. Electronic Privacy Information Center, *Statement of U.S. Senator Russ Feingold on the Anti-Terrorism Bill from the Senate Floor October 25, 2001.* [online] [cited 18 November 2003]; available on World Wide Web @ http://www.epic.org/privacy/terrorism/usapatriot/feingold.html.

31. Omnibus Crime Control and Safe Streets Act of 1968 (18 USC 2510-2522).

32. Electronic Communications Privacy Act (18 USC 2701-2712).

33. Pen Register Statute (18 USC 3121-3127).

34. Foreign Intelligence Surveillance Act (FISA) (50 USC 1801-1863).

35. Paul T. Jaeger, John Carlo Bertot, and Charles R. McClure, "The Impact of the USA Patriot Act on Collection and Analysis of Personal Information under the Foreign Intelligence Surveillance Act," *Government Information Quarterly* 20 (2003): 295-314, 297.

36. Ibid.

37. See Jaeger, Bertot, and McClure, "The Impact of the USA Patriot Act on Collection and Analysis of Personal Information under the Foreign Intelligence Surveillance Act," 297; Report of a AAUP Special Committee, "Academic Freedom and National Security in a Time of Crisis," *Academe.* 89 No. 6 (November-December 2003): 34-59, 40; and Electronic Privacy Information Center, *Foreign Intelligence Surveillance Act Orders: 1979-2002.* [online] [cited 18 November 2003]; available on World Wide Web @ http://www.epic.org/privacy/wiretap/stats/fisa_stats.html.

38. Tracy Mitrano, "Taking the Mystique Out of the USA Patriot Act: Information, Process and Protocol," *IT Policy Advisor* (Office of Information Technologies, Cornell.) [online] [cited 7 March 2003]; available on World Wide Web @ http://www.cit.cornell.eud/oit/PatriotAct/article.html.

39. See Jaeger, Bertot and McClure, "The Impact of the USA Patriot Act on Collection and Analysis of Personal Information under the Foreign Intelligence Surveillance Act," for a listing of Law Review articles relating provisions of Patriot Act to FISA, 313.

40. Reporters Committee for Freedom of the Press, *Homefront Confidential: How the War on Terrorism Affects Access to Information and the Public's Right to Know*, 3rd ed. (March 2003): 1-74, 39. [online] [cited 6 August 2003]; available on World Wide Web @ http://www.rcfp.org/homefrontconfidential/.

41. Report of AAUP Special Committee, "Academic Freedom and National Security in a Time of Crisis," 40.

42. Charles Doyle, "The USA PATRIOT Act: A Legal Analysis," *CRS Report for Congress: RL31377*. Congressional Research Service, The Library of Congress. (15 April 2002): 1-24, 2; and Electronic Privacy Information Center. *The USA PATRIOT Act*.

43. Mary Minow, "The USA Patriot Act." *Library Journal*. 127 No. 16 (October 1, 2002): 52-55.

44. Ibid.

45. Electronic Privacy Information Center, *The USA PATRIOT Act*.

46. Charles Doyle, "Terrorism: Section by Section Analysis of the USA PATRIOT Act." *CRS Report to Congress: RL31200*. Updated December 10, 2001. Congressional Research Service, The Library of Congress, 1-59, 9.

47. Electronic Privacy Information Center, *The USA PATRIOT Act*.

48. Ibid.

49. Leigh S. Estabrook, *Public Libraries and Civil Liberties: A Profession Divided.* The Library Research Center, University of Illinois at Urbana-Champaign. Last updated on 22 January 2003. [online] [cited 2 December 2003]; available on World Wide Web @ http://alexia.lis.uiuc.edu/gslis/research/civil_liberties.html.

50. Minow, "The USA Patriot Act," 53.

51. American Civil Liberties Union, *The Government's Response*. [online] [cited 3 December 2003]; available on World Wide Web @ http://www.aclu.org/patriot_foia/foia3.html.

52. Minow, "The USA Patriot Act," 52; Rice, "The USA PATRIOT Act and American Libraries," 3; and Krug, "ALA and Intellectual Freedom: A Historical Overview," 12.

53. Krug, "ALA and Intellectual Freedom: A Historical Overview," 12.

54. American Library Association, *Resolution on the USA PATRIOT Act and Related Measures That Infringe on the Rights of Library Users*. [online] [cited 2 December 2003]; available on World Wide Web @ http://www.ala.org/PrinterTemplate.cfm?Section=The_USA_Patriot_Act_and_Libraries&Te . . .

55. "Ashcroft Mocks Librarians in Patriot Act Defense." *American Libraries*. 34 No. 10 (November 2003): 10-12; Linda Feldman, "Ashcroft's Lightning-rod Role." *Christian Science Monitor*. 24 September 2003: 1; Eric Lichtblau, "U.S. Says It Has Not Used New Library Records Law." *New York Times*. 19 September 2003: A1; and Dan Eggen, "Patriot Monitoring Claims Dismissed; Government Has Not Tracked Bookstore or Library Activity, Ashcroft Says." *Washington Post*. 19 September 2003: A02.

56. American Library Association, *Confidentiality and Coping with Law Enforcement Inquiries: Guidelines for the Library and Its Staff*. [online] [cited 2 December 2003]; available on World Wide Web @ http://www.ala.org/Template.cfm?Section=Intellectual_Freedom_Issues&Template=/ContentManagement/ContentDisplay.cfm&ContentID=21654.

57. For an explanation of these legal processes see Mary Minow, *Library Records Post-Patriot Act (Federal Law)*. Law Library Resource Exchange. [online] [cited 13

December 2003];, available on World Wide Web @ http://www.llrx.com/features/ libraryrecords.htm; Wiley Rein & Fielding LLP, *The Search & Seizure of Electronic Information: The Law Before and After the USA PATRIOT Act.* [online] [cited 13 December 2003]; available on World Wide Web @ http://www.arl.org/info/frn/other/ matrix.pdf; and Lee Strickland, "Responding to Judicial Process: A Guide to the Unexpected for Search Warrants, Subpoenas and Otherwise." *Virginia Libraries* 49:1 (January-March 2003): 13-23.

58. Jaeger, Bertot, and McClure, "The Impact of the USA Patriot Act on Collection and Analysis of Personal Information under the Foreign Intelligence Surveillance Act," 310.

59. For a listing of such legislation see American Library Association, *Pending Legislation Concerning the USA Patriot Act.* [online] [cited 4 December 2003]; available on World Wide Web @ www.ala.org/Template.cfm?Section=Related_Links6& Template=/ContentManagement/ContentDispl; and American Library Association, *Privacy Related Legislation.* [online] [cited 4 December 2003]; available on World Wide Web @ http://www.ala.org/Content/NavigationMenu/Our_Asociation/Offices/ ALA_Washington/Issues2?Civil_Lib . . .

60. Reporters Committee for Freedom of the Press, *Homefront Confidential: How the War on Terrorism Affects Access to Information and the Public's Right to Know*, 45.

61. Cited in Report of an AAUP Special Committee, "Academic Freedom and National Security in a Time of Crisis," 42.

62. Jaeger, Bertot, and McClure, "The Impact of the USA Patriot Act on Collection and Analysis of Personal Information under the Foreign Intelligence Surveillance Act," 310.

63. Thomas Blanton, *National Security and Open Government: Striking the Right Balance*, Campbell Public Affairs Institute; The Maxwell School of Syracuse University; 2003, 33-73, 63.

64. Reporter's Committee for Freedom of the Press, *Homefront Confidential: How the War on Terrorism Affects Access to Information and the Public's Right to Know*, 1.

65. Blanton, *National Security and Open Government: Striking the Right Balance*, 66.

The Online Government Information Movement: Retracing the Route to DigiGov Through the Federal Documents Collection

Jan Jorgensen

SUMMARY. The National Commission on Libraries and Information Science published recommendations for a national information policy in 1976, and concerns regarding the protection of privacy and equal public access to online information were introduced. From the mid 1970s to the early 1990s, federal government agencies were beginning to publish materials and maintain records electronically. Most current U.S. government information was available on the Internet by the late 1990s, and depository libraries were required to provide workstations that would facilitate access to documents. Documents librarians, already concerned with the lack of attention to archiving online federal information, were provided with an example of the vulnerability of online publications in the early 2000s when federal agency Web sites were made inaccessible–quickly and easily. The possibility that too much government information was available to anyone with access to the Internet was becoming

Jan Jorgensen is Documents Librarian and Associate Professor of Library Science, Brooks Library, Central Washington University, Ellensburg, WA 98926-7548 (E-mail: jorgenja@cwu.edu).

[Haworth co-indexing entry note]: "The Online Government Information Movement: Retracing the Route to DigiGov Through the Federal Documents Collection." Jorgensen, Jan. Co-published simultaneously in *The Reference Librarian* (The Haworth Information Press, an imprint of The Haworth Press, Inc.) No. 94, 2006, pp. 139-162; and: *The Changing Face of Government Information: Providing Access in the Twenty-First Century* (ed: Suhasini L. Kumar) The Haworth Information Press, an imprint of The Haworth Press, Inc., 2006, pp. 139-162. Single or multiple copies of this article are available for a fee from The Haworth Document Delivery Service [1-800-HAWORTH, 9:00 a.m. - 5:00 p.m. (EST). E-mail address: docdelivery@ haworthpress.com].

a national concern. Using government documents as resources, this article retraces the events that were occurring in federal government agencies during the movement of government information to the Internet. *[Article copies available for a fee from The Haworth Document Delivery Service: 1-800-HAWORTH. E-mail address: <docdelivery@haworthpress.com> Website: <http://www.HaworthPress.com> © 2006 by The Haworth Press, Inc. All rights reserved.]*

KEYWORDS. Electronic government information, online federal information, digital government documents

INTRODUCTION

To perform this study, the evolution of electronic government information was traced from magnetic tapes to present day Web sites, using only government documents as a resource. This quest through the U.S. depository collection was undertaken to illustrate the unique informational qualities of government publications, while examining an issue that affected how these federal information materials were made accessible for research.

The fluid nature of federal government agencies, due to the fact that the missions of Executive Departments change whenever a new President takes office, provides a challenge for anyone tracking a topic through "federal government time." Even the roles of the Government Printing Office (GPO) and the Federal Depository Library Program (FDLP) are redirected when a newly elected President appoints a new Public Printer to office. It is, however, the fact that significant federal government documents reflect the prevalent political opinion at the time they were published that makes these materials such an essential primary resource.

An informed public has been declared a basic requisite for democracy, assuring that public access to federal information will continue to be heralded as a fundamental right. The United States has assumed a strong economic and military position internationally through the development and utilization of technology, guaranteeing ongoing funding for technological advancement. However, the other elements required for libraries to provide free and equal public access to vast amounts of electronic federal government information are open to interpretation. Determination of whether or not particular information constitutes a threat to national security, how access to federal information will be funded, where information archives will be located, and if the right to privacy is violated by disclosing the information resources used by an individual, are all issues that continue to be unresolved.

1970s:
FEDERAL INFORMATION
IN THE MACHINE-READABLE ERA

Two government agencies that produced technical information in the late 1960s, the Department of Defense (DOD) and National Aeronautics and Space Administration (NASA), were credited with developing the first computer systems utilized to store and retrieve information. During the 1970s, the Census Bureau also began storing statistical data on magnetic tapes, using computer programs to compile tables. One of the first guides to machine-readable information, published in 1977, provided access to Department of Health, Education and Welfare databases containing poverty statistics.[1] Information providers were able to acquire copies of federal agency magnetic tapes containing raw data, but very few libraries had equipment, or personnel, to facilitate the use of machine-readable formats. It was only after computer technology had been effectively employed by government and business to manage their own information for several years that the potential for using electronic systems to expand public access to information was explored.

In 1970, the U.S. Congress passed Public Law 91-345, the *National Commission on Libraries and Information Science Act*.[2] This legislation provided appropriations to establish and support a new independent agency, the National Commission on Libraries and Information Science (NCLIS), charged with the task of developing a national information policy. One of the primary concerns leading to this act was the fact that citizens who were economically or socially disadvantaged did not have adequate access to information services. The passage of this act substantiated the importance of maintaining public access to information and supported the use of technology as a tool for facilitating the sharing of information resources among libraries.

By the mid 1970s, at least one third of the U.S. gross national product was attributable to the production and distribution of information. At this time computers were being used in libraries to assist with bibliographic control, circulation, and acquisition procedures. When the first annual report to the President was published by NCLIS in 1976, the proposed national information policy was unveiled and some of the technological challenges federal agencies and libraries would face with the use of technology were predicted:

> The advent of computer and communications technology is causing a quiet revolution to occur in the field of information. It is quiet because the signs of change are subtle and not always visible. It is a revolution because the rate of change is very rapid. Our country now possesses new information technology that can retrieve and distribute information faster, with greater facility to more people than ever before in history. But information technology has brought problems as well as opportunities. Inadequate protection of the privacy of individuals, ineffective handling of computerized information systems, and uncertain relationship between public and private sector groups involved in information activities, have all raised difficulties.[3]

It was not until 1979 that NCLIS emphasized the need for access to government documents, specifically, by publishing a report entitled *Government Publications: Their Role in the National Program for Library and Information Services.*[4] This report claimed the inability for libraries and individuals to find out what materials government agencies were publishing caused as much concern as the formats in which they were published. The role of government information, allowing citizens to acquire the information necessary to participate in democratic processes, was stressed and a comprehensive study of public access to documents was suggested. Since libraries were having difficulty acquiring paper copies of documents from noncompliant federal agencies, it was feared that the change to electronic formats would cause government information to become even more difficult to trace. If allowed, technology could actually eliminate public access to numerous government publications.

1980s:
THE GOVERNMENT INFORMATION TECHNOLOGY AGE

The Government Printing Office (GPO) continued to deal with problems revolving around public access issues during the 1980s, but it was the economic effects of technology that caught the attention of our nation's leaders. By the early 1980s it had become apparent that U.S. citizens were not adequately prepared for the overwhelming amount of information being produced, nor was the use of basic information technology taught as a part of the normal school curriculum. The United States was an electronic information society consisting of a large number of citizens without access to the hardware or training to obtain information in electronic formats.

In 1982, the Office of Technology Assessment (OTA) completed a report for Congress describing the crisis the U.S. would face if citizens were not provided with the knowledge and education necessary to remain economically stable and internationally competitive. Libraries, according to this report, should redefine their roles and charge patrons for computer use, if necessary. "Libraries that fail to adopt these new technologies for information services may risk becoming irrelevant,"[5] OTA warned. The solution for one library mentioned in this report was to set up a rented, self-service microcomputer in the library, allowing patrons to pay by the hour to use the equipment. In this case, librarians did not need any additional training because the computer came from the vendor with instructions. Since this placed electronic access to information into vending machine status, it was not a solution adopted by very many libraries.

Libraries that had not yet faced the challenges of using technology to retrieve information were forced to do so when private companies, such as BRS and DIALOG, developed fee-based online search systems. The ability to search multiple indexes and abstracts covering long time periods by simply typing in subject words one time, was well received by users willing to pay the cost. Librarians learned how to mediate searches, becoming adept at determining which databases to search, what terminology to use, and how to perform online searches for patrons. As many of these databases contained government publications, it was the private companies who first supplied expedient methods for searching government information.

The landmark federal document for the 1980s was *A Nation at Risk: The Imperative for Educational Reform.* This 1983 report from the National Commission on Excellence in Education provided evidence that our nation's education system was failing to keep up with changes in technology, stating:

> The people of the United States need to know that individuals in our society who do not possess the levels of skill, literacy and training essential to this new era will be effectively disenfran-

chised, not simply from the material rewards that accompany competent performance, but also from the chance to participate fully in our national life.[6]

Two 1984 publications from the Department of Education mentioned libraries when the issue of providing additional technological training for adults lacking skills was discussed. Libraries were established as the institutions responsible for supporting adult learners and self-learners attempting to upgrade skills and needing access to computers.[7] The surveys included in these documents showed that technology was taking away jobs, due to improved efficiency requiring fewer workers, and the limited supply of workers with technology skills available to fill necessary positions.[8] These federal documents, and others, illuminated the role education plays in national economics and recognized libraries as educational institutions.

The Office of Technology Assessment (OTA) published a study conducted for the U.S. Congress in 1988 on teaching technical information. The need for federal employees with technical knowledge could not be met, and OTA reported that one of the primary roadblocks for technology education was the lack of a lead agency. Individual agencies had training programs, but there was limited funding, no consistency in training, and no cooperation between agencies. Most of the government funding provided to schools for technology training came from the Department of Defense, an agency that needed to recruit well-trained high school graduates.

Some of the problems reviewed by OTA were attributed to administrative changes that took place in 1984. Apparently, the newly selected Department of Education Secretary did not share the vision of improving education through technology that had been expressed by his predecessor. When *A Nation at Risk* was published, there had been a great fanfare, publicity, and nationwide distribution. However, when a follow-up report, *Transforming American Education: Reducing the Risk to the Nation*, was given to the new Secretary of Education by the National Task Force on Educational Technology, this was held for three months, and, when finally released, it was not printed or made available to the public through GPO.[9]

A second report published by OTA in 1988, *Informing the Nation: Federal Information Dissemination in an Electronic Age*, brought legislative focus directly on issues related to the electronic publishing of government publications. This document began by clearly explaining why federal government information was an essential tool for relaying information about national issues to the public, and then described how access to this information could be helped or hindered by the use of technology. This report warned that technological advances could allow government information to be distributed in a more efficient and less costly manner, but equity in access would need to be maintained. Changes would also need to be made in the roles performed by the GPO, the Superintendent of Documents, the Depository Library Program, and the National Technical Information Service. In addition, the *Freedom of Information Act* (FOIA) would need to be amended as quickly as possible to include electronic formats.[10]

Most federal agencies had been utilizing electronic methods for storing and distributing information within their departments for many years before public dissemination of electronic government information was discussed. Even if everything placed in a database could or should be made accessible to the public, there was a great deal of variation between formats and types of information contained in each agency's databases. In March 1989, the Federal Library and Information Center Committee (FLICC) held it's sixth annual forum, and the discussion topic was Federal Information Policies.[11] It was pointed out during this forum that it had taken eleven years for FOIA to pass, from 1955 to 1966, and several agencies continued to object to this particular act. These issues needed to be resolved before electronic information could be acquired under FOIA in the same manner that paper documents were provided. During his presentation at the FLICC forum, consumer advocate Ralph Nader pointed out that people had to pay for information accessed through FOIA. He stated that a broader definition of information posing a threat to national security was now being utilized, increasing the number of documents accessible only through FOIA. In addition, government agencies were publishing fewer publications in compliance with the Paper Work Reduction Act.[12] FLICC presentations included other statements regarding classified information, such as the following statement:

> Better use of security classification could command congressional attention in various regards. For example, millions of federal documents are security classified every year and added to the growing mountain of officially secret material. To facilitate use of this volume of classified literature (some in electronic formats), over four million individuals have been cleared for access to such protected records. It has been argued that this is a system of excess involving

too much information, too many people, and too great a cost in terms of both money and public confidence.[13]

In April of 1989, a symposium was sponsored by NCLIS to discuss the concept of information literacy. The conclusion of these discussions was a call for reforming education to include teaching students how to access, evaluate, and analyze information as a part of the daily school curriculum. With overwhelming amounts of information readily available, the ability to succeed as a student, employee, or even a citizen participating fully in a democratic society, depended upon an individual's capacity for gathering and synthesizing appropriate information on a topic.[14] As electronic information became more and more prevalent, information access and evaluation skills would become more and more necessary.

1990s:
GOVERNMENT ON THE INFORMATION SUPERHIGHWAY

Government Information on topics related to electronic publishing and use of the Internet were extremely prevalent during the 1990s. The electronic dissemination of information was a requirement for all federal agencies, and reports during the 1990s included descriptions of how technological goals were being achieved. It was during the 1990s that providing public access to online government information became essential rather than simply possible. In 1991, GPO began to develop an electronic bulletin board that could be used by federal depository libraries.[15] Although the original purpose for this system was to accommodate record keeping, it was the first step toward providing libraries with access to online materials. CD-ROMs containing issues of the *Congressional Record* were the first electronic publications GPO distributed to depository libraries. Most documents librarians do not have fond memories of these difficult to use CDs, but the effort was appreciated.

Annual reports from the GPO for 1990, 1991, and 1992 described GPO as an agency addressing issues related to: cost cutbacks, modernizing technology, gaining cooperation from federal agencies, and meeting public demands for electronic government publications. During 1990 twelve new electronic products were added to the Depository Library Program (DLP), primarily in the form of CDs, with bulletin board access to full-text available through pilot projects.[16] GPO's report for 1991 stated there were [approximately] 1,400 federal depository libraries receiving a total of 29.6 million copies of 57,700 document titles, including 116 CD-ROMs and 53 diskettes.[17]

The 1992 annual report from GPO announced that the Federal Bulletin Board (FBB) was available as of September 1992, enabling users to have

> immediate self-service public access to Federal information in on-line format at reasonable rates. It permits users to identify, select, and transfer electronic files to their own personal computers quickly and easily, thereby offering Federal publishing agencies the opportunity to expand the dissemination of their publications in on-line format.[18]

The number of documents distributed to depository libraries in 1992 was 29.7 million–71% on microfiche, 29% in paper format, and less than 1% in electronic format.

At the end of 1991, GPO published a strategic planning document covering departmental expectations for the next ten years. This document implied that GPO would have changed radically by 2001, but changes would be made gradually over the next ten years as technology and government procedures changed. GPO's mission would be

> to assist Congress and Federal agencies in the cost-effective creation and replication of information products and services, and to provide the public with the most efficient and effective means of acquiring Government information products and services. . . . The electronic information era, however, requires that we embrace, adopt, and advance the use of electronic methods and formats to accomplish our mission.[19]

The dissemination activities that would take place, according to the strategic plan, included using a system named SEND (Satellite Electronic Network Dissemination). SEND would be a method for fulfilling GPO's responsibility to distribute electronic federal documents to depository libraries. Information would be relayed daily via satellite from the GPO to a receiving station located at each depository library.

The Federal Library and Information Center Committee (FLICC) held forums in 1990 and 1991 discussing access to federal information, the development of networks, and what came to be called "information superhighways." The preface to this publication states that 317 public laws had been enacted between the 95th and 100th Congresses

(1978-1988) that involved information policies. The act that was under discussion during the forum was the High Performance Computing Act of 1991, which had been reintroduced at the beginning of the 102nd Congress by Senator Albert Gore. This Act proposed the establishment of NREN (National Research and Education Network), which would link together supercomputers and digital libraries throughout the nation. The responsibilities of GPO to the public were discussed during this forum, and left no doubt that changes would need to be made at GPO and throughout the federal agencies to accommodate electronic formats.[20]

During the 1991 White House Conference on Library and Information Science, the challenges libraries would face during the Information Age were discussed. These key issues were listed as literacy, productivity, and democracy. Although the issues themselves were not new, the implications of electronic information presented a different perspective and unique problems libraries could not ignore.[21]

Hearings held before the House Government Information, Justice, and Agriculture Subcommittee in 1992 had the interesting title (and topic) of *Creative Ways of Using and Disseminating Federal Information.* The purpose of these hearings, according to the opening statement made by Subcommittee Chairman Robert E. Wise, was to highlight "enterprising, inventive, and imaginative ways that people use, and agencies disseminate, public information." The use of creativity was encouraged because the federal budget could not support high cost equipment. New technologies, such as CD-ROMs, GIS software, and networks created for in-house use by organizations and agencies, were presented as alternatives to expensive databases. Examples discussed included federal agency databases that were being sold primarily to businesses, such as: the *National Trade Data Bank* CD-ROM, containing export and trade information (costing $360 for an annual monthly subscription) and the online *Economic Bulletin Board* ($.05 to $.20 per minute or $35 per year to log on) from the Department of Commerce, and the *CASSIS* Patent CD-ROMs with information from the Patent and Trademark Office ($210 for an annual quarterly subscription).[22]

The Office of Technology Assessment continued to provide Congress with research reports on various aspects of technology during the first half of the 1990s. The OTA was disbanded in 1995, so these reports were some of the last to be issued by this agency. Two separate reports focused on legal issues related to electronic information, such as copyright, proprietary software, intellectual property rights, privacy, international policy, and information security. In 1993, OTA published a report discussing the use of technology to support adult literacy. OTA was responsible for examining implications of technology from various aspects, and in the process verified the fact that many issues had been overlooked prior to embracing the use of electronic systems for government information.

The *Government Printing Office Electronic Information Access Enhancement Act of 1993*[23] provided GPO with a legal mandate to pursue the goal of providing electronic access to federal government information. In June of 1994, GPO published a status report, a statutory requirement, on *GPO Access*, GPO's online database for the distribution of official documents. This report details the plans for the type of hardware and software to be utilized, the funding necessary, the documents and information to be included, and how the database would be made accessible. This database was considered to be a depository item, giving all federal depository libraries and their users free access to official government information. Other users would be required to pay a minimal charge for access.[24] GPO had now officially entered into the realm of digitizing and Web site maintenance.

In 1993, the Clinton Administration conducted a National Performance Review headed by Vice President Albert Gore. Federal agencies were examined and methods for improving services and lowering costs were recommended. One of the many volumes that comprised this report was focused on the use of information technology to expedite services. By this time the private sector had used technology successfully, and, as it was pointed out in this report, government was lagging far behind. The report also mentioned that government information and services were not coordinated with one another (between agencies) and citizens seeking assistance were met with unfriendly and inadequate responses. Overall, it became apparent that major changes needed to be made in federal agency services so taxpayers could retrieve necessary information. The primary solution suggested to rectify this situation was a system of kiosks (customer-activated terminals) to be stationed throughout the country, and a central 800 (toll-free) telephone number where cooperative government employees would provide basic information and make referrals.[25]

The Information Infrastructure Task Force, appointed by President Clinton in 1993, was assigned responsibility for developing a plan describing how the National Information Infrastructure (NII) would be implemented. The NII was considered a top priority among Presidential goals, because it was a necessary prerequisite for other changes in government procedures. In the Executive Summary of the Task Force's proposal for action, the administration pledged to "seek to ensure that

Federal agencies, in concert with state and local governments, use the NII to expand the information available to the public, ensuring that the immense reservoir of government information is available to the public easily and equitably."[26]

GPO's report to Congress on the status of *GPO Access* in 1996, as required by Public Law 103-40, provided evidence that GPO's database, containing thirteen titles by December 1995, was quite successful. The success of this database was attributed to feedback from depository librarians prior to its implementation, and the ability to allow free access to Internet/dial-in users. With the easily obtained Adobe Reader software, users could view current pages of primary documents published daily, such as the *Federal Register* or the *Congressional Record*, almost immediately after publication.[27] However, the Wide Area Information Server (WAIS) used to retrieve documents on GPO was not as user friendly as the subscription databases most librarians had been using in their libraries. GPO facilitated the use of *GPO Access* by distributing training materials and setting up training sessions upon request.[28]

It was Congressional legislation that served as the prod to increase the pace and move the Federal Depository Library Program toward disseminating electronic publications more quickly. Public Law 104-53, *Legislative Branch Appropriations Act, 1996*, directed the Public Printer to initiate a study of the Federal Depository Library Program (FDLP) and develop a strategic plan to be completed by March 1996. To conduct a study that was as informative as possible, the legislature suggested gathering input from bodies participating in all aspects of the depository program, federal agencies, depository libraries, public users, Depository Library Council members, etc. The final document resulting from the study was intended to describe the most cost-effective program for distributing federal documents while utilizing services and programs already in place. The adding of advanced technology as a means of distribution was expected to save costs and expedite services.

The original version of the study, as submitted for comment to members of the FDLP community, stated that the majority of documents distributed through the depository library program would be published only in electronic formats by 1999, two and one-half years from the time the announcement was made. Government information librarians, already struggling with format changes requiring new equipment and additional training, uniformly objected to this time frame. The positive aspects of electronic access were obvious, but questions regarding archiving, assurance of accuracy, agency compliance, costs to libraries, user assistance, disability access, and other issues related to maintaining public access were mentioned. Librarians also feared that electronic formats would encourage agencies to either disregard publishing requirements (which had not been changed to include online formats), or comply but send information in inaccessible or illegible formats. Since the purpose of changing the depository program to electronic formats was aimed at improving access, more flexibility was put into the time frame. The final version of the report submitted to Congress in June 1996 allowed a five to seven year period for conversion. GPO's funding, however, had already been cut back drastically earlier in the year when the legislature concluded electronic materials would save a great deal of expense.[29]

Meanwhile, back in the Executive Branch, teams focused on developing the nation's information superhighway and "reinventing government." The Interagency Kiosk Committee published a report in 1995 describing why the U.S. needed to set up one-stop interactive government service stations that would be available twenty-four hours per day, seven days per week. The kiosk solution would deploy information technology to "bring government closer to the people it is meant to serve" by improving delivery of government services through the use of an interactive system accessible from a home PC or by using a kiosk available in the local U.S. Post Office. Since most people were comfortable with ATMs, this would provide an equivalent transaction, only customers would receive information rather than money.[30]

The Advisory Council on the National Information Infrastructure was created by Executive Order 12864 in 1993. This Council published several reports in 1995 and 1996. The first report to the Secretary of Commerce in March 1995 set goals for the National Information Infrastructure (NII), including a description of how NII would be used, methods for access, the maintenance of privacy and integrity of data, and the overall social purposes to be upheld in an online environment.[31] The Council's next report to the Secretary of Commerce, at the beginning of 1996, provided a more focused look at NII benefits for education, lifelong learning, electronic commerce, health, public safety, and government information and services.[32] A companion report from the council discussed how to establish connections to the information superhighway in communities. This was a call for neighborhood access via museums, libraries, and community centers.[33] A June 1995 publication from the National Communications and Information Administration discussed the need for connecting public organizations, specifically schools, libraries, and healthcare organizations, to a national information and telecommunications system. Since the private sector would also utilize this system, a cooperative effort between the private and public sectors was suggested. This document expressed a desire to maintain equal access and avoid "evolving into a nation of information 'haves' and 'have nots.'"[34]

President Clinton signed Executive Order 13011 on July 16, 1996, declaring his vision for "Federal Information Technology." He began by stating:

> A Government that works better and costs less requires efficient and effective information systems. The Paperwork Reduction Act of 1995 and the Information Technology Management Reform Act of 1996 provide the opportunity to improve significantly the way the Federal Government acquires and manages information technology. Agencies now have the clear authority and responsibility to make measurable improvements in mission performance and service delivery to the public through the strategic application of information technology.[35]

Agencies were mentioned generally and specifically, by name, in the Executive Order, with priorities and areas of responsibility outlined.

Falling Through the Net was one of the more publicized documents of the decade. This government publication from the National Telecommunications and Information Administration was published in 1999 and contained data that showed how electronic publishing had created unequal access to information. Computers were not something everyone had available at home. In fact, many people had no access to the Internet readily available anywhere close by. The division was along economic lines; people with higher incomes could afford to have computer equipment and online access, while people with low incomes could not afford computers.[36]

GPO was actively involved in disseminating electronic federal information products and databases by the end of the 1990s. In 1998, *GPO Access* contained over 116,000 individual titles that were maintained and archived on a GPO server. In a document published by the Library Programs Service in 1998, GPO's charge, as interpreted from Public Law 103-40, was to operate an electronic storage facility where documents would remain permanently available. Since funding would not allow the creation of a single GPO-operated storage facility for all depository documents, partnerships with other institutions were sought. Information could then be networked from a locator service, such as the

GILS (Government Information Locator Service) tool currently in use, to the server containing a document.[37]

The National Commission on Libraries and Information Science (NCLIS) held a hearing at the end of 1998 on some of the problems encountered when children took advantage of public access to the World Wide Web. The majority of people testifying and submitting materials at the hearing were librarians struggling with a problem associated entirely with the national policy of providing public access to electronic information. Many libraries had been forced by adult users to formulate policies, and these were also discussed during the testimony and in written supplementary materials.[38]

During 1998, NCLIS was commissioned by GPO to perform a survey of electronic information products produced by federal government agencies and to determine what changes were necessary to complete a transition to electronic formats. This research was performed as a further response to Public Law 104-53, which charged the GPO with successfully converting the majority of materials in the Federal Depository Library Program to electronic formats. The final report published March 1999 contained information compiled from written surveys and personal visits to producers and users of government information. Documents librarians who were surveyed agreed that users preferred paper and microfiche products over electronic resources, and CD-ROMs were the least useful format received. Concerns regarding the ability of libraries to purchase appropriate hardware and software to access electronic information while continuing to provide free public access were expressed. NCLIS found that agency policies were lacking, materials were not archived, and many electronic documents were not disseminated. Responsibility for electronic publishing was not assigned to an individual position within the departments, so each subagency was responsible for making copies of reports available for public use. NCLIS stated it was also necessary to develop a clearer definition of what was meant by "ensuring authenticity" of electronic government information.[39]

According to the GPO 1998 *Annual Report*, about 34 percent of the titles received by Federal Depository Libraries at the end of the fiscal year were in electronic format. Partnerships with libraries, government agencies, and non-profit organizations were being developed to provide free, permanent access to government information. Agreements had also been made with the Department of Energy (DOE) and National Technical Information Service (NTIS) to allow direct public access to information contained on their databases.[40]

2000 + :
E-GOVERNMENT INFORMATION

The Bush Administration brought a new focus on government information and a new course of action. This was the beginning of e-government (electronic government). However, the Bush Administration suddenly became the "Homeland Security Administration" after the acts of terrorism occurred on 9/11/01, removing any government information with potential for misuse from public access. Electronic government was placed on hold, temporarily.

At the end of 2000, the National Telecommunications and Information Administration (NTIA), an agency within the Department of Commerce, re-addressed the issue of unequal access to technology and digital information. This topic had been reported earlier during three separate studies on the "digital divide." NTIA had determined that the U.S. was a nation of "haves and have nots" where access to digital information was concerned. The fourth study found that there had been a significant increase in the number of individuals using the Internet over the past year, with 51 percent of all households now having computers with Internet access. However, those households that did not have Internet access could still be categorized within the same socio-economic groups as in the past. This last study also surveyed household access to high-speed Internet services, with the intention of tracking use of this type of access over time.[41]

NCLIS published a report at the beginning of 2001 describing the methods that were currently in use for distribution of government information. This document provided an overview of the problems associated with electronic formats. Electronic dissemination methods allowed government agencies to load information directly on to their own Web sites, bypassing any government body responsible for standardizing, indexing, or archiving government information products. This method of distribution saved a great deal of time and money, but the documents were not easy to find or use. National Technical Information Service (NTIS), an agency within the Department of Commerce, had previously been responsible for indexing and publishing government reports, but funding was no longer available. The findings reported by NCLIS in their final report on the dissemination of government information included thirty-six separate recommendations.[42]

The Clinton Administration and the government information infrastructure program concluded their efforts with the development of *FirstGov.gov*, "the U.S. Government's official Web portal." Originally developed in ninety days in response to an offer of private funding, *FirstGov.gov* went online September 22, 2000 with very little advance notice. This database provided a user-friendly, cost-free, and somewhat commercialized interface with government information sites. The first significant problem developed when database managers discovered that users sent them e-mail questions regarding government information instead of comments on the database (this was of no surprise to Documents Librarians . . .). As a result of this confusion, *FirstGov* now has a link to contacts for users with questions.[43]

Three Acts (available on *GPO Access* and *Thomas.loc.gov*) with the potential for causing changes in access to government information have been passed during the Bush Administration, so far:

1. Public Law 107-56, *Uniting and Strengthening America by Providing Appropriate Tools Required to Intercept and Obstruct Terrorism (USA PATRIOT Act of 2001)* allows government officials to obtain information that has been protected by libraries under individual privacy rights in the past.[44]
2. Public Law 107-296, *Homeland Security Act of 2002*, states government information to be suppressed by an information officer if there is any potential for violating national security by making the information available to public users.[45]
3. Public Law 107-347, *E-Government Act of 2002*, established a Federal Chief Information Officer within the Office of Management and Budget to oversee and encourage all agencies to enhance public services by relaying information through the Internet. President Bush described the purpose of this act in a statement accessible online:

    This legislation builds upon my Administration's expanding E-Government initiative by ensuring strong leadership of the information technology activities of Federal agencies, a comprehensive framework for information security standards and programs, and uniform safeguards to protect the confidentiality of information provided by the public for statistical purposes. The Act will also assist in expanding the use of the Internet and computer resources in order to deliver Government services, consistent with the reform principles outlined on July 10, 2002, for a citizen-centered, results-oriented, and market-based Government.[46]

The Chief Information Officer at the U.S. Department of Agriculture, prepared for addressing the use of electronic information dissemination, published a five-year strategic plan for developing and using e-government in USDA in 2002. During 2002 to 2006 the primary mission of the Department and its agency, according to this plan, would be to utilize electronic communications as a means of reaching out to farmers, rural businesses, low-income families, schoolchildren, and rural communities.[47]

The Department of Justice (DOJ) published a strategic plan for information technology in July 2002. New priorities were in place at DOJ and the mission of the Department had changed. The number one goal now was to "protect America against the threat of terrorism." Since the Department has branches and employees located in various capacities throughout the country, the ability to share information quickly with other branches would be the most obvious use of information technology.[48]

The Library of Congress, working with the National Science Foundation, sponsored a workshop on research possibilities leading to the development of an advanced technology for digital archiving. This innovative method of preservation could solve many ongoing problems related to the preservation of government information, and funding is available for research.[49]

The White House was responsible for a publication released February 2003 on securing cyberspace. This recent document calls for "developing a comprehensive national plan for securing the key resources and critical infrastructure of the United States, including information technology . . ."[50]

An electronic publication dated April 2003, *Implementing the President's Management Agenda for E-Government: E-Government Strategy*, lists further development of the *FirstGov* interface as one of the government's highest priorities for maintenance and ongoing improvements. According to the President's Management Agenda, which details the plan for e-government, information should never be more than three clicks away. Several new e-government projects and plans, falling under the new motto of "my government my terms," are also described in this recent electronic document.[51]

One of the most easily observed changes that occurred with the Bush Administration was the creation of the Department of Homeland Security. The establishment of this new executive agency caused a rearrangement in the line-up of former agencies, changes in funding, changes in policies and regulations, and changes in both the focus and the sources for federal information.

Several examples of how quickly and easily government information can "disappear" from the Web were observed during the past few years, but the Bureau of Indian Affairs (BIA) Web site is probably the most notable. BIA's Web site has been inaccessible since 2001 when litigation on a court case began, and agency records will be unavailable for public access until the final decision is handed down. Paper documents from the BIA were not re-collected from library shelves, providing evidence that this was an unforeseen problem unique to electronic resources. It has served to provide libraries with an example of how vulnerable information becomes when its components are all so efficiently stored in one (easy to remove) location.

CONCLUSION

Few of the issues regarding electronic government information have been resolved as of this writing. Questions asked in the 1970s, '80s, and '90s concerning archiving, right to privacy, national security, and equal access are still being asked today. The right to free public access to government information continues to need advocates; we live in an information society where information will always be seen as a commodity.

U.S. government information resources are a very diverse collection of materials that in combination can cover a topic from every perspective. Examining the same issue using documents from two very different, and very outspoken, Presidential Administrations is particularly enlightening. The information was readily available, easy to understand, and paper is still much more rewarding to use than the other formats.

NOTES

1. U.S. Department of Health, Education and Welfare. *Inventory of Federal Data Bases Related to the Measurement of Poverty.*

2. "National Commission On Libraries and Information Science Act" (P.L. 91-345), *United States Statutes at Large*, 84 Stat. 440.

3. U.S. National Commission on Libraries and Information Science. *National Information Policy: Report to the President of the United States*, p. 3.

4. U.S. National Commission on Libraries and Information Science. Government Publications: Their Role in the National Program for Library and Information Services, p. 34.

5. U.S. Congress. Office of Technology Assessment. *Information Technology and Its Impact on American Education*, p. 238.

6. U.S. National Commission on Excellence in Education. *A Nation at Risk: The Imperative for Educational Reform*, p. 7.

7. U.S. Department of Education. *Alliance for Excellence: Librarians Respond to a Nation at Risk.*

8. U.S. Department of Education. *The World of Work.*

9. U.S. Congress. Office of Technology Assessment. *Power on! New Tools for Teaching and Learning.*

10. U.S. Congress. Office of Technology Assessment. *Informing the Nation: Federal Information Dissemination in an Electronic Age.*

11. U.S. Federal Library and Information Center Committee. Forum on Federal Information Policies: The Congressional Initiative. The sixth annual forum held March 22, 1989.

12. Ibid, pp. 15-16.

13. Ibid, p. 64.

14. U.S. National Commission on Libraries and Information Science. *Information Literacy and Education for the 21st Century.*

15. U.S. Government Printing Office. Library Programs Service. *Electronic Bulletin Board System for the Federal Depository Library Program: A Study.*

16. U.S. Government Printing Office. *Annual Report 1990.*

17. U.S. Government Printing Office. *Annual Report 1991.*

18. U.S. Government Printing Office. *Annual Report, 1992*, p. 20.

19. U.S. Government Printing Office. GPO 2001: Vision for a New Millennium: Strategic Planning. *GPO 2001: Vision for a New Millennium*, p. 3.

20. U.S. Federal Library and Information Center Committee. *The Seventh and Eighth Annual FLICC Forum on Federal Information Policies.* 1992.

21. White House Conference on Library and Information Services. Information 2000: Library and Information Services for the 21st Century.

22. U.S. House. Committee on Government Operations. *Creative Ways of Using and Disseminating Federal Information: Hearings.*

23. "Government Printing Office Electronic Information Access Enhancement Act of 1993" (P.L. 103-40), *United States Statutes at Large*, 107 Stat. 112.

24. U.S. Government Printing Office. Status Report: GPO Access, a Service of the U.S. Government Printing Office.

25. U.S. Office of the Vice President. *Reengineering Through Information Technology: Accompanying Report of the National Performance Review.*

26. U.S. Information Infrastructure Task Force. The National Information Infrastructure: Agenda for Action.

27. GPO. *Biennial Report to Congress on the Status of GPO Access.*

28. U.S. Superintendent of Documents. Office of Electronic Information Dissemination Services. *Helpful Hints for Searching Federal Databases Online via GPO Access.*

29. U.S. Government Printing Office. *Study to Identify Measures Necessary for a Successful Transition to a More Electronic Federal Depository Library Program.*

30. U.S. Interagency Kiosk Committee. The Kiosk Network Solution: An Electronic Gateway to Government Service.

31. U.S. National Information Infrastructure Advisory Council. Common Ground: Fundamental Principles for the National Information Infrastructure.

32. U.S. Advisory Council on the National Information Infrastructure. *A Nation of Opportunity: Realizing the Promise of the Information Superhighway.*

33. U.S. Advisory Council on the National Information Infrastructure. KickStart Initiative: Connecting America's Communities to the Information Superhighway.

34. U.S. Department of Commerce. National Telecommunications and Information Administration. *Connecting the Nation: Classrooms, Libraries, and Health Care Organization in the Information Age*, p.1.

35. "Federal Information Technology" (Executive Order 13011, 16 July 1996) *Federal Register,* 61 F.R. 37657.

36. U.S. Department of Commerce. National Telecommunications and Information Administration. *Falling Through the Net: Defining the Digital Divide.* <http://www.ntia.doc.gov/ntiahome/fttn99/contents.html>.

37. U.S. Government Printing Office. Library Programs Service. *Managing the FDLP Electronic Collection: A Policy and Planning Document.*

38. U.S. National Commission on Libraries and Information Science. *Kids and the Internet: The Promise and the Perils.*

39. U.S. National Commission on Libraries and Information Science. *Report on the Assessment of Electronic Government Information Products.*

40. U.S. Government Printing Office. *Annual Report Fiscal Year 1998.*

41. U.S. Department of Commerce. National Telecommunications and Information Administration. Falling Through the Net: Toward Digital Inclusion. A Report on Americans' Access to Technology Tools.

42. U.S. National Commission on Libraries and Information Science. *A Comprehensive Assessment of Public Information Dissemination: Final Report, Volume One.*

43. *FirstGov.gov (Database)* <http://www.firstgov.gov/index.shtml>.

44. "USA PATRIOT Act of 2001" (P.L. 107-56), *United Statutes at Large,* 115 Stat. 272.

45. "Homeland Security Act of 2002" (P.L. 107-296) *United Statutes at Large,* 116 Stat. 2135.

46. "E-Government Act of 2002" (P.L. 107-347) *United Statutes at Large,* 116 Stat. 2899.

47. U.S. Department of Agriculture. *eGovernment Program: eGovernment Strategic Plan FY 2002-FY 2006.*

48. U.S. Department of Justice. *Information Technology Strategic Plan.*

49. U.S. Library of Congress and U.S. National Science Foundation. *It's About Time: Research Challenges in Digital Archiving and Long-Term Preservation.*

50. National Strategy to Secure Cyberspace.

51. U.S. Executive Office of the President. *Implementing the President's Management Agenda for E-Government: E-Government Strategy.* <http://www.whitehouse.gov/omb/egov/2003egov_strat.pdf>.

REFERENCES

"E-Government Act of 2002" (P.L. 107-347) *United Statutes at Large,* 116 Stat. 2899.

"Federal Information Technology" (Executive Order 13011, 16 July 1996), *Federal Register*, 61 F.R. 37657.

FirstGov.gov (Database) <http://www.firstgov.gov/index.shtml> (5 December 2003).

"Government Printing Office Electronic Information Access Enhancement Act of 1993" (P.L.103-40), *United Statutes at Large,* 107 Stat. 112.

"Homeland Security Act of 2002" (P.L. 107-296) *United Statutes at Large,* 116 Stat. 2135.

"National Commission On Libraries and Information Science Act" (P.L. 91-345), *United States Statutes at Large,* 84 Stat. 440.

National Strategy to Secure Cyberspace, Washington: Government Printing Office, 2003.

"USA PATRIOT Act of 2001" (P.L. 107-56), *United Statutes at Large,* 115 Stat. 272.

U.S. Advisory Council on the National Information Infrastructure. *KickStart Initiative: Connecting America's Communities to the Information Superhighway.* Washington: Government Printing Office, 1996.

U.S. Advisory Council on the National Information Infrastructure. *A Nation of Opportunity: Realizing the Promise of the Information Superhighway.* Washington: Government Printing Office, 1996.

U.S. Congress. Office of Technology Assessment. *Adult Literacy and New Technologies: Tools for a Lifetime.* Washington: Government Printing Office, 1993.

U.S. Congress. Office of Technology Assessment. *Finding A Balance: Computer Software, Intellectual Property and the Challenge of Technological Change.* Washington: Government Printing Office, 1992.

U.S. Congress. Office of Technology Assessment. *Information Security and Privacy In Network Environments.* Washington: Government Printing Office, 1994.

U.S. Congress. Office of Technology Assessment. *Information Technology and Its Impact on American Education.* Washington: Government Printing Office, 1982.

U.S. Congress. Office of Technology Assessment. *Informing the Nation: Federal Information Dissemination in an Electronic Age.* Washington: Government Printing Office, 1988.

U.S. Congress. Office of Technology Assessment. *Power on! New Tools for Teaching and Learning.* Washington: Government Printing Office, 1988.

U.S. Department of Agriculture. *eGovernment Program: eGovernment Strategic Plan FY 2002-FY 2006.* Washington: Government Printing Office, 2002.

U.S. Department of Commerce. National Telecommunications and Information Administration. *Connecting the Nation: Classrooms, Libraries, and Health Care Organization in the Information Age.* Washington: Government Printing Office, 1995.

U.S. Department of Commerce. National Telecommunications and Information Administration. *Falling Through the Net: Defining the Digital Divide.* 1999. <http://www.ntia.doc.gov/ntiahome/fttn99/contents.html> (9 December 2003).

U.S. Department of Commerce. National Telecommunications and Information Administration. *Falling Through the Net Toward Digital Inclusion: A Report on America's Access to Technology Tools.* 2002. <http://search.ntia.doc.gov/pdf/fttn00.pdf> (12 December 2003).

U.S. Department of Education. *Alliance for Excellence: Librarians Respond to a Nation at Risk.* Washington: Government Printing Office, 1984.

U.S. Department of Education. *The World of Work.* Washington: Government Printing Office, 1984.

U.S. Department of Health, Education and Welfare. *Inventory of Federal Data Bases Related to the Measurement of Poverty*. Washington: Government Printing Office, 1977.

U.S. Department of Justice. *Information Technology Strategic Plan*. Washington: Government Printing Office, 2002.

U.S. Executive Office of the President. *Implementing the President's Management Agenda for E-Government: E-Government Strategy*. Washington: Government Printing Office, 2003. <http://www.whitehouse.gov/omb/egov/2003egov_strat.pdf> (12 December 2003).

U.S. Federal Library and Information Center Committee. *Forum on Federal Information Policies: The Congressional Initiative. The sixth annual forum held March 22, 1989, a Summary of Proceedings*. Washington: Government Printing Office, 1989.

U.S. Federal Library and Information Center Committee. *The Seventh Annual FLICC Forum on Federal Information Policies, March 20, 1990: Access Is the Key. The Eighth Annual FLICC Forum on Federal Information Policies March 21, 1991: Building Information Superhighways: Supercomputing Networks and Libraries*. Washington: Government Printing Office, 1992.

U.S. Government Printing Office. GPO 2001: Vision for a New Millennium: Strategic Planning. Washington: Government Printing Office. 1991.

U.S. Government Printing Office. Library Programs Service. *Electronic Bulletin Board System for the Federal Depository Library Program: A Study*. Washington: Government Printing Office, 1991.

U.S. Government Printing Office. Library Programs Service. *Electronic Bulletin Board System*.

U.S. Government Printing Office. Library Programs Service. *Managing the FDLP Electronic Collection: A Policy and Planning Document*. Washington, D.C.: U.S. Government Printing Office, 1998.

U.S. Government Printing Office. *Status Report: GPO Access, a Service of the U.S. Government Printing Office*. Washington: Government Printing Office, 1994.

U.S. Government Printing Office. *Study to Identify Measures Necessary for a Successful Transition to a More Electronic Federal Depository Library Program*. Washington: Government Printing Office, 1996.

U.S. Government Printing Office. *United States Government Printing Office Annual Report Fiscal Year, 1990, 1991, 1998*. Washington: Government Printing Office.

U.S. House Committee on Government Operations. *Creative Ways of Using and Disseminating Federal Information: Hearings June 19, 1991, February 19 and June 4, 1992*. Washington: Government Printing Office, 1992.

U.S. Information Infrastructure Task Force. *The National Information Infrastructure: Agenda for Action*. Washington: Government Printing Office, 1993.

U.S. Interagency Kiosk Committee. *The Kiosk Network Solution: An Electronic Gateway to Government Service*. Washington: Government Printing Office, 1995.

U.S. Library of Congress and U.S. National Science Foundation. *It's About Time: Research Challenges in Digital Archiving and Long-Term Preservation, Final Report, Workshop on Research Challenges in Digital Archiving and Long-Term Preservation April 12-13, 2002*. Washington: Government Printing Office, 2003.

U.S. National Commission on Excellence in Education. *A Nation at Risk: The Imperative for Educational Reform*. Washington: Government Printing Office, 1983.

U.S. National Commission on Libraries and Information Science. *A Comprehensive Assessment of Public Information Dissemination: Final Report, Volume One.* Washington: Government Printing Office, 2001.

U.S. National Commission on Libraries and Information Science. *Government Publications: Their Role in the National Program for Library and Information Services.* Washington: Government Printing Office, 1979.

U.S. National Commission on Libraries and Information Science. *Information Literacy and Education for the 21st Century: Toward an Agenda for Action: A Symposium.* Washington: Government Printing Office, 1989.

U.S. National Commission on Libraries and Information Science. *Kids and the Internet: The Promise and the Perils, an NCLIS Hearing in Arlington, Virginia November 10, 1998.* Washington: Government Printing Office, 1999.

U.S. National Commission on Libraries and Information Science. *National Information Policy: Report to the President of the United States.* Washington: Government Printing Office, 1976.

U.S. National Commission on Libraries and Information Science. *Report on the Assessment of Electronic Government Information Products.* Washington: Government Printing Office, 1999.

U.S. National Commission on Libraries and Information Science. *Toward a National Program for Library and Information Services: Goals for Action.* Washington: Government Printing Office, 1975.

U.S. National Information Infrastructure Advisory Council. *Common Ground: Fundamental Principles for the National Information Infrastructure: First Report of the National Information Infrastructure Advisory Council.* Washington: Government Printing Office, 1995.

U.S. Office of the Vice President. *Reengineering Through Information Technology: Accompanying Report of the National Performance Review.* Washington: Government Printing Office, 1993.

U.S. Superintendent of Documents. Office of Electronic Information Dissemination Services. *Helpful Hints for Searching Federal Databases Online via GPO Access.* Washington: Government Printing Office, 1996.

White House Conference on Library and Information Services. *Information 2000: Library and Information Services for the 21st Century.* Washington: Government Printing Office, 1991.

GOVERNMENT INFORMATION MANAGEMENT

Documents Data Miner©: Creating a Paradigm Shift in Government Documents Collection Development and Management

Nan Myers

SUMMARY. In April 1998, the Documents Data Miner (DDM) was announced as a partnership site of the Government Printing Office's Federal Depository Library Program (FDLP), with an enhanced proto-

Nan Myers is Associate Professor and Librarian for Government Documents, Patents and Trademarks, Wichita State University Libraries, 1845 Fairmount, Wichita, KS 67260-0068 (E-mail: nan.myers@wichital.edu).

The author wishes to thank the following institutions for their ongoing support of the DDM/DDM2 projects: Wichita State University Libraries, the National Institute for Aviation Research, University Computing and Telecommunications Services, and the Government Printing Office.

[Haworth co-indexing entry note]: "Documents Data Miner©: Creating a Paradigm Shift in Government Documents Collection Development and Management." Myers, Nan. Co-published simultaneously in *The Reference Librarian* (The Haworth Information Press, an imprint of The Haworth Press, Inc.) No. 94, 2006, pp. 163-190; and: *The Changing Face of Government Information: Providing Access in the Twenty-First Century* (ed: Suhasini L. Kumar) The Haworth Information Press, an imprint of The Haworth Press, Inc., 2006, pp. 163-190. Single or multiple copies of this article are available for a fee from The Haworth Document Delivery Service [1-800-HAWORTH, 9:00 a.m. - 5:00 p.m. (EST). E-mail address: docdelivery@haworthpress.com].

type version (DDM2) announced in October 2001. Documents Data Miner 2 is located on the Internet at http://govdoc.wichita.edu/ddm2. DDM was originally developed in 1995-1996 as a research project which attempted to eliminate labor-intensive tasks in processing and collection development of government documents at Wichita State University's Libraries by developing in-house technology, resulting in a relational database built using Paradox. The development team quickly understood the potential for mounting a nationally useful set of tools on the Internet, utilizing Government Printing Office (GPO) legacy metadata which were emerging simultaneously as files available for download from the Federal Bulletin Board. The data mining capabilities of DDM/DDM2 incorporate tabular data available in the *List of Classes*, *Discontinued List*, *Superseded List*, *Item Lister*, *Federal Depositories Library Directory*, the GPO Shipping Lists, and GPO MARC Records. Union lists of documents are available to users categorized by geographic area (in miles), by state, and by national region. Use data collected by *WebTrends* documents over 11,000 unique users of the DDM2 set of Web tools in 2003. The emergence of the Documents Data Miner products single-handedly moved issues of collection development, processing and cataloging of government documents from a 19th century paper-based environment to a 21st century data mining model. *[Article copies available for a fee from The Haworth Document Delivery Service: 1-800-HAWORTH. E-mail address: <docdelivery@haworthpress.com> Website: <http://www.HaworthPress.com>* © *2006 by The Haworth Press, Inc. All rights reserved.]*

KEYWORDS. Documents Data Miner, DDM, Documents Data Miner 2, DDM2, *List of Classes*, shipping lists, MARC Records, *Item Lister*, government documents, Government Printing Office, GPO, Federal Depository Library Program, FDLP, Library Program Service, LPS, electronic transition, collection development, data mining, data warehousing

INTRODUCTION

The Documents Data Miner products DDM and DDM2 provide a library management system for U.S. government documents distributed by the Federal Depository Library Program of the Government Printing Office.[1] As Web-based relational database systems, DDM and DDM2 assist depository libraries in processing, cataloging, bibliographic control, and collection management of federal documents collections by providing a sophisticated set of customizable data mining tools.

Data mining is a process that uses advanced information technologies to extract valid and comprehensible information from large, frequently diverse datasets. The information or knowledge extracted can then be used to support crucial decision-making. The methodology that "combines and coordinates many sets of diversified data into a unified and consistent body of useful information"[2] is called data warehousing. The data warehouse architecture consists of a relational database and an information management system server hosting end user queries.

The Documents Data Miner products are large relational databases, in which specific information can be extracted from numerous tables and assembled in meaningful ways. The tables are linked by the use of a primary key which provides a common link. In the DDM products, the primary key is the Item Number/SuDoc Number pair. When we began working with the DDM tables, we did not know all of the potential relationships among the tables. As we "dug" for valid data relationships, we employed techniques referred to as "discovery-driven data mining" (which refers to seeking unknown but valid information or patterns) and "drill-down technology" (which suggests searching deeply into the information).

While data mining techniques had been widely touted in the business arena for several years, by the mid-1990s they had not been used by the FDLP to support depository libraries in decision making. The depository management environment, in fact, was still primarily paper-based, with separate and disparate tools, such as item cards, computer-generated library profiles with lists of item numbers only, and various print publications, such as the *List of Classes*, the *Discontinued List*, and the *Superseded List*.

A search of library literature supports the fact that by the mid- to late 1990s, the understanding of how data mining could add value to library decision-making was just beginning to emerge in library management circles. The Association of Research Libraries' recently published *Spec Kit* titled *Data Mining and Data Warehousing* (July 2003) documents some of that progress and offers a list of articles and papers which have surfaced largely from 1998 to the present. In the conclusion to the Executive Summary, the editors state: "Libraries are discovering, as businesses have, the value of merging existing data or full-text resources to form a very large data warehouse that can be mined for analytical purposes."[3]

RESPONSES TO THE ELECTRONIC TRANSITION

The mandate to the Government Printing Office to comply with the transition to digitized publication of information came in 1993 with Public Law 103-40, known as the Government Printing Office Electronic Information Enhancement Act of 1993.[4] That transition was begun in 1994 and is continuing today at an accelerating rate. The public impact hit first with the introduction of *GPO Access* in 1994 and its subsequent development into a massive full-text finding aid and permanent archive. However, for depository libraries, the electronic transition in Government publishing produced substantial change without a well-planned infrastructure. The daily workload of processing, cataloging, and collection development remained paper-based. In addition, until 1999, there was little reduction in the physical selection list available from the FDLP. In fact, the development of electronic access to government titles for the first five years after the announcement of the "electronic transition" seemed to be running parallel to publication in physical formats rather than supplanting them. This compounded workload creates problems for depository staffs struggling to juggle their traditional workloads with the emerging growth of the government's new online bibliographic agenda.

The national mandate to GPO was concurrent with a local mandate at Wichita State University's Libraries to downsize the government documents collection to conserve space. The WSU Library has been a federal depository since 1901, selecting at the 55-60% level, with approximately 500,000 items in paper, 250,000 microfiche titles, about 20,000 maps, and 2,000 CD-ROMs in its collection. In 1994-1995, access to the collection had been enhanced by the tapeloads of cataloging records and the move of both cataloging and processing to Technical Services. Then, in 1996, came the mandate from Library Administration to address: (1) space issues in the Documents collection, which was 86.4% full; (2) place a greater emphasis upon electronic access to documents; and (3) market the documents collection to increase its use. Since weeding and deselection were the only options for addressing the first part of this mandate (the Administration having ruled out outside storage, compact shelving, and a building initiative), the Project Team Leader[5] sought decision-making assistance–what to weed and what to deselect?[6]

Ideally, a university depository library should weed and deselect materials which least contribute to its programs, and which are readily available elsewhere in the state. The Wichita State University Libraries' long-established collection development policy for government documents made it clear which materials should be protected for the sake of program support; however, it was no simple task to determine what was being collected regionally. In short, there was no union listing utility in any format at the national level.

Union listing is an old methodology that allows for cooperative collection development among participating libraries. The Government Documents Project Team Leader felt the damage of collection reduction would best be avoided if deselection could occur with knowledge of other state libraries' profiles. At the same time, in Technical Services, the Government Documents Group[7] needed a tool to assist with both cataloging and processing issues. Specifically, at the top of the wish list were a searchable *List of Classes* and way to affiliate the printout of the Library's item number profile with the titles and SuDoc numbers in the *List of Classes*. The author and the Head of Acquisitions[8] began to work on the development of an in-house government documents relational database with a preliminary design accomplished through a partnership between Library faculty and staff and the faculty and graduate students of the University's Departments of Electrical Engineering, Computer Science, and Decision Science.[9] Thus was born GPRD (Government Documents Processing Relational Database), which was pronounced "jeopardy."

PART I:
CASE STUDY DEVELOPMENT OF A PROTOTYPE

Development of GPRD occurred between Fall 1995 and Spring 1997, culminating in a presentation at the Federal Depository Library Conference in April 1997 shared with Thomas G. Tyler, Associate Director of the University of Denver, who in 1996 had published his *Basic Depository Library Documents: The Unauthorized HTML Editions* (*BDLD*) site on the Internet.[10] The presentation title, "Managing the Depository Database: Some Opportunities with Shared Technology," emphasized one of the best survival tactics in the depository environment–sharing and the formation of institutional relationships. With a similar intent to ease workload, the two initiatives held common objectives. However, Tyler's BDLD concentrated on adapting FDLP documents for republication on the Web and consisted of flat files, while the goal of GPRD (and later DDM) was to create searchable files in a relational database management system (RDBMS).

GPRD evolved from flat files, or a simple data warehouse, into a complete relational database. Over an 18-month period, it became an information management system with data mining programs, which provided a platform for report generation and a decision-support system. Initially, GPRD was created to serve our needs for easy storage and retrieval of item file information, for warehousing map holdings, and for tracking unresolved claims and rainchecks. Because the initial work in the Fall of 1995 predated the ASCII text files available online from the Government Printing Office, much of the data in the tables was derived from legacy systems or keyed in manually. We acquired an item file from the University of California/Riverside, on diskettes for $100.00.[11] Then, we imported the State of Kansas Union Listing of Government Documents distributed to us on diskettes by Washburn Law Library.[12] Washburn had been maintaining Kansas depository selection profiles for several years, but was dependant on depository librarians to send updates and becoming discouraged with its lack of cooperation. Our GPO profile was pre-Item Lister and was originally keyed in by a student. Other data keyed in included information in the map file and unautomated check-out data for the use file. Finally, to obtain an initial sample of about 400 LC subject headings from our Government Document bibliographic records, a programmer ran extract programs written in COBOL from our NOTIS system.

The platform for GPRD was Borland's Paradox 7 for Windows 95. Software included Paradox Application Language for the database (creating the forms or views from the tables) and Borland's C++ Compiler for Windows 95 for the data mining. The primary key (unique identifier) for the database, or the common denominator of all the tables, was the Item Number *and* SuDocs Number pair–a compound key. Development continued such that information in these tables (essentially a data warehouse), could be associated using a query generator (Paradox's Query by Example) to achieve a discovery-driven data mining system. A team of four graduate students working in Acquisitions was assembled to create the database and design the views (or forms) for their Master's project in Computer Science.[13]

By the fall of 1996, we replaced the data in the GPRD tables via the BDLD Web site. With permission from Tyler, we used the BDLD as a value-added network (VAN) to import the following data into GPRD:

- WSU's List of Item Selections (profile).
- The Kansas Union List (profiles of the 18 other Kansas depository libraries).

- The List of Classes.
- The List of Discontinued Items.

In order to implement the BDLD to GPRD data migration, Tyler provided access to his source code. A professor in the WSU Computer Science Department agreed to do the C++ programming required for the data transfer. All the text files were converted into tables in a temporary directory and then derived over to the permanent project directory after we verified the accuracy of the files.

It was clear immediately that GPRD would allow us to manage cumbersome tasks which had previously been handled manually. In addition, GPRD provided a platform for report generation and a decision-support system for collection development. GPRD provided the Library the abilities:

- To reduce labor-intensive tasks in a period of reduced staffing;
- To accomplish inspection requirements;
- To address issues of public access in an electronic era;
- To focus on pro-active rather than re-active decision making; and
- To facilitate statewide depository goal-setting.

The development of GPRD represented a proactive stance during a period of uncertainty and change in the history of Federal documents. The work on GPRD confirmed the viability of the Design Team's techniques and, because of the cooperation and interest of faculty and students in the University's Computer Science and Electrical Engineering Departments, the costs were affordable. GPRD clearly pointed to a national need for a standardized set of electronic tools for working on documents. The designers decided to use GPRD as a prototype for an Internet-based utility so that other depository libraries throughout the United States could have access to a set of tools for processing documents and managing collection development.

IMPLEMENTATION OF DOCUMENTS DATA MINER

The Design Team determined to migrate the GPRD information system to the Web. By early 1997, sufficient Federal documents metadata was available to begin building a set of documents Web tools using official data from the Government Printing Office files at the Federal Bulletin Board File Libraries. Files created by the GPO/LPS for downloading were the *List of Classes* (in CSV format) and Profiles (the *Directory of Depository Libraries* in dBase format). In addition, the Item Lister had been introduced by GPO/LPS in December 1996, allowing online access to the current item selection profiles of the approximately 1,400 depository libraries in the Federal Depository Library Program. Since the *Inactive/Discontinued List* did not become available in an official file until the spring of 1999, we initially retained the data we had derived from the BDLD with a data mining program and later overlaid it. Files developed in GPRD which were specific to WSU information needs did not migrate (for example, WSU's map holdings and user data).

In order to rapidly implement the development of the Web site, the Library's Design Team was fortunate to be able to capitalize on the expertise of colleagues at Wichita State's National Institute for Aviation Research (NIAR).[14] Initially, NIAR was willing to lease space on their server to the Library for the Documents Data Miner project. Then the Operations Director at NIAR became interested in prototyping a database for a large body of metadata because of similarities to some other projects they were working on. In exchange for a nominal monthly storage fee, they contributed time, expertise, hardware and software, and student hours for the project. The Library also hired a graduate student to work on the project.

During the summer and fall of 1998, the Web data mining prototype was developed. Nan Myers and John Williams of the Library provided the overall project conception and management. Myers also contributed the name and acronym for the utility ("Documents Data Miner" or "DDM") and the layout for the home page, which was implemented by a computer graphics undergraduate employed at NIAR. John Ellis developed the architecture for Documents Data Miner. He provided SQL Server database implementation, query algorithms, and Web database publication. If properly billed to the Library, initial development of the Documents Data Miner would have cost in excess of $25,000.

Official Databases

There are five official GPO databases in Documents Data Miner: *List of Classes*, Government Authors File, Item Lister's *Current Item Number Selection Profiles for Depository Libraries*, the *Federal Depository Library Directory*, and the *Inactive or Discontinued Items List*. The initial development goals for the Documents Data Miner were:

- A searchable *List of Classes,*
- A searchable *Inactive/Discontinued List,*
- Union lists which could be associated with the *List of Classes,*
- Collection profiling tools,
- Depository directory and e-mail access,
- Mirroring, security and user profiling,
- Open system follow-ons, such as export of query/profile results.

The home page design provides four modules for key tasks and a frame for navigation. At the frame, users can see the latest date that files have been refreshed.

List of Classes and Inactive/Discontinued

In the *List of Classes* module, users can search the current *List of Classes* by field, search the *Inactive/Discontinued List* by field, or merge the searches by choosing "all" at the "Status" box. Choices in the search grid include Agency, Item Number, SuDocs Stem, Title, Format, and Status. A pop-up box at "Agency" provides a list of government agencies with the sum of active item number stems for each agency. A drop-down box at "Format" provides the formats used by the GPO: Paper, Microfiche, CD-ROM, Electronic, or Electronic Library (i.e., online).

The *Inactive/Discontinued List* feature, offered separately as well as combined with the LOC search, contains unique data mined from the BDLD in the "Notes" fields–manually entered annotations from Shipping Lists, additions and changes to the LOC, surveys, and other LPS sources. From 1999 on, the official GPO data overlaid that of the introductory version; however, the Notes mined from BDLD have been retained.

Depository Selection and Directory

Module three is called "Depository Selection and Directory," and merges profile data from the Item Lister with the *List of Classes*. This allows the user to view complete item information for the selections in their own profile. It also provides directory information for each depository and e-mail functions for ease in communicating. The search parameters allow users to query by single library, by geographic patterns (by city, by state), or by type of library (Community College, Academic, Law, State Libraries, etc.). Each depository library's profile search screen has an Agency drop-down box with item number totals by agency selected by that depository.

Tools

The "Union Listing" tool, which was developed to assist depositories with building and/or downsizing their collections, can be accessed by clicking on any Item Number in a depository library's profile, after setting an appropriate filter. Module four, titled "Tools–Configuration," provides the filter for creating union lists. Users can filter in three ways: by state, by region, or by distance from a depository. Often, viewing the item number holdings of an entire state is the methodology in selection or deselection decision-making. But, in large cities with numerous depository libraries within a small radius, the distance-setting feature is most useful for consortial collecting or shared housing agreements. A Gazetteer, with longitude and latitude information extracted from a CD-ROM published by the U.S. Geological Survey, was added to the tables of the Documents Data Miner to allow this customization.

When a user sets up a "Session Configuration," a shortcut to their depository profile is automatically configured on the frame of the DDM homepage. This shortcut persists on DDM for several days, deriving from the "cookies" required from the user's computer for accessing DDM. Also at the "Session Configuration" page is the mechanism for changing the number of records per page in a query return from the default of 25 to another number, allowing scrolling through lengthy returns.

Exports and Downloads

DDM was designed to allow users to build their own inhouse databases with files from the Tools page. The comma delimited ASCII files from the FBB are available in ASCII text or Excel. If the user sets up a "Session Configuration," then DDM recognizes the depository number and also provides customized files available for export into Excel. All files are dated. Available are:

- Your Depository's Selected Item List
- Your Depository's Non-Selected Item List
- Your Selects and Non-Selects Together
- GPO's Current *List of Classes*

- GPO's Current *Inactive/Discontinued List*
- GPO's Depository Directory (profiles)

An added enhancement is the ability to export a query into Excel or CSV. This feature is available from the Tools page, but is also available at the bottom of every query return from the various modules of DDM.

Profile Status Option

By using the "Status" feature in a library's depository profile screen, a user may query for five options:

- Active
- Dropped
- Unselected
- Active + Dropped
- Active + Dropped + Unselected

Thus, a library can pinpoint exactly what their status is with regard to the active *List of Classes*. This feature is particularly useful during the GPO's Annual Update Cycle, when depository libraries are scrutinizing their profile selections for potential "adds" or "drops." A larger depository which involves subject librarians in the collection development process can make use of printouts agency by agency in order to clearly capture what is already being received and what titles potentially could be selected.

ARCHITECTURE AND FUNCTIONALITY

The design parameters for DDM were as follows:[15]

- Use only GPO data as provided with no scrubbing of data.
- Use low cost "wintel" (Windows OS and Intel cpu) database servers and Microsoft Operating Systems.
- Use low cost "wintel" Web server. The IIS 4.0 server from Microsoft came bundled with NT server 4.0 and was therefore free. It is also extremely powerful and easy to use. There are about four sets of ASP (active server pages) which are the core components of the DDM. The Microsoft paradigm for serving dynamic data on Web pages is elegant and simple. It takes very little (but finely tuned)

code to produce the pages that pop up when those queries are submitted.
- Use only Web-based clients. The development of the Web browser made the problem of distributing DDM moot.
- Target both Netscape and IE browsers. We were very careful to make sure that our programs would work equally well on either Netscape 3.0 or IE 3.0 or better.
- Make it flexible and keep it simple. The programming for the project was completed using only Microsoft VB 5.0, Microsoft Access 97, and Microsoft Interdev. There were no C++ scripts, no special libraries, and no custom CGIs.

At the time of DDM's announcement at the 7th Annual Federal Depository Library Conference in April 1998, there were 1,364 active depositories in the FDLP. DDM also showed five inactive depositories from data retained since the initial loading of files in the fall of 1997. There were 9,507 active GPO items and 8,158 inactive GPO items. The active Union List held 2,718,126 data elements, while the inactive Union List already held 225,754–another example of data retention in DDM, which has enabled us to reconstruct prior profiles for some depositories during the past six years. The Design Team determined never to delete data and, in the summer of 1998, a system was initiated to date-tag every data element in the database.

There were other considerations, caused by the lack of uniformity and consistency of GPO legacy data. For example, since the *List of Classes* and *Inactive/Discontinued List* are published by different departments within the FDLP, a time lag occurs between an item number dropping off the LOC and being published as inactive or discontinued. Because DDM still retains data for these item numbers, a way was devised to reflect this temporary status. Officially, in DDM, these item numbers are designated as "undefined." Unofficially, they are referred to as "orphans." After monthly updates to DDM, the "orphans list" report is sent to the appropriate person at the FDLP.

Numerous enhancements have been made to the Documents Data Miner since its debut. Most notable are the features that allow exporting of files and query returns. The Design Team intended from the outset that users of DDM would be able to extract files (normalized on DDM) and use them to build their own in-house databases. These files are available from the Tools page of DDM. The comma delimited ASCII files from the FBB are available in ASCII text or Excel (our conversion). In addition, one can export any query return into Excel or CSV.

This feature is available from the Tools page, but is also available at the bottom of every query return from the various modules of DDM2. It is thus possible for users to use DDM data exports for short-term projects (such as examining their selections from a certain agency in Excel, while adding their own in-house project-related data) or for creation of a full database for long-term project work or as a permanent record.

PARTNERSHIP WITH GPO

By the fall of 1997, the Design Team was ready to approach the FDLP regarding a partnership arrangement for DDM, and by December 1997, the general agreement for the partnership was in place between the WSU Libraries and the GPO. We determined that only a partnership arrangement would afford the publicity and use compliance necessary to justify the efforts of the WSU Libraries and NIAR in the development of DDM. Documents Data Miner became an official partnership site of the Government Printing Office on April 15, 1998 and was announced in a presentation before an audience of over 200 depository librarians at the 7th Annual Federal Depository Library Conference in Washington, D.C.[16] A link was established from the FDLP Desktop to the Documents Data Miner as an official partner and dozens of depositories linked DDM to their Web sites. The positive response was immediate, as reflected in use data collected by *WebTrends* since the announcement date.[17]

Another demonstration of the positive response was the instant workload created for the developers in responding to e-mail and phone messages requesting assistance with use of DDM and setting up of in-house projects, as well as the request for state-level presentations. From Fall 1998 through 2000, the author gave invited presentations at meetings of Government Documents Round Tables in Ohio, Michigan, Louisiana, Georgia, Minnesota/North Dakota, and the MPLA Conference in Arizona. There was also an invited instructional session given at the 1999 Depository Council Meeting in Kansas City, Missouri. Dozens of messages with instructional explanations and monthly reports were posted by the author on the Govdoc-L and, later, the DocTech-L listservs. The give-and-take from communications with library staff working with government documents led to many of the improvements in the DDM during this time; and, DDM's programmer, John Ellis, was persistent and enthusiastic in making changes.

DEVELOPMENT OF DOCUMENTS DATA MINER 2

In December 1998, the GPO began posting the monthly cataloging records produced by the FDLC's Cataloging Branch in the SPCMOCAT files at the Federal Bulletin Board. The records are available in one, long datastream requiring conversion to MARC format (parsing), but once that was accomplished, it became possible for the first time to tie the full bibliographic records of government publications to the *List of Classes* and to depository profiles. The DDM Design Team envisioned an array of new features, including: providing free access to batched or single downloadable records, and designing a public access catalog for the use of smaller libraries without government documents records in their OPACs. Added to this was the potential of the Shipping Lists, which had been posted at the FBB since 1997, but which were not available in a searchable utility. Extraction of titles at the piece level from the Shipping Lists would support development of a shelflist of documents actually shipped to depository libraries. These new pieces of the Federal depository workload puzzle made it possible to provide, in one online location, a complete Library Management System for United States Federal documents. The project designers turned their attention to a new version of DDM titled Documents Data Miner 2.

Documents Data Miner 2 (DDM2) was initially announced and demonstrated as a pilot project in October 2001 at the Federal Depository Library Conference. By this time, DDM2 had become a collaboration between Wichita State University Libraries and the University Computing Center.[18] The Libraries' Project Team remained the same.

Retaining all the capabilities of the original data mining utility, DDM2 also introduced new modules for:

- Shipping List Services
- GPO MARC records in the MARC LOCATOR and URL LOCATOR
- Shelf Lists
- Superseded List
- DDM2 Catalog

As mentioned above, the conception of the new features was informed by the appearance of additional data files from the GPO. GPO presented shipping list files from 1997 to date and the output of MARC records created by GPO's Cataloging Division from December 1998 to date. In addition, the GPO posted the 2000 edition of the *Superseded List* as a pdf file, which was the first electronic version of this title.

There was some disappointment in the depository community that GPO failed to deliver a file of the *Superseded List* suitable for data mining; however, it was not much work to convert this to Access and create a searchable data product. This list is one of many files on the Tools page of DDM2 which are available for download by the depository community.

Work on DDM2 development was initially regarded as a pilot project in 2000-2001, as the Libraries searched for possible avenues of cost recovery. The development goals for DDM2 were ambitious enough to require substantial new design work, a more robust platform, and more extensive oversight and maintenance. The development goals for Documents Data Miner 2 were:

- Searchable Shipping Lists
- National shelf listing capability, recording items shipped to depositories from GPO
- Searchable *Superseded List*
- Provide export of USMARC records from GPO Cataloging (available at the FBB from 12/98 to present
- Identify the subset of records with URLs
- Full-text indexing of GPO MARC Records
- Provide bulk export of GPO MARC Records
- Develop an online national public access catalog to government information, which can be profiled for individual libraries' selections.

The list of value-added features for DDM2 grew rapidly. For example, the design of searchable Shipping Lists also made the creation of a national Shelf Listing tool possible because of the piece level description in the lists and the extensions of SuDoc numbers beyond the stem. It is now possible to look up the title of a journal and see exactly which issues have actually shipped. Monographic series titles such as the *Water Supply Papers* (I 19.13:) can be tracked. Also, for the first time, it is possible to review the monographic titles issued and shipped in the general publications numbers (such as the Department of Agriculture's general publications classed at A 1.2:).

Searchable Shipping Lists

Documents Data Miner 2 provides the only searchable depository shipping list utility, allowing users to search by: Shipping List number, title, fiscal year and month, shipping year and month, item number, SuDoc number, and media (all or to filter for paper, microfiche, electronic, separates). In addition, it is possible to set a depository filter which eliminates from the query return shipping lists with no item numbers selected by that depository. For example, in September 2003, 74 shipping lists were issued by the GPO. Depository number 0204A (Wichita State) only received items on 60 of those lists, thus minimizing the number of lists to review.

When a shipping list is opened, two additional features are available. First, a link is provided to the official pdf file from the GPO, making claiming easier. Second, a column titled "MARC" is added to the shipping list information providing links to any MARC records which are warehoused in the DDM2 database for that title (actually for that Item Number/SuDoc pair). One click provides access to the MARC record citation. Once there, the user can view the MARC record and/or download the record directly into the local institution's OPAC. Header information added to the MARC record includes a designation of the record as "Monograph" or "Serial," the MARC Revision Date, which is the date of the latest GPO Cataloging revision to the records, and finally, the DDM2 Revision Date, which is the date of download into DDM2.

If the user prefers to batch load all monograph records or all serial records from a certain shipping list, it is possible to scroll to the bottom of the shipping list and do so. The MARC record feature works well for monographs, where the database provides an exact match on the Item and SuDoc Numbers for the title. However, with serial titles, the match cannot always be exact and the user may need to scroll through multiple MARC records in the query return. The algorithm for display of serials is to first run the query for an exact match of an Item Number and SuDoc Number stem. Then, if nothing is found, the algorithm makes a second pass for a match on the Item Number and the SuDoc Number and a wildcard. For example, the 086 field for the SuDoc Number in the MARC record only provides the SuDoc stem for serials such as NAS 1.15: (NASA Technical Memorandum). On Shipping List 2003-0426-m, one of the titles is "The Evaluation and Implementation of a Water Containment System to Support Aerospace Flywheel Testing," a NASA Tech Memo classed at NAS 1.15:. The DDM2 MARC feature attaches 95 records to this SuDoc stem, providing an index in alphabetical order when opened. It is possible that none of the list of records will match the sought after title.

The Shelf List Module

In DDM2, a separately searchable Shelf List module ties individual pieces on the shipping lists to the MARC records and offers the only existing automated shelf-listing of multi-part titles and the general publications classes of the SuDoc class system. As of October 2003, this module held data elements for 154,100 individually shipped pieces. The Shelf List can be searched by item number, SuDoc Number, or title. It can also be filtered by format category (any category, paper, microfiche, separates, electronic) and by the depository's number. A search for the title *Internal Revenue Bulletin* produces a list of 206 holdings shipped beginning in 1997. Along with the title, Item Number, and SuDoc Number, the query return provides each shipping list number and ship date for the 206 holdings. The shipping lists are hotlinked, allowing the user to navigate to other pieces of information about that item.

MARC Locator and URL Locator

The MARC Locator warehouses MARC records created by GPO Cataloging and extracted from their monthly files posted at the Federal Bulletin Board. The URL Locator is a subset of the MARC Locator, representing records with an 856 field for online access. Thus, users can access only records for online resources if they prefer. The records in both MARC and URL Locator modules are searchable using: OCLC number, Item or SuDoc Numbers, agency author (draws from the 1xx fields), title, title key words, subject (draws from the 6xx fields), or publication type (monograph, serial, or map). It is also possible to filter the query return by depository profile. The query return provides the title, Item Number, SuDoc Number, hotlinked PURLs, OCLC number, access to the MARC view of the record, the GPO timestamp, and the option to download the record. If the search is done on "agency," the agency name also appears in the results screen.

Full Text Indexing

In the Spring of 2003, full text indexing was added to the MARC and URL Locator and the Catalog modules. In those modules, DDM2 searches on "words" rather than letters, with search logic. DDM2 can search for: a word or phrase, the prefix of a word or phrase, a word near another word, a word inflectionally generated from another, or a word that has a higher designated weighting than another word.

DDM2 Catalog

This feature is still in development, but the framework of a public access catalog is firmly in place. The DDM2 Catalog offers both public and MARC views of the GPO records in its database. The Design Team has long had a number of ideas for enhancing this feature, but the resources to accomplish this (time and money) have not yet been available. The DDM2 Catalog could serve as an individual library's catalog, whether or not they were a designated depository library. For small libraries which do not have government document records in their OPAC, the availability of a customizable screen providing entrée for searching government information could indeed be an asset. The intention would be to allow institutions to apply their names to the home screen (as in "Haysville Public Library's Government Information Catalog"). Projected design work at one time included plans to offer leased space at a modest fee to depository libraries on Wichita State University's servers for check-in and holdings purposes. The Design Team refers to this concept as a "fourth generation catalog," with the first generation being the card catalog, the second being a mainframe-based catalog, and the third, the client-server catalog. The "fourth generation catalog" will be purely Web-based.

PART II:
KNOWLEDGE DISCOVERY USING DDM2

An examination of the data elements warehoused in DDM2 provides a number of discoveries. The total active item numbers in the *List of Classes*, for example, declined 24% in the past two years, from a total count of 8,534 in October 2001 to a total of 6,476 in October 2003.[19] This information either supports those who are aware of the shrinking of the physical depository system, or concerns those who know that the FDLP assigns item numbers even to virtual resources and wonder if the FDLP acquisitions and cataloging staffs are keeping up. In fact, it may reflect long overdue weeding of the *LOC*. Information from the Shipping List data and the MARC Record data offer interesting insights.

Shipping List Data–Demonstration of the Decline of the "Physical FDLP"

By October 2003, there were a total of 8,166 shipping lists in DDM2. However, an examination of the chronology of the lists and volume of items shipped since 1997, clearly demonstrates the decline of the "physical FDLP." From the advent of shipping list availability in 01/01/97 to 10/15/01, a total of 6,278 shipping lists were posted at the FBB. In FY2002, 980 lists were added for a total of 7,258. And in FY2003 only 908 lists were added, bringing the total to 8,166.

A review of the actual items shipped against these shipping lists from 1997 to 2003 illustrates the significant decline in the volume of materials flowing towards depository libraries during that time:

- 1997:   28,087
- 1998:   32,499
- 1999:   27,342
- 2000:   21,984
- 2001:   16,523
- 2002:   15,767
- 2003:   11,351

From 1997-2003, the volume shipped decreased 60%. And, between 2000-2003, the decrease was 48%. Workload in processing of physical government documents has thus decreased overall by 60%, with an accelerating decline during the past three years.

Even more telling is a look at the number of supposedly active Item Numbers in the *List of Classes* which have not been shipped in years. When these statistics were gathered in October 2003, the current active Item Number total was 6,476.

- Item #s not shipped since 9/1/1997 = 3,176
- Item #s not shipped since 9/1/2000 = 4,282
- Item #s not shipped since 9/1/2001 = 4,655
- Item #s not shipped since 9/1/2002 = 5,028

Thus, in FY2003, GPO did not ship against 5,028 Item Numbers, which is 78% of the total active Item Number count of 6,476. In other words, depositories have the potential to receive physical items for only 22% of active Item Numbers.

Depository libraries should ask the question "What is our *actual* depository profile percentage?" In the past six years, 3,176 item numbers were not shipped, which is 51% of the total current active item number count of 6,476. There will be some deviation from these figures, because the active item number count changes from year to year. However, it is probably fair to say that about 50% of GPO item numbers have not shipped in six years.

Using the Wichita State University Libraries' profile of 65% selection rate of item numbers as an example, a query was run to determine how many of the 3,176 unshipped item numbers were in their active profile. The response was that 2,104 of the unshipped item numbers were in the WSU profile, about half of its 4,208 selected items. Is WSU really a 34% depository instead of a 65% depository? It depends on how many of the 2,104 item numbers in the WSU profile that did not ship are for online-only titles. It also depends on how many records are in the WSU catalog for online titles.

MARC Record Data–Demonstration of the Rise of the "Virtual FDLP"

The MARC Locator module of DDM2 warehouses MARC records created by GPO Cataloging and posted at the FBB from December 1998 to the present. It also warehouses 131,464 MARC records created by GPO Cataloging from 1991 through November 1998, which were loaded into DDM2 as a batch file in October 2002. By October 2003, MARC records in DDM2 totaled 207,000.

The growth of MARC records containing PURLs in the 856 field illustrates the explosion of government resources available on the Internet, as well as the determination of GPO's Cataloging Division to devote resources to creation of MARC cataloging records for online titles. The progression in cataloging statistics for MARC records with PURLs is as follows:

- Total October 2001 = 14,215
- Total October 2002 = 25,475
- Total October 2003 = 38,565
- Total January 2004 = 45,586

Between 2001 and 2003, GPO Cataloging Division added 24,350 MARC records with PURLs, for an increase of 171%. Production appears to be accelerating, as in the four-month span between October 2003 and January 2004, there was an 18% growth rate.

Another point of measurement for GPO MARC records is the rising rate of cataloging produced for online-only titles. These are titles which exist only online and have no physical distribution. In October 2003, the DDM2 held 10,443 records for online-only titles. Again, using Wichita State as an example of a library which may want to filter record downloads against their 65% FDLP profile, the total records for online-only titles related to the WSU profile total 8,047–or, 77% of the total online-only records available in DDM2. Whether Wichita State would want to regard itself as a 34% depository library (for physical items) or a 77% depository library (for virtual items), two conclusions can be suggested. First, the concept of a depository "profile" needs to be defined. Second, libraries may wish to concentrate heavily on cataloging online titles, and especially online-only titles, in order to fulfill their mission as depository libraries.

PART III:
DEMOGRAPHICS AND COSTS

Data on the use of Documents Data Miner and DDM2 has been gathered in *WebTrends* since the utility was announced in April 1998. The heaviest use has always been in the two-month period in June and July during the GPO's Annual Update Cycle. The addition of the modules in DDM2 led to a significant jump in use statistics between 2000 and 2003. Total hits in 2003 reflect more than eight times the usage in 2000. There are close to five times the average number of visitors per day and about four times the number of visitor sessions. Not surprisingly, the most active identifiable user organization, after America Online, is the U.S. Government Printing Office. With DDM2, the FDLP staff have access for the first time to searchable shipping lists and electronic shelflisting of document titles, as well as the convenience of the other DDM2 features. Other very active users in 2003 include Arizona Public Service, Rutgers, University of Wyoming, Excalibur Group, Georgia Tech, West Texas A&M, Buffalo & Erie County Public, Berkeley, and the University of Minnesota.

WebTrends Use Statistics for DDM in 2000:

- Total hits   179,437
- Average per day   1,080

- Visitor sessions   10,950
- Average per day   65
- Average visitor session length   07:02
- Unique visitors   3,839
- Visitors who visited once   2,446
- Visitors more than once   1,393

WebTrends Use Statistics for DDM in 2003:

- Total hits   1,495,627
- Average per day   5,122
- Visitor sessions   41,960
- Average per day   143
- Average visitor session length   10:55
- Unique visitors   9,292
- Visitors who visited once   6,230
- Visitors more than once   3,062

ISSUES OF COST RECOVERY

The two current partners for DDM2 are Wichita State University Libraries and University Computing. Partnership with the Government Printing Office is pending a Memorandum of Understanding. As with most collaborations, especially where a significant investment has been made in time, staff, and money, there are the inescapable politics to consider. After the announcement of Documents Data Miner in April 1998, the situation at the WSU Libraries changed with the retirements by the summer of 1998 of two supportive administrators, the Dean and Associate Dean of Libraries. A year's search concluded in the hiring of a new Dean in July 1999. In addition, the DDM2 programmer moved from NIAR to a position as Web Applications Manager for University Computing in January 2000. By the fall of 2002, the WSU Libraries were again searching for a Dean, with the current incumbent arriving in September 2003. These administrative changes have required several periods of transition and education, as well as changes in outlook regarding cost recovery for DDM2.

By 2001, all discussions about completion of DDM2 led to the need for an Oracle platform in order to provide a sound national-level utility for the future. Redesign work using newer tools and technologies was desirable. It was also clear that maintenance requirements even at the most basic level for DDM2 would require daily oversight. Since such an expense could not be absorbed by either University Libraries or University Computing, it became apparent that cost recovery would be required to complete the vision of DDM2.

Following is a cost summary for development of both DDM and DDM2 between 1997 and 2001:

- Actual costs to date $10,000
- Unbilled costs–Fair Market Value $200,000
  1997-2001 (DDM and DDM2)
- Unbilled costs (DDM2)– $75,000
  Fair Market Value 2000-2001
- Projected annual maintenance of current $30,000
  DDM2 design–Fair Market Value

  TOTAL $315,000

Cost recovery revenue streams would allow completion of all the modules for DDM2 and provide for the ongoing operation of the site. This revenue could derive from user fees, from a contract with GPO or other vendor, or from grants. DDM's partner, the GPO, had been approached in early 2001, but declined to negotiate any cost recovery assistance. In the summer of 2001, it was decided that a survey should be conducted of the over 1,300 Federal depository libraries in order to determine whether or not users would be willing to pay modest fees to use DDM2. In fact, DDM2's homepage was designed with a Log-In feature, which would be crucial to a fee-based utility.

The survey was announced on the GOVDOC-L and the DocTech-L discussion lists, as well as through a batched direct e-mailing to the depository library addresses in the directory of DDM. The DDM2 Survey was available on the Web from July 13 to August 10. There were 243 responses, a response rate of about 18.5%. Responders represented a satisfactory cross-section of the depository library community, from major universities and small colleges, to law, military, and professional libraries. Complete details of this and a later survey will be detailed in a forthcoming article. But, basically, University Libraries was seeking information regarding (1) whether the libraries were interested in the DDM2 prototype features, and (2) whether the libraries were willing to reimburse Wichita State's costs in making the service available to them. The Shipping List Services and the URL Locator were requested by over 75% of responding libraries. Over 45% of those surveyed wanted the MARC records utility and shelf-listing. And between 30-40% wanted a Public Access Catalog and spine labeling.[20]

The positive response to this survey, along with a reluctance of the Design Team to charge for the DDM2 utility, encouraged the current Dean to apply for a grant from the Institute of Museum and Library Services to assist with the costs of ongoing development. The grant was submitted in January 2002, but it was not until September 2002 that the Design Team learned the grant would not be funded. In the meantime, the Team had been steadily working on its design goals and had fulfilled much of the plan for DDM2. There would be no move towards a more robust (and more expensive) platform, but new and long-desired features were available for use in DDM2.

At this point, in the Fall of 2002, the Library's Dean resigned to accept another position, and the Design Team simply marked time, made the DDM2 resource available, and maintained updates to the system until the arrival of a new Dean (in September 2003) could provide direction. They also dismantled (at least temporarily) the Login mechanism to allow more immediate user access to DDM2. Currently, the Library's Dean has mandated both the development of a business plan for DDM2 and the submission of another grant to the IMLS, which has been accomplished. The Memo of Understanding on a partnership for DDM2 between the WSU Libraries and the GPO is still pending.

CONCLUSION

Today, DDM2 warehouses nearly four million item lister elements, nearly 215,000 MARC records, over 8,400 shipping lists, and 158,000 shelf list entries. The subset of MARC records providing online access through URLs totals nearly 46,000, with close to 14,000 of them representing online-only titles. As of January 2004, there are 6,729 active item numbers and 8,587 inactive item numbers in DDM2. Pending upgrades include: the addition of approximately 100,000 GPO MARC records dating from 1976 through 1990, design of a platform for batched download of records, and an enhanced training module.

The key concepts for development of DDM2 have remained the same during its six years of operation: build on the work of others, maintain collaborative professional relationships, get the politics right, provide high standards for maintenance, offer quick response time to problems, track the use statistics, design frequent upgrades, focus on continued marketing, and plan to evolve for the future. Through hard work and consistency of operation, the designers for DDM and DDM2 have built and maintained a valuable national-level tool for the government documents community. The true challenge, however, involves securing a fate that DDM2 deserves. As the engine now exists, it is the backbone of a completely integrated, fourth generation catalog of government publications, an identifiable inventory of all libraries subscribing to these publications, and a dynamic registry of pieces sent by GPO and received by libraries. Very little remains to design in order to allow for centralized predictive check-in of physical materials and dynamic updating of links to digitized materials. Documents Data Miner has clearly created a paradigm shift in government documents collection development and management, altering the way in which documents professionals address their workload and offering new paths for the future.

NOTES

1. For a full discussion of the development of the GPRD relational database, see Nan Myers, "GPRD–Institutional and Statewide Benefits of an Internet-Accessible Relational Database," in Myers, Nan and Thomas G. Tyler, "Managing the Depository Database: Some Opportunities with Shared Technology," *Proceedings of the 6th Annual Federal Depository Library Conference, April 14-17, 1997,* http://www.access. gpo.gov/su_docs/fdlp/pubs/proceedings/97pro.html (accessed January 21, 2004).

2. Michael L. Gargano and Bel G. Raggad, "Data Mining–a Powerful Information Creating Tool," *OCLC Systems and Services* 15, no. 2 (1999): 81-90.

3. Barbara Mento and Brendan Rapple, eds. *Data Mining and Data Warehousing,* SPEC Kit 274 (Washington, D.C.: Association of Research Libraries, July 2003) 13.

4. See *Study to Identify Measures Necessary for a Successful Transition to a More Electronic Federal Depository Library Program: as Required by Legislative Branch Appropriations Act, 1996, Public Law 104-53: Report to the Congress* (Washington, DC, U.S.G.P.O., 1996).

5. In 1994, the author was hired at Wichita State University Libraries as Government Documents Cataloger, responsible for ongoing and retrospective tapeloads of government documents records into the ILS and subsequently placed in charge (as Project Team Leader) of every additional enhancement to the Government Documents program.

6. For a detailed description of Wichita State University Libraries' initiatives in management of government documents, see Nan Myers, "Models of Depository Management: from Archive to Access," *Proceedings of the 7th Annual Federal Depository Library Conference, April 20-23, 1998,* http://www.access.gpo.gov/su_docs/fdlp/pubs/proceedings/98pro.html (accessed January 21, 2004).

7. From 1994-1999, the Government Documents Group in Technical Services consisted of one FTE Librarian (the author) and percentages of position descriptions of five classified staff. Documentation of the management of the government documents

tapeloads and cleanup at the WSU Libraries using in-place staff is available in the un-published presentation titled "The Tip of the Iceberg: Mainstreaming Government Documents into the Automated Library Materials Flow," Kansas Library Associa-tion/College and University Libraries Section Annual Meeting, Hutchinson KS, Octo-ber 26, 1995.

8. The Head of Acquisitions at Wichita State University Libraries is John Wil-liams, who has been instrumental in the development of both GPRD and the DDM products. John Williams, programmer John Ellis and the author constitute the Design Team for Documents Data Miner products.

9. From 1995 to 2000, eleven graduate students from the Departments of Electrical and Computer Engineering and Computer Science worked to develop parts of GPRD and the Documents Data Miner. Ten of these students incorporated this work into their Master's or final projects. For the design start-up of DDM, one received a graduate assistantship from the Library. In addition, faculty relationships in the departments of Computer Science and Decision Science, and at NIAR (National Institute for Aviation Research) were instrumental in providing support and skills needed by the DDM De-sign Team.

10. The BDLD is still updated regularly and available online at http://www.du.edu/bdld/bdldhome.htm.

11. Margaret Mooney, Government Documents Librarian at the University of Cali-fornia/Riverside, is a pioneer in workload issues for library government documents and/or cataloging departments. She described her check-in utility in "Depository Pro-cessing Made Easy: A One Keystroke Automated Check-in System for U.S. Govern-ment Documents," *Documents to the People* 22 (September 1994): 211-12.

12. Paul Arrigo was the Law Librarian at Washburn University who had the vision to collect item profiles from the 18 selective depositories in Kansas and make this in-formation available to Kansas depositories on diskettes. The process involved manual labor, was only available in flat files, and relied on submission of updated information from the Kansas depository community. Arrigo is currently Library Director at Penn-sylvania State University at Shenango and a member of the GPO Council.

13. Details of the development of GPRD are available in an unpublished paper by Nan Myers and John Williams, "Placing Ourselves in GPRD: Using a Relational Data-base to Manage Information for a Government Documents Depository Collection," 1996 Tri-Conference: A Joint Conference with Mountain Plains Library Association, Wichita KS, April 11, 1996.

14. Dr. John Hutchinson, Associate Vice President for Academic Affairs and Re-search, and Professor of Mathematics at Wichita State University, was then Director of Operations at the University's National Institute for Aviation Research (NIAR). He and John Ellis, Senior Program Analyst for NIAR, were veterans at building relational databases on contracts from the Federal Aviation Administration. That they were seek-ing a large body of untapped metadata for use in design prototyping for an FAA con-tract, and that, at the same time, the DDM Design Team needed server space and expertise in Web implementation was pure serendipity.

15. The description of design components for DDM is found in John Ellis, "Archi-tecture and Functionality of Documents Data Miner," *Proceedings of the 7th Annual Federal Depository Library Conference, April 20-23, 1998*, http://www.access.gpo.gov/su_docs/fdlp/pubs/proceedings/98pro.html (accessed January 21, 2004).

16. The announcement of the Documents Data Miner Partnership at the FDLC on April 15, 1998 was accompanied by three presentations. Design Team members Nan

Myers and John Ellis presented respectively on "Collection Management Using the Documents Data Miner" and "Architecture and Functionality of Documents Data Miner." Cathy Hartman of the University of North Texas had been recruited to test the utility in its last phase of development and report on the results with "Documents Data Miner: A Resource for Collection Development and Management." All three presentations are available in *Proceedings of the 7th Annual Federal Depository Library Conference, April 20-23, 1998*, http://www.access.gpo.gov/su_docs/fdlp/pubs/proceedings/98pro.html (accessed January 21, 2004).

17. See the section later in this article titled "Part III: Demographics and Costs."

18. In January 2000, John Ellis accepted a position as Manager of Internet Applications for the WSU Computing Center. With the cooperation of the University Computing Center, he moved the DDM applications to UCC servers and remained the programmer for DDM and DDM2.

19. Data in this section was gathered for the Federal Depository Library Conference in October 2003, and reflects the GPO's fiscal year timeframe.

20. Additional information on this survey can be found in Nan Myers, "Documents Data Miner 2: Demonstration of a Pilot Project: http://govdoc.wichita.edu/ddm2," *Proceedings of the 10th Annual Federal Depository Library Conference, October 14-17, 2001*, http://www.access.gpo.gov/su_docs/fdlp/pubs/proceedings/01pro.html (accessed January 21, 2004).

REFERENCES

Ellis, John. "Architecture and Functionality of Documents Data Miner," *Proceedings of the 7th Annual Federal Depository Library Conference, April 20-23, 1998*, http://www.access.gpo.gov/su_docs/fdlp/pubs/proceedings/98pro.html (accessed January 21, 2004).

Gargano, Michael L. and Bel G. Raggad, "Data Mining–a Powerful Information Creating Tool," *OCLC Systems and Services* 15, no. 2 (1999): 81-90.

Hartman, Cathy. "Documents Data Miner: A Resource for Collection Development and Management," *Proceedings of the 7th Annual Federal Depository Library Conference, April 20-23, 1998*, http://www.access.gpol.gov/su_docs/fdlp/pubs/proceedings/98pro.html (accessed January 21, 2004).

Mento, Barbara and Brendan Rapple, eds. *Data Mining and Data Warehousing*, SPEC Kit 274. Washington, D.C.: Association of Research Libraries, 2003.

Mooney, Margaret T. "Depository Processing Made Easy: A One Keystroke Automated Check-in System for U.S. Government Documents," *Documents to the People* 22 (September 1994): 211-12.

Myers, Nan. "Collection Management Using the Documents Data Miner," *Proceedings of the 7th Annual Federal Depository Library Conference, April 20-23, 1998*, http://www.access.gpo.gov/su_docs/fdlp/pubs/proceedings/98pro.html (accessed January 21, 2004).

Myers, Nan. "Documents Data Miner 2: Demonstration of a Pilot Project: http://govdoc.wichita.edu/ddm2," *Proceedings of the 10th Annual Federal Depository Library Conference, October 14-17, 2001*, http://www.access.gpo.gov/su_docs/fdlp/pubs/proceedings/01pro.html (accessed January 21, 2004).

Myers, Nan. "Documents Data Miner 2: Search Strategies and Statistics," *Proceedings of the 12th Annual Federal Depository Library Conference, October 20-22, 2003*, http://www.access.gpo.gov/su_docs/fdlp/pubs/proceedings/03pro.html (accessed February 9, 2004).

Myers, Nan. "Documents Data Miner 2 Searching Strategies," *Proceedings of the 11th Annual Federal Depository Library Conference, October 20-23, 2002*, http://www.access.gpo.gov/su_docs/fdlp/pubs/proceedings/02pro.html (accessed January 21, 2004).

Myers, Nan. "Models of Depository Management: From Archive to Access," *Proceedings of the 7th Annual Federal Depository Library Conference, April 20-23, 1998*, http://www.access.gpo.gov/su_docs/fdlp/pubs/proceedings/98pro.html (accessed January 21, 2004).

Myers, Nan and Thomas G. Tyler. "Managing the Depository Database: Some Opportunities with Shared Technology," *Proceedings of the 6th Annual Federal Depository Library Conference, April 14-17, 1997*, http://www.access.gpo.gov/su_docs/fdlp/pubs/proceedings/97pro.html (accessed January 21, 2004).

Study to Identify Measures Necessary for a Successful Transition to a More Electronic Federal Depository Library Program: as Required by Legislative Branch Appropriations Act, 1996, Public Law 104-53: report to the Congress. Washington, D.C.: U.S.G.P.O., 1996.

Catalogs, Indexes, and Full Text Databases: An Integrative Approach to Accessing Government Literature

John D. Kawula
Arlene Weible

SUMMARY. Persistent themes in modern librarianship have included the importance of online catalogs in recording local holdings, the ability of indexes to extend the subject and descriptive analysis of these catalogs, and the desirability of mainstreaming government publications with non-governmental literature. These themes have been reaffirmed, but in another sense challenged by recent developments in online public access catalogs (OPACs), commercial indexing services such as Lexis/Nexis, and government produced full text databases such as GPO Access.

Recent professional literature often recommends compressing and integrating bibliographic description and access without adequately addressing the methods or problems of the process. The management of

John D. Kawula is Government Documents and Maps Librarian, University of Alaska Fairbanks, Fairbanks, AK (E-mail: ffjdk@uaf.edu). Arlene Weible is Head, Government Documents Department, University of North Texas, Denton, TX (E-mail: aweible@library.unt.edu).

[Haworth co-indexing entry note]: "Catalogs, Indexes, and Full Text Databases: An Integrative Approach to Accessing Government Literature." Kawula, John D., and Arlene Weible. Co-published simultaneously in *The Reference Librarian* (The Haworth Information Press, an imprint of The Haworth Press, Inc.) No. 94, 2006, pp. 191-206; and: *The Changing Face of Government Information: Providing Access in the Twenty-First Century* (ed: Suhasini L. Kumar) The Haworth Information Press, an imprint of The Haworth Press, Inc., 2006, pp. 191-206. Single or multiple copies of this article are available for a fee from The Haworth Document Delivery Service [1-800-HAWORTH, 9:00 a.m. - 5:00 p.m. (EST). E-mail address: docdelivery@haworthpress.com].

records in an OPAC centering on the use of direct links to online resources is one of the more concrete and practical forms of such integration. However, the required maintenance may not be a cost effective or desirable use of staff time. *[Article copies available for a fee from The Haworth Document Delivery Service: 1-800-HAWORTH. E-mail address: <docdelivery@haworthpress.com> Website: <http://www.HaworthPress.com> © 2006 by The Haworth Press, Inc. All rights reserved.]*

KEYWORDS. Catalogs, indexes, portals, government publications, online public access catalogs, cataloging, electronic resources

INTRODUCTION

It is self-evident that electronic formats and Web oriented technology have changed the nature of government publications collections. In addition to tangible formats, libraries now have complex mixtures and blends of OPACs, electronic indexes, and full text databases. All of these in one sense or another provide satisfactory access to government literature with some overlap and redundancy.

Most libraries continue their tradition of maintaining a local catalog indicating ownership of material. Increasingly, these catalogs include some direct links to Web-based resources thus extending the concept of a catalog beyond the recording of tangible items owned by that institution. Indexes such as *Lexis/Nexis Congressional, Lexis/Nexis Statistical,* and their printed counterparts add details, analysis, and interpretation unobtainable with traditional library descriptive cataloging or subject analysis based on Library of Congress subject headings. Many depository Web pages prompt users to these indexes as well as the local catalog. Full text material is provided from a variety of sources including GPO Access, commercial indexes, and the Web pages from individual agencies. These three methods of access, catalogs, indexes, and full text databases are becoming intertwined, yet extended analysis and local availability remain major concerns. The integration or mainstreaming of governmental with non-governmental literature has been facilitated by retrospective conversion of pre-1976 records by many libraries and the inclusion of government publications in popular indexing services such as EbscoHost.

Although these developments are all positive, ironically, they create uncertainties among patrons and librarians alike. It is often unclear which access point will be most effective or desirable under which circumstance. A whole series of management questions also arises. For example, how much time and effort should be spent editing catalog records when the same library pays for several online indexes that include citations and links to full text? Is there a point in selecting depository item numbers for electronic resources when they can be obtained just as easily by linking directly to federal government agency Web sites? How should electronic titles be represented especially given the Public Printer's current estimate that 95% of new titles will be electronic only? (Russell 2003). Are detailed statements in the OPAC necessary when indexes may provide better description and direct linkage to the specific parts?

Ultimately, each library has to determine its own answers to these kinds of questions. To do so, it is helpful to consider the present situation in light of contemporary literature as well as the practicalities of using different avenues of access in modern depository libraries.

RECENT TRENDS AND INTERPRETATIONS

"In the pre-Internet age," a recent book states regarding the depository program, "public access was equated with the number of member libraries; the more libraries in the program, the better was public access. In other words, members of the public need not travel far to use depository collections" (Hernon et al. 2002, 352). Although there is validity to this point, realistically, the emphasis began to shift away from the physical location of depositories even before the advent of the Internet. As interlibrary loan services expanded, material could be made available between libraries in a faster and more efficient manner. As a result, bibliographic representation of government publications in catalogs and indexes, although always an issue, increased in importance.

A search through *Library Literature* reveals a long history of institutional and professional self-doubt concerning appropriate representation of government publications. Even the titles of articles are sometimes revealing. "GPO Cataloging: Is It a Viable Current Access Tool for U.S. Government Documents?" "GPO Access: Government At Its Best?" and "The Perils of Being Ahead of the Curve" are among the literature on the subject.

A noticeable and important trend is toward the view that standard monographic and serials entries do not constitute adequate control, and in some cases their details hinder or even burden the search process. Initially the assumption, often unstated, was that treating government publications like everything else would be sufficient. A dozen years ago Bolner and Kile wrote in their abstract: "Poor bibliographic control of government publications has plagued the depository library system almost from its inception . . . The promise of the GPO/MARC tapes has remained largely unfulfilled–problems with the tapes have prevented libraries from taking advantage of this cost-effective way to acquire full cataloging for U.S. government publications" (Bolner and Kile 1991, 51). The bulk of the article outlines the bibliographic control felt necessary for government publications and describes a joint project of several libraries to clean up the GPO/MARC catalog records in accordance with these guidelines. Unstated in this and similar articles is the implication that traditional cataloging with appropriate technological adaptations constitute adequate access. But this implication was countered with the warning that: "A commonly held assumption that increasing bibliographic control automatically leads to increased accessibility and availability must be re-examined" (Hernon and McClure 1988, 13).

One author describes several creative approaches to item representation including the sole reliance on indexes and abstracts for the identification of government publications. He concludes that selective cataloging using an OPAC as the major access point is a desirable compromise (Oliva 2000). Another author in an editorial piece advocates a thesaurus for government Web sites stating, "I am not suggesting that we force Library of Congress Subject Headings onto the federal Web pages. LCSH was a 19th-century solution to 19th-century problems. It is time to fundamentally rethink our approach to the whole issue of controlled-vocabulary access systems and apply that new thinking to provide access to the Web" (Seavey 1998, 35).

One of the best and most clearly articulated reconsiderations of these concepts is presented in a 1996 article by Dena Hutto. She reaffirms the importance of high quality locally maintained catalogs but notes that GPO catalog records form the backbone of many indexing systems, blurring the distinction between catalogs and separate indexes. Citing technical advances, Hutto advocates the linking of items, finding aids, and databases via standard identification numbers. This would be accompanied by a decrease in descriptive notation and LC subject headings. The concluding paragraph of this article is one of the more succinct statements of this concept:

> the potential now exists to transform the local catalogs, union catalogs, and bibliographic databases of specific collections into

linked components of comprehensive networks capable of describing, locating, and retrieving items from a broad range of government information resources . . . some elements of cataloging have little or no value in evolving systems of bibliographic control. Cooperation will be required in order to create networks that are comprehensive in scope, that uniquely identify resources, and that effectively show relationships within the virtual collection of available government resources. (Hutto 1996, 342)

A hindrance to the implementation of this strategy is the lack of comprehensiveness or permanency in many governmental Web sites. A number of authors, especially those using technical and grey literature, are documenting serious omissions in the theoretically complete Web sites. In two somewhat similar articles, Derksen (2001) and Jensen (2001) both note that not only are depositories missing a lot of tangible items in key series, many of these items are not represented in library catalogs, indexes, or agency Web sites. Taking a slightly different angle to this same issue, Lopresti and Gorin (2002) note that about a third of their sampled material from federal depository distribution did not appear on government Web sites even two years after the tangible format was sent to libraries.

By the late 1990s, many authors were openly questioning some of the traditional elements of catalogs, cataloging, and bibliographic control. These concerns were not restricted to government publications and were discussed and expressed in a variety of contexts. In a serials cataloging workshop, "it was suggested that catalogers consider the option of attempting only to adequately *identify* the nature and scope of online sources rather than attempting to exhaustively describe them in an environment where change is the norm" (Banach 1997, 248). In comparing Web lists to OPACs one author advocates an integrated ". . . collection of compatible databases, some more complete than others, some in MARC format and others in various flavors of metadata, some generated and maintained locally and others provided by external sources" (Anderson 1999, 315-316). Several authors take this idea further and recommend restructuring traditional library catalogs, not simply combining them with other search methods. "It is particularly important that we end our dependence on systems based solely on authority control and Boolean searching . . . MARC has proved to be a remarkably robust data format, but we will need to find ways to incorporate other data structures into the catalogs we build. AACR2, while it represents a century of cataloging practice, is based on print documents, and its governance structures make it unresponsive and slow to adapt as the nature of documents change. In a world where the full document is a couple of clicks away from the bibliographic citation or catalog record, insistence on complete descriptive cataloging seems silly" (Lewis 1999, 266-267). Finally, even the titles of three editorial pieces by Roy Tennant, "MARC Must Die," "MARC Exit Strategy," and "Library Catalogs: The Wrong Solution" forcefully convey dissatisfaction with the rigidity of AACR oriented descriptive cataloging, MARC format, and the limited capabilities of library catalogs.

The call for flexibility in bibliographic description and encoding, even if it means dramatic overhauling of current practices, is a unifying theme of the reform oriented literature. This literature also expresses inadequacy in the cataloging and indexing of government publications, and calls for better integration of the various elements of access without specifying what this integration would look like. Anecdotal observations suggest that many patrons do conduct their research without traditional catalogs, librarians' instructions, or direct assistance. Under these circumstances, and in the absence of concrete examples in the literature, how should the effective integration of catalogs, indexes, and full text databases proceed?

MANAGING ELECTRONIC RESOURCES IN THE ONLINE CATALOG

Integration can and probably should begin with providing access to both tangible and electronic government publications through a library's OPAC. Despite possible inadequacies of the traditional catalog record, a well constructed and maintained OPAC remains a major if not dominant access point for most library collections. The OPAC can provide bibliographic description of both types of resources, links to full text electronic resources, and holdings statements for the tangible depository collection through a single interface. However, the inclusion of records and links to electronic resources requires some consideration of a number of issues and concerns.

Initial Considerations

Libraries regularly provide catalog access to resources they purchased. They may not feel obligated to provide catalog access to free online resources such as government publications they do not "own" or "subscribe" to in the same sense. The degree to which they are a legitimate part of the library's collections may still need to be debated at any given institution.

Another problem concerns the catalog's ability to retain accuracy in catalog records for government online resources given the changeability of agency Web sites. No matter what procedures are used to verify data, there will always be inaccurate links or outdated statements in some catalog records. This illustrates an important point: modern catalogs contain a degree of uncertainty, sometimes even a high degree of uncertainty. Even by doing nothing, libraries implicitly accept this uncertainty. They can try to manage the uncertainty, but they can never eliminate it altogether.

Resource Identification

GPO item selection profiles don't allow for a title by title selection of resources or catalog records. If GPO catalog records are purchased from a vendor, this inevitably leads to the receipt of records for electronic resources not desired for the collection. Furthermore, multiple records for a single title, reflecting tangible and electronic formats, can inadvertently enter the catalog. A depository wanting more selectivity in their catalog records may decide not to select electronic only item numbers, and instead regularly review the New Electronic titles service provided by GPO (http://www.access.gpo.gov/su_docs/locators/net/index.html). Another option would be to use the URL Locator service available on the Documents Data Miner 2 (http://govdoc.wichita.edu/ddm2/urllocator.asp). Both provide lists of GPO catalog records containing links to electronic resources. The lists can be reviewed, and the desired records can be manually added to the library's catalog. This may give more control over records, and less revision may be necessary once the records are added. Clean up is pretty much inevitable if records are batch loaded from a vendor.

Choice of Links

It is also important to consider the type of links to be provided. GPO catalog records with the 856 MARC field, indicating electronic resource linking data, will contain a link to a PURL record. Acting as an intermediary resolution service, PURL records are created and maintained by GPO. PURLs redirect the user to the URLs for the specific resources. In effect, the URLs are updated without individual libraries having to update their catalog records. Thus, GPO takes responsibility for maintaining the links. However, there are drawbacks. One is that the links in the library's catalog have to pass through GPO servers before connecting to the resource. If the GPO server is down, access to all those links in the library's catalog also goes down. Furthermore, the PURL used in a particular catalog record may not point to the best link for that resource. At times, GPO will point to a Web site that provides a list of publications, rather than to the specific publication. Using PURLs means that the library must live with GPO's decisions about appropriate points of access, and some libraries would prefer to have more control. Some may choose to use both URLs and PURLs. Despite their drawbacks, it is unlikely that a library would want their staff to replace every PURL with a URL. A compromise position might be to systematically review the links for items of particular importance to the library's user community.

OpenURLs provide a new approach to establishing links to electronic resources. This standard is now being used by many aggregators and electronic journal vendors and has considerable promise for government electronic resources (Rossmann 2003). Like PURLs, OpenURLs use a secondary resolution server. However, an OpenURL contains embedded metadata that can be used to search for the source and create an appropriate link. Additional options for linking to electronic resources are being developed, and the depository community should pay attention to their potential applications.

Checking Links

Some online catalog systems have a link checking program. For example, the Innovative Interfaces Millennium product has a feature called URL Checker. It provides a report and displays the non-functional links offering substitute links when redirects have occurred. Links may thus be checked and records edited. But URL Checker has its drawbacks. It does not check links such as PURLs that redirect to other resources. Instead, it lists them as errors. The system does allow certain addresses to be blocked from link checking reports, which is what most libraries would want to do with PURLs. Hopefully, library users can continue to work with Innovative Interfaces and other vendors to further develop the functionality of such software.

Obviously, it would be ideal to have electronic depository links accurate all the time. Unfortunately, this is an unrealistic goal in most depositories. The time devoted to checking links increases accuracy, but should be balanced with available staff resources and a realistic appraisal of patron usage.

Multiple Formats

One of the big challenges in managing electronic resources in the catalog is determining how their records will interact with the records for tangible resources. Most depository collections have both monograph and serial titles that are available in paper, microfiche, and electronic formats. Cataloging rules generally recommend separate bibliographic records for each format. Recent interpretations by GPO and other national cataloging agencies have allowed flexibility, particularly when the electronic resource is identical in content to the tangible version. However, in practice, there is a lot of variation depending on the specifics of a given title. For example, if GPO can determine that the paper or microfiche version of a serial is no longer published, it will "close" the record for the tangible version, and create a new record for the online version, even if the title is identical. While this is a technically correct cataloging practice, it often creates confusion because two records for the same title appear in the catalog. Depending on how the records display in a particular OPAC, this may or may not be a problem.

Some libraries may decide to combine holdings statements for all versions of a title on a single record. This approach requires a lot of maintenance, particularly as records are sometimes received in multiple formats from vendors. The library may feel this work is worth the effort if it results in a single, straightforward statement of which issues are available in each format. The point to emphasize is that individual depositories do not have to follow GPO cataloging practice regarding resources in multiple formats if they feel an alternative will be more helpful to their patrons. However, these issues will also need to be addressed with colleagues who establish cataloging standards for the whole library.

Measuring Usage

Creating and maintaining links to electronic depository resources in online catalogs can involve a great deal of work, applied uniformly over a long period of time. It is therefore helpful to assess the usage of these records in the catalog in order to justify the use of staff resources. Presently, no major online catalog system provides an automated method for keeping statistics on the number of times a given link is used. There are some substitutable options available. GPO can provide statistics on the number of times a particular IP address links to the PURL server. Libraries using PURLs in their catalogs can sign up to have these statistics collected. All they need to do is provide GPO with their catalog's IP address.

Another way of tracking catalog link usage is to create a local database for collecting statistics. Such a system has been developed by Chris Brown at the University of Denver. A Cold Fusion database interacts with the catalog and collects the data. A locally developed Microsoft Access database then matches URLs to the titles of resources being used. A presentation regarding this method was made at the Federal Depository Library Conference, Arlington, Virginia in October 2003. The presentation will be available at a Web site that is under production by GPO, but not available at the time of this writing.

Finally, another option for collecting link usage data is to gather feedback from library staff and users. Reference librarians can be consulted to find out if they use the catalog for identifying government publications on the Internet. It may also be possible to include appropriate questions into library-wide usability studies.

BEYOND THE ONLINE CATALOG

As far as government publications are concerned, providing access to electronic depository resources in OPACs is the most concrete example of widespread integration of access to electronic and tangible collections. But this concept is taken further in the recent literature on library portals. Although there is no agreed upon definition, portals are usually conceived to be systems that are capable of gathering access points, searching numerous sources, and fusing results. "Portals are more than enhanced Web pages, although some have evolved from library Web sites . . . The core feature of any portal will be integrated, cross-database searching of a local catalog, other library catalogs, selected Web sites, locally licensed full-text and abstracting/indexing databases, and public domain or publicly accessible abstracting and indexing services" (Jackson 2002, 37-38). Narrow discussions of portals sometimes limit the term to systems that customize and individualize displays permitting library patrons alerting and recommendation services. However, most discussions focus on the integrative functions and fusibility potentials (partial de-duplication of results, etc.). In addition, "Portals can also offer the ability to transfer captured citations into ILL requests, commercial document delivery requests, or requests for the library to purchase the item. Portals that do this eliminate the current need to search in one tool and enter ILL requests using another. It is the seamless flow from discovery to requesting that will make for a successful portal" (Jackson 2002, 39).

Currently, portal technology and literature is "hot." Much of the attention is centered on the specifics of certain commercial products and how they have been implemented by larger libraries. In some cases, the technology is purchased and used at a university wide level, and the library's portal is a sub-portion of a campus system. Federated searching, distributed searching, and broadcast searching are terms for related technologies and techniques for cross searching from a single interface that would be employed in portals.

It is interesting and relevant that this literature makes relatively little mention of applications to government publications collections, and the literature on government resources seems to make relatively little mention of these technologies. This is ironic because GPO Access and FirstGov are often viewed as portals. On the whole, federated searching and portal applications have not been prominent topics among government publications librarians. One article that does discuss governmental portals notes that the focus is moving away from GPO Access and related databases to agency maintained sites that have their own style of consolidation (Shuler 2002).

MANAGED LOCAL INTEGRATION

These ideas can be amalgamated and taken one step further. Realistically, they have been in embryonic form for some time but not consolidated in the government publications literature. For lack of a better term, the phrase "managed local integration" is suggested to describe applications of such a consolidation.

Most librarians that manage government publication collections maintain a Web page with various kinds of explanatory assistance, connections to the local OPAC, and links to online indexes and full text databases. By definition, this packages and integrates the various methods of access. In the absence of direct linkage where users can search these sources simultaneously, the manner in which each library constructs their Web page, prompts their users, and manipulates data and records within their OPAC all constitute local integration. The next step is to manage this integration in a more deliberative manner.

For example, a library could choose to emphasize a strategy of using the OPAC to locate government electronic resources. They could write a one or two sentence recommendation that their patrons start their searches by looking for both tangible and Web based material in the OPAC. Another library may not want to spend the time on catalog maintenance and instead emphasize the portal applications of GPO Access and FirstGov. Another may feel GPO Access is not adequate for the kind of searching they do and direct patrons to the Lexis/Nexis indexes, deliberately omitting any mention or link to GPO Access. Any of these libraries may want to draw attention to specialized indexes such as PAIS and Agricola, by placing links on their Web page more or less in order of importance to their institution.

Literature on such topics as information architecture, Web page design, and even principles of art and photographic composition that were developed decades ago can assist in this integration. In other words, libraries have the opportunity to unify local interpretations, representations, and adaptations of national level cataloging and indexing, emphasizing some aspects and deemphasizing others, and to do so in a creative, innovative, and professional manner. This constitutes managed local integration.

Although some of this may be self-evident or intuitively obvious, it is worth mentioning for several reasons. A high percentage of activity in the library field now takes place outside of libraries *per se*. Outsourced cataloging, most indexing, and some portal development are such examples. The relationships between libraries and private sector companies are deeper, stronger, and more important than ever before. Economic trends of the past decade or more have indicated that the boundary between profit and non-profit activity is murky and constantly in flux. Creative innovations and developments often occur at this boundary area. Two examples that impact libraries are the development of maps that are manipulated enhancements or reconfigurations of governmental surveys, and amalgamated indexing of journals, governmental data, and Internet material from various sources.

Realistically, libraries have for a long time been maintaining their catalogs and Web pages to partially reflect what is referred to here as managed local integration. What is advocated is a clearer and stronger recognition of the triangular relation between government publication activity, private sector indexing and related activity, and deliberative interpretations and management at the local level.

It is helpful to briefly look at how this has been implemented and where libraries can go from where they are now. A cursory non-scientific, non-random viewing was made of the depository library Web pages that are directly linked from GPO Access (http://www.gpoaccess. gov/libraries.html). At least one Web page per state was viewed, with representative samples from regional depositories, institutions of various sizes, academic libraries, community and technical college libraries, public libraries, law libraries, and other special libraries.

The Web pages had many similarities, yet some libraries have designed pages that stand out for their focus on interpretative aids or noteworthy way of listing and grouping material. Almost all libraries link to their OPAC but few, if any, explicitly recommend a search strategy of following the links embedded in their OPAC or key indexes. As would be expected, the larger libraries of all types tend to have more extensively developed sites with several subsections. Some libraries emphasize locally written finding aids; some offer an alphabetical listing of indexes, agencies, or selected titles organized separately or interfiled; others prefer subject groupings. Many of the more extensively developed sites have direct links to selected new titles, or hot topics.

It is interesting to note some examples of Web pages reflecting considerable thought to the manner library patrons select and use specific sources. The Eleventh Circuit U.S. Court of Appeals library (http://www.ca11.uscourts.gov/library/Government.html) links to the court's most often used Internet sites; Berry College (http://www2.berry.edu/library/govdoc) displays their own annotations for frequently requested government publications; Dartmouth College (http://www.dartmouth.edu/~govdocs) has an extensive section for searching social science statistics. Rice University (http://www.rice.edu/fondren/gov/index.html) has one of the more interesting features, a special search engine for uncataloged Texas state publications.

No matter how a depository library maintains its catalog, organizes its Web page, or constructs its links, some other depository library has likely tried a similar approach. Even so, this should not deter creative ideas or their implementation. Additional work interpreting catalog and Web linkage does seem appropriate. There is no ideal model suggested here. Any library's emphasis should be on human mediation that implements subjective interpretations of the value and significance different sources and search strategies have for their patrons.

CONCLUSION

In a modern Web-oriented environment, access to government publications relies on overlapping and partially redundant OPACs, indexes, and full text databases. OPACs maintained at the local level continue their traditional function of describing and indicating where a publication is located, physically or on the Web. Governmental and commercial indexes now provide search and full text features that transcend traditional indexing functions. Although the professional literature is often uncomfortable with bibliographic description and control of government publications in this environment and recommends compressing and integrating description and access, it does not adequately address methods or problems concerning this process.

Presently, local management of MARC records within an OPAC to include URLs and/or PURLs is the most common method combining description and access. Continued development of OpenURL technology by GPO and other cataloging sources could provide a more sophisticated and efficient variant of this process. Portal and federated searching technology offers the potential to more effectively combine search results.

However, most discussions of these processes ignore an extraordinarily important point: Excessive maintenance and manipulation of catalog records or the creation of access that is not used may be a waste of time and money. The patrons in many if not most libraries are using traditional access methods less, and non-traditional, such as Google, more. What is cost effective in one library may not be cost effective in another. The term "managed local integration" is used to encourage libraries of all types and sizes to carefully consider the alternatives for item description, access, and retrieval, and subjectively combine them in a manner which is meaningful and useful to their patrons, without unnecessary expenditures of staff time and money.

REFERENCES

Anderson, Barbara. 1999. Web lists or OPACs: Can we have our cake and eat it too? *Library Computing* 18 (4): 312-16.

Bahr, Alice H. 1986. Cataloging U.S. depository materials: A reevaluation. *College & Research Libraries* 47 (6): (November): 587-95.

Banach, Patricia S. 1997. Finding the missing link: How cataloging bridges the gap between libraries and the Internet. *The Serials Librarian* 31 (1-2): 245-49.

Bolner, Myrtle S., and Barbara Kile. 1991. Documents to the people: Access through the automated catalog. *Government Publications Review* 18 (1) (January/February): 51-64.

Bushing, Mary C. and Bonnie Johnson. 1994. Control of government document serials in local electronic and organizational systems. *Cataloging & Classification Quarterly* 18 (3-4): 85-95. (co-published in *Cataloging Government Publications Online* edited by Carolyn C. Sherayko. New York: The Haworth Press, Inc.: 85-95).

Cochrane, Pauline A. 1985. *Redesign of catalogs and indexes for improved online subject access: Selected papers of Pauline A. Cochrane.* Phoenix: Oryx Press.

Derksen, Charlotte R.M. 2001. USGS publications: Current access via the Web and via catalogs. *Geoscience information: A dynamic odyssey: Proceedings of the 36th meeting of the Geoscience Information Society,* edited by Michael M. Noga: 107-16.

Hernon, Peter and Charles R. McClure. 1988. *Public access to government information: Issues, trends, and strategies.* 2d ed. Norwood N.J.: Ablex Publishing Corp.

Hernon, Peter, Harold C. Relyea, Robert E. Dugan, and Joan F. Cheverie. 2002. *United States government information: Policies and sources.* Westport, Conn.: Libraries Unlimited.

Hutto, Dena H. 1996. Old solutions in a new age: Cataloging and the future of access to government information. *Journal of Government Information* 23 (3) (May/June): 335-44.

Jackson, Mary E. 2002. The Advent of Portals. *Library Journal* 127 (15) (September 15, 2002): 36-9.

Jensen, Kristi L. 2001. Providing access to online government documents in an academic research library collection: A case study in the geosciences. *Science and Technology Libraries* 20 (2/3): 15-25. (co-published in *Electronic resources and services in sci-tech libraries,* edited by Mary C. Schlembach and William H. Mischo. New York: The Haworth Press, Inc.: 15-25).

Keating, Kathleen and Linda St. Clair. 1993. The perils of being ahead of the curve: Impact of *GPO Monthly Catalog* records on a university library. *Government Publications Review* 20 (5) (September/October): 523-29.

Kinney, Thomas and Gary Cornwall. 1991. GPO cataloging records in the online catalog: Implications for the reference librarian. *The Reference Librarian* 32: 259-75.

Laskowski, Mary S. 2000. The impact of electronic access to government information: What users and documents specialists think. *Journal of Government Information* 27 (2) (March/April, 2000): 173-85.

Lewis, David W. 1999. Where will the catalog go? *Library Computing* 18 (4): 263-68.

Lopresti, Robert, and Marcia Gorin. 2002. The availability of US government depository publications on the World Wide Web. *Journal of Government Information* 29 (1): 17-29.

McKay, Beatrice and Norma Carmack. 1994. Sharing expertise to mainstream government documents cataloging. *Cataloging & Classification Quarterly* 18 (3-4): 57-74. (co-published in *Cataloging government publications online,* edited by Carolyn C. Sherayko. New York: The Haworth Press, Inc.: 57-74).

Macomber, Nancy. 2001. Taking stock and making plans: Providing access to Web-based federal government periodicals. *The Serials Librarian* 40 (3-4): 309-15 (co-published in *Making waves: New serials landscapes in a sea of change,* edited by Joseph C. Harmon and P. Michelle Fiander. New York: The Haworth Press, Inc.: 309-15).

Mooney, Margaret T. 1989. GPO cataloging: Is it a viable current access tool for U.S. documents? *Government Publications Review* 16 (3) (May/June): 259-70.

Oliva, Victor T. 2000. Bringing federal documents to the forefront for library users: Selective cataloging using an OPAC. *College & Research Libraries* 61 (6) (November): 555-64.

Platt, Nina. 1998. GPO Access: Government at its best? *Database* (Weston, Conn.), v. 21 (2) (April/May): 41-3.

Plaunt, James R. 1985. Cataloging options for U.S. Government Printing Office documents. *Government Publications Review* 12 (5) (September/October): 449-56.

Redmond, Mary. 1989. From backwater to mainstream: Government documents in the online catalog. *The Bookmark* (Albany, N.Y.) 47 (Spring): 161-65.

Rossmann, Brian W. 2003. OpenURL: Is GPO paying attention? *DttP* 31 (3/4) (Fall/Winter): 7-8.

Russell, Judy C. 2003. Information Dissemination Operations. *Administrative Notes* 24 (13) (November 15): 7.

Schottlaender, Brian E.C. and Mary E. Jackson. 2003. The current state and future promise of portal applications. *The Bowker Annual Library and Book Trade Almanac* 48th edition: 279-90.

Seavey, Charles A. 1998. Accessible government information: A three step proposal. *American Libraries* 29 (February): 34-5.

Shuler, John A. 2002. Of Web portals, e-gov, and the public's prints. *The Journal of Academic Librarianship* 28 (6) (November): 410-13.

Strauss, Howard. 2003. Web portals: The future of information access and distribution. *The Serials Librarian* 44 (1/2): 27-35.

Tennant, Roy. 2002. MARC must die. *Library Journal* 127 (17) (October 15): 26, 28.

_____ 2002. MARC exit strategies. *Library Journal* 127 (19) (November 15): 27-8.

_____ 2003. Library catalogs: The wrong solution. *Library Journal* 128 (3) (February 15): 28.

Tseng, Sally C. 2001. Cataloging government online serials: Challenges and prospects. *The Serials Librarian* 40 (3/4): 237-44. (co-published in *Making waves: New serials landscapes in a sea of change*, edited by Joseph C. Harmon and P. Michelle Fiander. New York: The Haworth Press, Inc.: 237-44).

Zhou, Joe. 2003. A history of Web portals and their development in libraries. *Information Technology and Libraries* 22 (3) (September): 119-28.

PRESERVATION AND AUTHENTICATION OF GOVERNMENT INFORMATION

Preserving Electronic Government Information: Looking Back and Looking Forward

Susan Lyons

SUMMARY. Over the last ten years the Government Printing Office has made a massive shift from print to electronic media as the preferred distribution medium for government documents. Federal agencies over the same period have created large numbers of electronic records that require long-term preservation under the law. This article examines how the National Archives and the Government Printing Office are responding to the technical, financial, legal, and political challenges of providing permanent public access to electronic government information. NARA efforts to collect, appraise, and preserve records following the mandates

Susan Lyons is Government Documents and Reference Librarian, Rutgers Law Library, Newark, NJ.

[Haworth co-indexing entry note]: "Preserving Electronic Government Information: Looking Back and Looking Forward." Lyons, Susan. Co-published simultaneously in *The Reference Librarian* (The Haworth Information Press, an imprint of The Haworth Press, Inc.) No. 94, 2006, pp. 207-223; and: *The Changing Face of Government Information: Providing Access in the Twenty-First Century* (ed: Suhasini L. Kumar) The Haworth Information Press, an imprint of The Haworth Press, Inc., 2006, pp. 207-223. Single or multiple copies of this article are available for a fee from The Haworth Document Delivery Service [1-800-HAWORTH, 9:00 a.m. - 5:00 p.m. (EST). E-mail address: docdelivery@haworthpress.com].

Available online at http://www.haworthpress.com/web/REF
doi:10.1300/J120v45n94_12

of the courts in the wake of the PROFS litigation in *Armstrong v. Executive Office of the President* are discussed. The work of the GPO to develop an electronic archive and develop electronic partnerships with depository libraries and federal agencies is also examined. *[Article copies available for a fee from The Haworth Document Delivery Service: 1-800-HAWORTH. E-mail address: <docdelivery@haworthpress.com> Website: <http://www.HaworthPress.com> © 2006 by The Haworth Press, Inc. All rights reserved.]*

KEYWORDS. Digital preservation, GPO, NARA, PROFS litigation, FDLP

INTRODUCTION

Work on the preservation of electronic government information has made great strides in the last decade but much remains to be done to insure permanent public access to the vast quantities of government records and documents that now exist in electronic form. The World Wide Web and e-mail have generated an explosive growth in electronic government information. Entirely new systems are required for preservation and access of digital information, but these systems are underfunded, understaffed, and remain very much in the formative stage. The continued development of these systems is vital to the survival of government information.

The bulk of responsibility for preservation of electronic government information falls on two government agencies: the National Archives and Records Administration (NARA) and the Government Printing Office (GPO). This article examines the history of NARA's and GPO's efforts to preserve electronic information over the last thirty years and identifies some of the technical, financial, legal, and political challenges they face going forward. Not addressed in this article, but also of major concern to the documents community, is the need for greater efforts toward preservation of state and local electronic information.[1]

DIGITAL PRESERVATION

Library courses on preservation have long dealt with the effects of humidity, mold, insects, and acid on paper, until recently the most popular medium for storing and preserving information. But as terabytes of digital information flow daily into computer servers, the preservation strategies of archivists and librarians require updating. As with paper and microform, caring for the physical media on which data is stored is part of the challenge. Tapes and disks can be damaged and must be properly stored. But the challenges of electronic preservation go far beyond protection of the physical media.

Four key differences are:

- Archivists need to ensure the integrity of the digital data on computer tapes or disks. Over time digital information may degrade and require refreshing by copying it onto new magnetic or optical media.
- Hardware obsolescence. When the Census Bureau turned over tapes from the 1960 decennial census to the National Archives in the mid-1970s, the Archives found that the tapes required a long obsolete UNIVAC computer to read the data. Heroic and costly rescue efforts were required to salvage the data.
- Software obsolescence. Many computer files can only be interpreted with the aid of a proprietary software program. When the manufacturer no longer supports the software, the information must be migrated to a new format. Software obsolescence is a concern not only for application programs such as spreadsheets or word processing programs, but operating systems as well. Two models for coping with technological obsolescence have been proposed: migration and emulation. The first requires migrating digital information to a new generation of software while the data bits are still readable. This is a workable but labor-intensive solution that requires constant attention. Emulation is an alternate solution that proposes new hardware and software be used to emulate the look and feel of the original program. It is not yet clear how well the emulation model will work. When considering preservation of electronic information over decades and even hundreds of years, both solutions fall short.
- The exponential growth of digital information. As computers become ubiquitous in every aspect of government, the amount and complexity of data produced threatens to overwhelm the ability of the government to preserve it. Efforts to preserve the e-mail records from the Reagan and first Bush Administrations (discussed infra) consumed enormous resources at the National Archives. Future preservation demands will require far greater resources. While long-term preservation of some government electronic informa-

tion is merely highly desirable, the preservation of electronic databases that record tax, economic, legal, social security, medical, public health, and scientific information is crucial to the operation of government.[2]

NICKEL, DIMED, RIFFED, AND PROFFED: ELECTRONIC RECORDS AND THE NATIONAL ARCHIVES

Long before most government agencies, the National Archives gave consideration to the preservation of machine-readable records. As early as 1939, punch cards (then used in tabulating machines, not computers) were included in the definition of records in the Record Disposition Act.[3] The National Archives' first substantial efforts to preserve electronic information date back to the mid-1960s when the Archives included tapes from the Census Bureau in its record retention schedule.[4] In 1968, Archivist James B. Rhoads assigned three people to a Data Archives Staff with the responsibility for managing all machine-readable records in the federal government. This small staff developed methods for inventorying all magnetic tape files held by agencies, developed recommendations for the proper handling and storage of tapes and devised the first General Record Schedule for computer files (GRS 20).[5]

At the time the Data Archives Staff was created the National Archives was part of the General Services Administration (GSA). The GSA had a centralized computer and data processing unit and thus initially denied the Archives request for data processing professionals and computer equipment. It would take five years for the Data Archives unit to acquire its own data processing abilities.[6]

The Data Archives Staff grew steadily throughout the 1970s. In 1972 it became the Data Archives Branch. In 1974 it was elevated to the Machine-Readable Archives Division and by 1981 the staff had grown to twenty-one people, including data processing professionals and several archivists holding doctorates. The division staff members were leaders in the nascent field of electronic record management and preservation, giving numerous presentations at professional meetings and active in professional societies. During the 1970s, the Division developed appraisal standards for electronic records and began accessioning electronic records from federal agencies.[7]

The progress of the Division was abruptly halted in 1981 when a new president took office. Ronald Reagan was elected on a pledge to trim the federal government. The Reagan Revolution hit the Archives first with a hiring freeze and then a reduction-in-force or RIF. As the employees of the Data Archives Division were among the most recent hires at the National Archives, the staff of the division was decimated. By 1983 the staff was reduced to seven employees and Data Archives was reduced in status from a division to a branch.[8]

Throughout the 1980s the Data Archives Branch slowly regained staff as existing Archives staff members were reassigned to the Branch. In 1988 the branch was transformed into the Center for Electronic Records and given additional funds and staff that enabled it to recruit skilled computer scientists, systems analysts, and computer literate archivists to the Center. By 1993 the Center's staff had grown to forty-eight.[9] And then a new president took office.

President Clinton began his administration with a pledge to "reinvent government," which meant another reduction-in-force and a halt to plans to expand the Center for Electronic Records.[10] This decrease in staff came at a time when the National Archives was confronted with its most serious challenge in electronic record management and preservation: the PROFS litigation.

THE PROFS LITIGATION

On January 19, 1989, the last full day of the Reagan Administration, a lawsuit was filed to prevent the destruction of the electronic records maintained with the Professional Office System (PROFS) computer system, "an inter-computer communications system marketed by the IBM Corporation,"[11] and serving the agencies within the Executive Offices of the President, including the National Security Agency. The PROFS system was essentially an e-mail system that also permitted users to do some word processing and maintain electronic calendars.

PROFS gained notoriety as it was used during the Iran-Contra affair for back channel communications between Lt. Colonel Oliver North and Admiral John Poindexter. While Colonel North destroyed many incriminating paper records, he failed to adequately delete the same electronic records in the PROFS system (i.e., he deleted but did not overwrite the computer files or destroy backup tapes), and these surviving electronic records were the basis for much of the congressional investigation and subsequent criminal trials against the Iran-Contra participants. As one court put it, "The exegesis of mysterious PROFS notes consumed much time during the congressional investigation of the matter."[12]

The electronic nature of the PROFS records was an important factor in the investigations of the Iran-Contra Independent Counsel. Admiral Poindexter, the National Security Advisor, held a doctorate in physics and was also a computer expert. He set up a special channel, known as "Private Blank Check" which allowed North and Poindexter to relay messages to each other without those messages being routed through channels accessible to other NSC staff. While the substance of these messages was important to investigators, so was the mode of communication and the special channel through which they were sent. The distribution list of the e-mail was not reflected in paper printouts of the messages, but only in metadata contained in the electronic file. This metadata was important in aiding the investigators' understanding of the conspiracy.[13]

Scott Armstrong, a journalist, who was then the director of the National Security Archives, an independent non-governmental research institute and library located at George Washington University in Washington, D.C., initiated the PROFS litigation. The American Library Association, the American Historical Association, the Center for National Security Studies and several private individuals, including former U.S. Senator Gaylord Nelson, joined Armstrong as co-plaintiffs in the suit. The plaintiffs were represented primarily by Ralph Nader's Public Citizen Litigation Group.

The plaintiffs survived attempts by the government to dismiss the suit based on lack of standing and whether there were any federal statutes that gave the courts jurisdiction in the matter. The D.C. Circuit Court of Appeals found the plaintiffs had standing, the records were protected under the Federal Records Act, and the National Archives would be charged with the custody and preservation of the records.

A key question for electronic records management was what constituted adequate protection of the records. The government argued that it did not have the resources to maintain the records in electronic form and could only preserve them by printing them out on paper. The Armstrong plaintiffs argued that key historical aspects of the records, such as who the messages were routed to, who opened the messages, and who replied, would be lost if the Archives were allowed to reduce the records to paper and discard the original electronic files. This information was contained in metadata in the computer files but did not appear on the paper printouts. Echoing the language of Watergate, the court agreed with the plaintiffs, stating: "Such information can be of tremendous historical value in demonstrating what agency personnel were involved in making a particular policy decision and what officials knew, and when they knew it."[14]

On appeal the D.C. Circuit Court of Appeals affirmed the distinctive qualities of electronic records:

> The mere existence of the paper printouts does not affect the record status of the electronic materials unless the paper versions include all significant material contained in the electronic records. Otherwise, the two documents cannot accurately be termed "copies"–identical twins–but are, at most, "kissing cousins." Since the record shows that the two versions of the documents may frequently be only cousins–perhaps distant ones at that–the electronic documents retain their status as federal records after the creation of the paper print-outs, and all of the FRA obligations concerning the management and preservation of records still apply.[15]

The scope of the PROFS litigation expanded in November of 1992 after President George H. W. Bush lost his bid for re-election. The Armstrong plaintiffs returned to court seeking a restraining order to protect electronic records of the Bush Administration from destruction and amend their original complaint to include the electronic records of the Bush Administration in addition to those from the Reagan years. District Court Judge Charles Richey attempted to have the parties work out an agreement to preserve the records and come up with a joint stipulation of facts. His efforts were unsuccessful. On January 6, 1993, Judge Richey issued an order on the merits of the original suit, holding that at least some of the PROFS e-mail constituted records under the Federal Record Act and merited preservation in electronic form.[16] Judge Richey also ruled that the record keeping practice of the National Security Council and Executive Office of the President were "arbitrary and capricious."[17]

A week before the Bush Administration was to leave office, the government filed papers saying it needed to purge the White House computers because there was a danger the computers would overload and shut down unless all the memory was erased. The action would have destroyed many records that may have been covered by the Presidential Records Act, the Federal Records Act, or the Freedom of Information Act.[18] Judge Richey, a Nixon appointee, issued his second order in a week to prevent the government's action. His concerns that the White House was going to defy his order led him to make an unsolicited phone call to the *New York Times*. In a front page story, Judge Richey described the government's position as "just outrageous" and "really egregious."[19] The following day an appeals court issued a compromise ruling that permitted the White House and NSA to purge their computers on the condition that they preserve identical electronic copies of the information it was destroying.[20]

Staff from the National Archives finally obtained physical custody of the PROFS records on the night of January 19, 1993 as White House staff turned over 5,000 to 6,000 backup tapes and hard drives removed from personal computers. The transfer required numerous trips that continued into the next day past the time of the inauguration of President Clinton. The hard drives were placed in boxes without padding and some of the materials were damaged in the hasty transfer.[21] Judge Richey would later cite this damage as a part of a basis for a contempt citation issued three months later.[22]

The delay in turning over records may have been the result of White House efforts to keep control of the records through a last minute memorandum of agreement between the White House and the Archivist of the United States, Don W. Wilson. Shortly before midnight on January 19, 1993, Wilson signed an agreement that had been drawn up by lawyers from the White House Counsel's office, the National Security Council, and the Justice Department.[23] The agreement gave President Bush "exclusive legal control" over all computerized records of his presidency as well as "all derivative information in whatever form."[24]

The agreement raised a firestorm of controversy as Wilson had been in job negotiations with the President's son, George W. Bush, over Wilson's appointment as the executive director of the George Bush Center for Presidential Studies at Texas A&M University. This Center would later become the home of the Bush Presidential Library. Wilson was appointed to the $129,000 post shortly after Bush left office. Despite threats of a congressional investigation and criminal investigation by the Justice Department, no formal investigation was ever undertaken as to whether Wilson had a conflict of interest.[25]

The agreement itself was invalidated two years later by Judge Richey who found "that the Bush-Wilson Agreement is inconsistent with the Presidential Records Act and Article II of the Constitution, and that the decision by the Archivist to enter into that Agreement notwithstanding the provisions of the PRA was arbitrary, capricious, an abuse of discretion, and contrary to law."[26]

How did the PROFS litigation shape the National Archives electronic record management policies? A powder keg of a case, involving questions of executive privilege, government secrets, and the complex interplay of government information statutes, the PROFS case may not have been ideal for establishing precedents in the law of electronic government information. Yet the case clearly did establish that electronic records are not identical to analog copies and they must be preserved in electronic form.

In the short run, the demands of the PROFS court orders and discovery request placed tremendous strains on the staff of NARA's Center for Electronic Records. A contempt citation from Judge Richey ordering NARA to do whatever was necessary to comply with a court order in thirty days required the center's staff to work seven days a week in two eight-hour shifts for three weeks.[27] Further processing of the PROFS materials continued throughout the 1990s, draining the center's resources.[28]

Despite the difficulties the PROFS litigation caused NARA, its outcome was not wholly unwelcome to some NARA staffers. While the government's lawyers in the PROFS case argued that electronic records were best preserved by printing them out on paper, maintaining the records in electronic format was supported by some NARA archivists, including Trudy Peterson who became the Acting Archivist after the departure of Don Wilson. Concerning the PROFS litigation, Peterson wrote: "I and most of the archivists believed from the beginning that e-mail messages were record material and that printing out messages was simply not an adequate method of preserving the evidential value. We believed what, at the core, the judge believed. . . ."[29] Indeed, in the 1980s, Peterson and other NARA archivists had opposed recommendations by consultants to preserve all electronic records on computer output microfilm because such a solution would sacrifice the flexibility of electronic records.[30]

Peterson's sympathy for the plaintiff's position on maintaining electronic records in electronic format was not shared by Archivist Don W. Wilson. Writing of the PROFS case in 1997, Wilson stated: "The Archives position had been that hard copies of all records already existed as provided by the Presidential Records Act and therefore it was appropriate, and in fact a requirement, that the President be vested with the title to the back-up computer tapes which may or may not contain both types of additional record material–a determination only the President could make under the provisions of the Presidential Records Act and under the doctrine of Executive Privilege. The Judge disagreed and held the Archives responsible."[31]

One positive result of the PROFS litigation was that it persuaded the incoming Clinton Administration to invest in an automated records management system (ARMS) to archive electronic records, including e-mail, produced by the Executive Office of the President at the time they are created.[32] While this system was not perfect, it represented a big step forward in electronic records management.

Preserving the damaged PROFS tapes and hard drives also gave NARA valuable experience in conservation of electronic media. Some of the tapes were "shedding"–that is, the magnetic layer that contained the data was separating from the tape substrate. Archivists at NARA cured the problem by baking the tapes in a convection oven designed for that purpose.[33]

Yet for all the experience NARA gained in processing the PROFS tapes, the task they face today is infinitely more complex. The PROFS tapes contained mainly text files with some metadata. There were no embedded digital objects, no Web pages with hyperlinks to outside material, no images, no GIS or CAD data, in short, nothing like the complex digital records that federal agencies now routinely create every day.

THE ELECTRONIC RECORDS ARCHIVE

To address the challenges of preserving today's more complex electronic records, NARA created the Electronic Records Archive (ERA) in 1998. After several years of research, NARA is now issuing Requests for Proposals and beginning the process of moving the ERA from a vision to a reality. It expects to have "a functional subset of the system operational in 2007."[34] Current plans call for the ERA to be developed in five increments with work on the last increment completed by December, 2010.[35] NARA is wisely leveraging its resources by partnering with other government agencies, academic researchers, and private organizations in the development of the ERA.[36]

One element of the ERA includes plans to adapt a system developed jointly by the Defense Advanced Research Project Agency (DARPA) and the U.S. Patent and Trademarks Office. The Distributed Object Computation Testbed (DOCT) is a high performance computing system used for the processing of patent applications.[37] Patent applications contain, at a minimum, text and images, but may also contain scientific formulae, engineering blueprints, and gene sequences. The ability of this system to cope with complex digital records makes it an attractive candidate for further development in the ERA program.[38]

Another key element of the ERA is its plan to embrace the Open Archival Information System (OAIS) reference model, developed by NASA and in conjunction with governmental agencies in the United States and abroad. The OAIS is now an ISO standard,[39] and has been adopted by other national efforts at digital preservation, including the NEDLIB project in the Netherlands,[40] the CEDARS project in the United Kingdom,[41] and the PANDORA project in Australia.[42] The ISO standard defines OAIS as "an archive, consisting of an organization of people and systems that has accepted the responsibility to preserve information and make it available for a Designated Community."[43] It is essentially a framework for long-term storage and preservation of digital information.

The ERA's collaboration with other institutions, its careful research and planning and adoption of accepted standards augers well for its success, yet the program has had its share of problems. In August of 2003, the General Accounting Office (GAO) released a report critical of the ERA project. The GAO report cited problems in the planning documents and a failure to conform to industry standards.[44] Archivist John Carlin accepted the report and its recommendations for corrective action.[45]

Another concern for the success of the ERA is adequate funding. NARA has long suffered from the vicissitudes of federal appropriations. In October of 2003, in search of some additional money to fund Amtrak, a senator removed all funding for the ERA from the Senate version of an appropriations bill.[46] Lobbying from the library and archives community encouraged Congress to restore full funding in the conference report, but securing adequate funding will likely remain an Achilles heel of the program. To succeed, the ERA needs to recruit a core of highly skilled information scientists and archivists capable of doing groundbreaking research and solving technical problems that are still being defined. Such individuals are likely to be in high demand in private industry. Budget freezes, reductions-in-force, or program shutdowns will seriously jeopardize NARA's ability to build an archive capable of preserving the government's vast quantity of digital records.

THE GOVERNMENT PRINTING OFFICE
AND ELECTRONIC PRESERVATION OF DOCUMENTS

Historically, preservation issues, electronic or otherwise, were not major concerns for the Government Printing Office (GPO). GPO has functioned as a printer, jobber, and shipper of documents, not a repository or archive of government documents. It provided access and preservation of documents through the Federal Depository Library Program (FDLP), a partnership between the federal government and over 1,250 libraries. Through this model the government transferred the considerable costs of providing shelf space, reference services, binding and technical processing costs to the depository libraries. The libraries benefited by receiving free documents. The public benefited by gaining free and open access to government documents and the specialized reference services that are sometimes necessary to make full use of those materials.

This model began to change slowly in the 1990s. An electronic bulletin board system was rolled out in 1991, used at first mainly to provide communication with depository libraries by posting shipping lists and other items related to depository administration.[47] Content of wider interest was gradually added to the system. In 1993 Congress passed a law requiring the Superintendent of Documents to provide electronic access to the Federal Register and Congressional Record, provide an electronic directory of Federal electronic information, and "operate an electronic storage facility to which online access is made available."[48] In his signing statement, President Clinton said: "With recent advances in information technology, we can go beyond the costly printing of tons of paper documents without diminishing the quick and accurate delivery of important information to the public."[49] Clinton's statement did not address the costs of electronic publication and permanent public access.

Pursuant to that law, GPO Access[50] was born in 1994. Today, GPO Access provides access to over 2,800 databases and 147,000 titles on GPO servers and over 93,000 additional titles through links to other federal agency Web sites.[51] Without question, GPO Access has greatly expanded public access to federal government information. And it has done so at a comparatively low cost thus far, making the utmost of outdated or "legacy" computer hardware and software. Like NARA, GPO has suffered over the years from hiring freezes, budget cuts, and occasional threats of catastrophic budget cuts beaten back by the outcry of GPO's many supporters.

In 1996, the GPO announced its plan to "Transition to a More Electronic Federal Depository Library Program." The plan stated that the FDLP would make available fifty percent of its information electronically by the end of fiscal year 1998 and increasing amounts thereafter.[52] The transition is proceeding on schedule. At the October 2003 Depository Library Conference, Superintendent of Documents Judy Russell announced that sixty percent of documents distributed through the FDLP in 2003 would be electronic documents and electronic documents will comprise ninety-five percent or more of the program within five years.[53]

To its credit, GPO has considered the issue of permanent public access (PPA) at every step in its transition to a more electronic depository program. Title 44 of the United States Code requires GPO to provide permanent access to documents in the program.[54] Central to achieving PPA is digital preservation. In furtherance of this commitment, GPO and NARA entered into an agreement in August of 2003 whereby GPO was made an "archival affiliate." The agreement covers all of the content provided through GPO Access. NARA will have legal custody of the content but GPO will "retain physical custody and be responsible for permanent public access and preservation of the records."[55]

How will GPO carry out its commitment to digital preservation and permanent public access? Thus far, the GPO has adopted a number of strategies to move toward digital preservation: partnerships with depository libraries to maintain and post elements of the electronic collection; creation of an in-house archive operated on GPO servers; purchase of backup servers that are physically distant from the primary servers; participation in a digital archive maintained by OCLC; and the creation of permanent uniform resources locators or PURLS to point to back up versions of documents that are removed from agency servers. GPO has also sought to establish agreements with federal agencies to keep information permanently available on agency servers.[56]

One type of federal agency unable to guarantee permanent access to its electronic publications is an agency that has gone out of existence. GPO's partnership with the University of North Texas preserves these orphan documents in a "CyberCemetery."[57] The site is currently hosting the Web sites of some twenty-five dead commissions and agencies. Who would want to read the publications of dead bureaucracies? After the terrorist attacks of September 11, 2001 the reports and hearings concerning aviation safety by the National Civil Aviation Review Commission were in very high demand. Through the CyberCemetery journalists and others had immediate access to these materials some four years after the Commission ceased to exist.

In addition to the CyberCemetery, GPO has established five other content partnerships, including agreements with the Department of Energy and the National Library of Medicine. A complete description of the partnership initiative is available on the GPO Web site at: http://www.access.gpo.gov/su_docs/fdlp/partners/index.html.

As GPO shifts from a distributor of information in tangible formats to a repository of electronic information with responsibility for providing permanent public access, how will it manage the costs? In part, GPO expects a diminishment of costs in the traditional program, as fewer items are shipped out to depository libraries. George Barnum, Electronic Collection Manager for the depository program, put it this way:

> It has been the assumption of the transition process that as the emphasis on tangible product distribution diminishes, GPO's resources will be redirected toward managing electronic files, coordinating the cooperative efforts that will facilitate preservation of electronic publications, and maintaining a standard or permanence, authenticity, and reliability comparable to the print-based program.[58]

The emphasis on tangible products certainly has diminished, but whether GPO can further reduce tangible distribution without destroying the program is questionable. Distribution of paper hit a high mark in 1993 when GPO distributed 20,755 paper titles. It has decreased every year since then reaching a low of 7,121 titles in paper in 2003, or about thirty-four percent of the titles shipped in 1993. The number of microfiche titles has declined even more steeply, from 29,070 titles in 1994 to 5,448 titles in 2002.[59]

While most depository libraries have accepted a program that offers leaner pickings of tangible products there is a tipping point that may soon be reached where the costs and responsibilities of remaining in the program outweigh the value of the tangible items received. Some would argue the electronic products are adequate replacements for the lost tangible items and we can all be "virtual depositories." Indeed one library vendor now markets its cataloging records of online GPO documents to non-depository libraries looking to reap the benefits of government information without any of the responsibilities of depository libraries.[60] Anyone with access to the Internet can be a virtual depository, but libraries that participate in the Federal Depository Library Program offer far more. They provide the public with librarians highly skilled in government information. If depository libraries fail to receive a sufficient number of tangible documents to justify the expense of remaining in the program, there is a real danger that many will drop out and the public will lose access to these services.

The depository library program also contributes to the goal of permanent public access. Paper is an accepted archival medium and paper documents shipped today will likely be in many libraries a hundred years from now. Preserving the electronic equivalents for a hundred years is a challenge that remains to be solved.

To successfully preserve government information for future generations, NARA and the GPO must educate decision makers in Congress and the Executive Branch on the true costs and challenges of electronic preservation. Congress has often viewed electronic dissemination of government information as a way to save money. This is short sighted. When one factors in the long-term costs of electronic preservation and access, centralized costs that will be borne by the government not by depository libraries, the mirage of savings evaporates. But the only alternative to full and continued funding of electronic preservation is a catastrophic loss of government information. Permanent public access requires full funding for both electronic access and preservation and the traditional depository library program. Anything less will imperil the public's right to government information.

REFERENCES

1. The Government Relations Committee of the American Association of Law Libraries recently completed a fifty state survey on permanent public access to the electronic records of state governments. The survey found that most states are doing a poor job. The survey is available at: http://www.ll.georgetown.edu/aallwash/PPAreport.htm.

2. Over the last ten years the subject of electronic preservation has generated a sizable body of literature. For a good overview of the subject see: Donald Waters and John Garret, *Preserving Digital Information: Report of the Task Force on Archiving of Digital Information*, 1996, available at: http://www.rlg.org/ArchTF/. Also recommended is an article by Margaret Hedstrom, "Digital preservation: A time bomb for Digital Libraries," available at: http://www.uky.edu/%7Ekiernan/DL/hedstrom.html.

3. Bruce I. Ambacher, ed., *Thirty Years of Electronic Records* (Lanham, MD: Scarecrow Press, 2003), ix.

4. Meyer H. Fishbein, "Recollections of an Electronic Records Pioneer." In *Thirty Years of Electronic Records*, ed. Bruce I. Ambacher. (Lanham, MD: Scarecrow Press, 2003), xv.

5. Thomas E. Brown, "History of NARA's Custodial Program for Electronic Records: From the Data Archive Staff to the Center for Electronic Records, 1968-1998." In *Thirty Years of Electronic Records*, ed. Bruce I. Ambacher. (Lanham, MD: Scarecrow Press, 2003), 3-4.

6. Idem., 4-5.

7. Idem., 6-8.

8. Idem., 8.

9. Idem., 15.

10. Idem.

11. *Armstrong v. Bush*, 721 F. Supp 343, 345 (D.D.C. 1989).

12. *Armstrong v. Bush*, 721 F. Supp 343, 345 (D.D.C. 1989).

13. *Public Citizen v. Carlin*, 2 F. Supp.2d 1 (D.D.C. 1997)., footnote 27.

14. *Armstrong v. Exec. Office of the President*, 810 F. Supp 335, 341 (D.D.C. 1993).

15. *Armstrong v. Exec. Office of the President*, 1 F.3d 1274, 1283 (D.C. Cir. 1993).

16. *Armstrong v. Exec. Office of the President*, 810 F. Supp 335 (D.D.C. 1993).

17. Idem., 344.

18. Philip G. Schrag, "Working Papers as Federal Records: The Need for New Legislation to Preserve the History of National Policy," 46 *Administrative Law Review* 95 at 95, Spring, 1994.

19. Stephen Labaton, "Judge Sees Plan by White House to Defy Order and Purge Data," *New York Times* (January 15, 1993), A1.

20. Stephen Labaton, "Court Says Bush Administration Can Erase Files if Copies Are Kept," *New York Times* (January 16, 1993), A8.

21. Schrag at 96.

22. *Armstrong v. Exec. Office of the President*, 821 F. Supp. 761, 769 (D.D.C. 1993).

23. Schrag at 96.

24. George Lardner Jr., "Eleventh-Hour Covenant: Lost Memory Computes to Gain for Bush," *Washington Post* (March 13, 1993), A12.

25. Idem.

26. *American Historical Association v. Peterson*, 876 F. Supp. 1300, 1322 (D.D.C. 1995).

27. Brown, 17.

28. Idem., 18.

29. Trudy H. Peterson, "Views of Managers: Which Drawer Do You Use?" In *Thirty Years of Electronic Records*, ed. Bruce I. Ambacher. (Lanham, MD: Scarecrow Press, 2003),151.

30. Idem., 148-149.

31. Don W. Wilson, "Presidential Records: Evidence for Historians or Ammunition for Prosecutors," 14 *Government Information Quarterly* 344 (No. 4, 1997).

32. Jason R. Baron, "The PROFS Decade: NARA, E-mail and the Courts." In *Thirty Years of Electronic Records*, ed. Bruce I. Ambacher. (Lanham, MD: Scarecrow Press, 2003), 114-115.

33. Peterson, 151.

34. NARA Web Site at: http://www.archives.gov/electronic_records_archives/about_era.html.

35. U.S. General Accounting Office, "Records Management: National Archives and Records Administration's Acquisition of Major System Faces Risks," GAO-03-880 (Washington, DC: August 2003), p. 19. Available at: http://www.gao.gov/new.items/d03880.pdf.

36. A list of the ERA partnerships can be found at: http://www.archives.gov/electronic_records_archives/research/partnerships.html.

37. Kenneth Thibodeau, "Building the Future: The Electronic Records Archive Program." In *Thirty Years of Electronic Records*, ed. Bruce I. Ambacher. (Lanham, MD: Scarecrow Press, 2003), 93-95.

38. Idem.

39. The full text of the OAIS ISO Standard can be viewed at: http://www.classic.ccsds.org/documents/pdf/CCSDS-650.0-B-1.pdf.

40. Titia van der Werf-Davelaar, "Long Term Preservation of Electronic Publications: The NEDLIB Project," D-Lib Magazine, Vol. 5, No. 9 (September 1999). Available at: http://www.dlib.org/dlib/september99/vanderwerf/09vanderwerf.html.

41. See: http://www.leeds.ac.uk/cedars/index.html.

42. See: http://pandora.nla.gov.au/index.html.

43. Supra Note 35 at page 1-1 (page 10 within the pdf document).

44. U.S. General Accounting Office, "Records Management: National Archives and Records Administration's Acquisition of Major System Faces Risks," GAO-03-880 (Washington, DC: August 2003), p. 19. Available at: http://www.gao.gov/new.items/d03880.pdf.

45. Idem., 49.

46. See AALL Action Alert at: http://www.ll.georgetown.edu/aallwash/aa10302003.html.

47. For a description of the bulletin board service see: *Electronic Bulletin Board System for the Federal Depository Library Program: A Study.* (Washington: Government Printing Office, 1991). [GP 3.2:EL 2].

48. Government Printing Office Electronic Information Access Enhancement Act of 1993, P.L. 103-40, 107 Stat. 112, codified at 44 U.S.C. 4101 et seq.

49. 29 *Weekly Compilation of Presidential Documents* 1043, June 8, 1993.

50. GPO Access is the Government Printing Office's main portal to online information. It is available at: http://www.gpoaccess.gov/.

51. Remarks by Ric Davis, "Current Status and Next Generation of GPO Access," 24 *Administrative Notes*, No. 5, p. 13. (Washington: GPO, May 1, 2003).

52. *Study to Identify Measures Necessary for a Successful Transition to a More Electronic Federal Depository Library Program.* (Washington: GPO, June, 1996), page E-23. [GP.2:EL 2/3 Final], available at: http://www.access.gpo.gov/su_docs/fdlp/pubs/study/studyhtm.html.

53. Remarks by Judy C. Russell, "Information Dissemination Operations," 24 *Administrative Notes*, no. 13, p. 7 (Washington: GPO, November 15, 2003).

54. U.S.C. §1911.

55. Press release: "The GPO and National Archives Unite in Support of the Permanent Online Public Access." Available at: http://www.gpo.gov/public-affairs/news/03news46.html (August 12, 2003). The release was also reprinted in the August 15, 2003 edition of *Administrative Notes*.

56. George Barnum, "The Federal Depository Library Program Electronic Collection: An Approach to Ongoing Access to Government Information," 2 *Of Significance . . . A Topical Journal of The Association of Public Data Users* No. 2, p. 37 (2000).

57. The CyberCemetary is available at: http://govinfo.library.unt.edu/.

58. Barnum, supra note 54 at p. 38.

59. The numbers are based on an e-mail sent by Judith C. Russell, Superintendent of Documents, to GOVDOC-L, November 19, 2003.

60. See the Marchive brochure promoting "Documents without Shelves at: http://www.marcive.com/HOMEPAGE/dwsl.pdf.

Providing Perpetual Access to Government Information

Suhasini L. Kumar

SUMMARY. The past few years have seen the Government Printing Office (GPO) move from managing predominantly paper based government publications to collecting, organizing, and disseminating government information electronically. Serious concerns have been raised about perpetual access and authentication of government information in the new digital environment. This article focuses on GPO's plans to preserve both electronic and tangible government information resources and the initiatives being taken by GPO in collaboration with the library community and other stakeholders to address these matters. *[Article copies available for a fee from The Haworth Document Delivery Service: 1-800-HAWORTH. E-mail address: <docdelivery@haworthpress.com> Website: <http://www.HaworthPress.com> © 2006 by The Haworth Press, Inc. All rights reserved.]*

KEYWORDS. Authentication, digital environment, electronic, dissemination, GPO, Government Printing Office, government information, perpetual access, preservation

Suhasini L. Kumar is Associate Professor and Head, Government Documents Department, and Coordinator, Information and Instruction Services Division, Carlson Library, The University of Toledo, Toledo, OH 43606 (E-mail: Skumar@utnet.utoledo. edu).

[Haworth co-indexing entry note]: "Providing Perpetual Access to Government Information." Kumar, Suhasini L. Co-published simultaneously in *The Reference Librarian* (The Haworth Information Press, an imprint of The Haworth Press, Inc.) No. 94, 2006, pp. 225-232; and: *The Changing Face of Government Information: Providing Access in the Twenty-First Century* (ed: Suhasini L. Kumar) The Haworth Information Press, an imprint of The Haworth Press, Inc., 2006, pp. 225-232. Single or multiple copies of this article are available for a fee from The Haworth Document Delivery Service [1-800-HAWORTH, 9:00 a.m. - 5:00 p.m. (EST). E-mail address: docdelivery@haworthpress.com].

INTRODUCTION

Keeping America informed has been the main mission of the United States Government Printing Office (GPO) since 1813 when Congress realized that it was vital to make the workings of the government available to the people of the United States. GPO's primary function has been to collect, organize, and preserve information, originating from Congress, the three branches of the government and other federal publishers, and disseminate this information to the public.

Apart from offering Congress, the courts, and government agencies services that would help them produce print documents cost effectively according to federal government stipulations, GPO also offered these publications for sale through its Sales Program and free of cost to the public through the Federal Depository Library Program.

GPO was always avant-garde in its attitude towards change and technology and was the first to embrace the latest technologies and formats such as microfiche, CD-ROMs, and DVDs when they were first introduced.[1] With the Paper Reduction Act of 1995 the electronic dissemination of documents on the Internet had arrived, but no one had anticipated the publishing revolution this was about to unleash and the far reaching impact this would have specifically on the creation, dissemination, and preservation of government information.

For the past few years GPO and the library community have been seriously contemplating many important issues relating to access and preservation of digital and tangible government information. This article aims to focus on current preservation issues relating to both electronic and tangible government resources, and concerns regarding authentication of digital resources, and initiatives GPO is taking to address these matters in an ongoing effort to provide perpetual access to authentic government information.

PROBLEMS RELATED TO GOVERNMENT INFORMATION ON THE INTERNET

The fact that documents can now be created and published on the Internet so effortlessly has tempted agencies to circumvent conventional printing services offered by GPO. Apart from having them printed within the agency or buying them locally, many agencies have resorted to publishing straight to the Web with the intention of saving both time and cost of printing. This, according to the Public Printer

Bruce James, "has led to the breakdown of government information standards and deprived the public of the uniform and predictable availability of official government documents. It also deprives future generations from having an accurate record of the work of our government."[2]

If a printed document is altered after it is published it can be detected, whereas one of the greatest challenges in preserving access to electronic publications on the Internet is its evanescent nature and the fact that it can be changed easily. "This inherent instability presents challenges of various kinds: instability of location or address, the ease with which information can simply disappear, and establishment and verification of 'officialness' which exists alongside the actual authenticity or integrity of the digital object."[3]

The instability of location has been resolved to a certain extent by the Persistent Uniform Resource Locator (PURL) which directs the user to the appropriate URL on the agency server site from where the information was originally published and can be accessed.

TOWARD PERMANENT ACCESS AND AUTHENTICITY OF INFORMATION ON THE INTERNET

The publishing agencies provide GPO with the documented assurance that the electronic publications will be made permanently available at the original site of publication, with the promise that the files would be given to GPO if for some reason the agency is no longer able to maintain them. "Where a documented agreement is not possible GPO harvests a copy of the publication for its own archive. These publications are retained, updated as needed and served up to users only when the agency version is no longer available. The archived information may be managed on in-house servers at GPO, or servers operated by FDLP partners which agree to maintain and migrate archival publications, or on vendor-operated servers."[4]

Apart from the concern over the preservation and availability of government information into perpetuity, information users are also greatly concerned about the authenticity of government information on the Internet. At the Depository Library Council (DLC) meeting in October 2003, the Public Printer asked DLC members to provide ideas on what constituted a version of information and how it should be authenticated and stored.

After debating these issues, DLC approached the depository library community, library associations, and information specialists outside the depository library program for their ideas and input on this subject and incorporated this information into their response to the Public Printer on January 22, 2004.

The DLC said that digital information is amenable to change and the two major issues of concern regarding this were version and authenticity control. Multiple versions of information were available on several public Web sites; this could not only be confusing but may also prove to be detrimental to the user who is unaware of the version being used. Various copies of government publications available on the Web and on other digital media profess to be the same version but some are authentic and some are not. This again can lead to serious repercussions.[5]

The question of validity and authenticity of government information on the Web can have far reaching consequences on its users. This is especially true for information products related to legal documents such as statutes, regulations, opinions, decisions, and guidelines as well as health related bulletins, census reports, datasets, business statistics, etc. It is also very important for researchers and historians to be able to verify versions of documents that have changed over time in order to trace their evolution.

In its response to the Public Printer, DLC advocated that the standard setting process to identify versions and authenticity of government information needed to begin immediately. GPO, as the agency responsible for dissemination of government information, should be among the lead agencies to formulate the standards for official documents of the U.S. government. DLC also recommended that tools for verifying authenticity be made available to Federal Depository libraries and the public.

IMPLEMENTING THE PUBLIC KEY INFRASTRUCTURE (PKI)

In February 2004, the Public Printer James Bruce, said that "GPO's critical role for the 21st century was to be the guarantor of authentic government information"[6] both now and into the future. GPO was preparing to implement a test-bed application of the Public Key Infrastructure (PKI) as a preliminary instrument for authentication. In April 2004 during the Depository Library Council meeting update, it was said that GPO had finalized the documents establishing the policies and practices for GPO's PKI. The hardware and software needed for the PKI operation was on site and the PKI implementation was underway.

When the PKI was fully in operation GPO would begin digitally signing electronic documents. The Public Key Infrastructure (PKI) technology would help safeguard data against unauthorized alteration or substitution of information. It would also allow GPO's patrons to confirm the authenticity and integrity of the information they were accessing from GPO. Users would be able to verify the fact that the information was approved for submission to GPO by the appropriate Federal agency and that it was not altered from the time it was signed.

Judy Russell, GPO's superintendent of documents and managing director of information dissemination, said GPO would apply the PKI technology to all documents submitted to GPOAccess by the agencies, content would be marked as they came in, and the final product digitally signed so users could determine that the product was indeed authentic. "Once a document is digitally signed, users can use a free software tool from the technology vendors to determine the document's authenticity. The digital signature can be visible or not."[7] Russell said that GPO is also considering digital watermarks for print publications or electronic master documents. Users could employ a reader to display the watermark to determine the document's authenticity.

DIGITAL PRESERVATION OF THE LEGACY COLLECTION

GPO was also planning to digitize the legacy collection of tangible United States government publications and was collaborating with the library community in this endeavor. Its aim was to provide permanent Web access to the digital collection at no cost to the public through the Federal Depository Program. The collection would be digitally reformatted in order to preserve it for future generations. The digital preservation masters and the metadata related to it would be archived in the GPO electronic archive and also at other host sites. There are nearly 2.2 million print publications that are estimated to be about 60 million pages with the availability of an electronic legacy collection, it is believed that it would allow depository libraries, including regional libraries, to manage their tangible collections more effectively, substituting electronic copies for tangible copies if they wished to do so.

DEVELOPING SPECIFICATIONS
FOR THE DIGITIZING PROJECT

GPO is involved in the process of developing specifications for the digitizing project. Experts in the digitization field both in digital format conversion and project development were invited to a conference held by GPO in March 2004. They discussed standards and specifications for creation of digital preservation masters and chalked out the minimum requirements for digitizing documents from the legacy collection. The second meeting was scheduled for June, 2004 and GPO was "reviewing the necessary processes to establish a basic metadata package for each item (artifact) in the digital collection, as well as the mandatory metadata to be submitted to GPO by digitization partners."[8]

SHARED REPOSITORIES

The Government Printing Office (GPO) is working together with the library community on several new initiatives involving access to and preservation of print and digital federal government documents. GPO is actively promoting the movement toward shared repositories or housing agreements that would help libraries reduce some of the superfluous items in their collections. This initiative is in its early stages of planning but it is hoped that this would facilitate active preservation of the government documents collections by enabling depository libraries to move toward smaller collections of complete sets of tangible government publications that could be easily preserved.

The Center for Research Libraries (CRL) was contracted to prepare a draft for a "Decision Framework for Federal Documents Repositories for the U.S. Government Printing Office." The decision framework was drafted in order to help the Superintendent of documents "evaluate the qualities, resources and capabilities of potential repository facilities and their governing organizations, and to identify the configuration of light and dark repositories most appropriate to ensure the persistent archiving and public availability of tangible federal documents."[9]

The repositories would include depository libraries that would make government documents available to the general public according to the federal depository rules. There would be the "light archives," a collection of tangible materials preserved under the best conditions so that the safety and integrity of the materials are not jeopardized while permitting ongoing use of these materials to the public. The "light archives" would be different from the regular collections because there is a concerted plan already laid out to actively preserve and protect this collection.

A collection of tangible materials called the "dark archives" would also be preserved under the best conditions "designed to secure the integrity and artifactual characteristics of the archived materials."[10] These materials would be brought to light only when the "service copy" of the materials failed or proved to be inadequate under other circumstances established under the "dark archives" contract.

THE NATIONAL COLLECTION OF U.S. GOVERNMENT PUBLICATIONS (FORMERLY COLLECTION OF LAST RESORT)

GPO planned to acquire and preserve tangible and electronic copies of government publications in all formats and provide comprehensive, permanent public access to them in what was termed a Collection of Last Resort. During the Depository Library Council Meeting, Fall 2004, the Depository Library Council agreed that it would be more appropriate to change the term "Collection of Last Resort" to National Collection. The National Collection would include preservation and access copies of digital publications and tangible publications and would be located at multiple sites. Access copies of the National Collection assets would be publicly accessible from the "light archives" for tangible publications or the service archives in the case of digital publications.

The National Collection assets in the "dark archives" would be held for preservation rather than public access. Preservation copies of digital publications in the "dark archives" would be "used to create access copies or derivatives for delivery from GPO service archives or partner sites";[11] these assumptions on the elements of the National Collection are still under discussion and might be further refined before they are eventually finalized.

CONCLUSION

GPO's efforts to move toward a more electronic Federal Depository Library Program (FDLP) continues to progress; during FY 2003 the percentage of online titles in the FDLP increased to 65%. This transition mandated by the Congress in the Legislative Branch Appropriations

Act (PL1-4-52, 19 November 1995) promises to continue, with the percentage of online information expected to approach 95% by 2005.[12]

GPO is shifting from managing resources in a predominantly print environment to being a manager of digital government information electronically collecting, organizing, disseminating, and ensuring continued security and access to government information. It has worked assiduously to identify initiatives that are required to modernize and enhance its current level of information technology capabilities and security. Advice and input has been widely sought by GPO from the library community and a variety of interested stakeholders. Initiatives for collection development, access, dissemination, authentication, and preservation of both print and electronic information have been drafted and designed with the help of experts in the field; comments are being requested from all stakeholders so that GPO will be in a position to make informed decisions. On the brink of a challenging new era, GPO shoulders a great responsibility as it moves forward into the 21st century.

REFERENCES

1. James, Bruce. 2004. U.S. Government Printing Office Keeping America Informed in the 21st Century a First Look at the GPO Strategic Planning Process. *Depository Library Council Meeting*, St. Louis, Missouri, 19 April.

2. Ibid.

3. Barnum, George. 2002. Availability, Access, Authenticity, and Persistence: Creating the Environment for Permanent Public Access to Electronic Government Information. *Government Information Quarterly* 19, n. 1: 37-43.

4. Ibid.

5. Depository Library Council. 2004. Depository Library Council's Advice to the Public Printer, 22 January.

6. James, Bruce. 2004. Reply to Depository Library Council, 18 February.

7. Russell, Judy. 2004. *Federal Library and Information Center Committee Conference*, Washington, 25 March.

8. U.S. Government Printing Office. Report from the Meeting of Experts on Digital Preservation. June, 2004. http://www.gpoaccess.gov/about/reports/preservation.html (accessed June 18, 2004).

9. Center for Research Libraries (CRL). 2004. Decision Framework for Federal Document Repositories (Discussion Draft), 12 April.

10. Ibid.

11. U.S. Government Printing Office. 2005. Council Briefing Topic–Spring 2005 National Collection of U.S. Government Publication.

12. MacGilvray, Marian W. (Editor). Information Dissemination Annual Report-Fiscal Year 2003. *Administrative Notes* 24 n. 12:3-9.

ANNOTATED RESOURCES

Information on Native Americans in U.S. Government Publications

Allison A. Cowgill

SUMMARY. This article is a selective annotated list of print and electronic sources that provide information on Native Americans and the United States Government. While most of these are issued by the federal agencies, there are also some commercially published works that cover government resources or describe and interpret federal activities. The bibliography is arranged in broad subject areas; headings include finding tools, federal policy, federal laws and regulations, treaties, statistics, history and culture, and contemporary issues. *[Article copies available for a fee from The Haworth Document Delivery Service: 1-800-HAWORTH. E-mail address: <docdelivery@haworthpress.com> Website: <http://www.HaworthPress.com> © 2006 by The Haworth Press, Inc. All rights reserved.]*

Allison A. Cowgill is Assistant Professor and Coordinator of Information and Reference Services, Colorado State University Libraries, 501 University Avenue, Fort Collins, CO 80523-1019 (E-mail: Allison.Cowgill@colostate.edu).

The author would like to thank Dorothy Leising, Information and Reference, Reference Services, Colorado State Library, for her valuable and insightful editorial assistance.

[Haworth co-indexing entry note]: "Information on Native Americans in U.S. Government Publications." Cowgill, Allison A. Co-published simultaneously in *The Reference Librarian* (The Haworth Information Press, an imprint of The Haworth Press, Inc.) No. 94, 2006, pp. 233-255; and: *The Changing Face of Government Information: Providing Access in the Twenty-First Century* (ed: Suhasini L. Kumar) The Haworth Information Press, an imprint of The Haworth Press, Inc., 2006, pp. 233-255. Single or multiple copies of this article are available for a fee from The Haworth Document Delivery Service [1-800-HAWORTH, 9:00 a.m. - 5:00 p.m. (EST). E-mail address: docdelivery@haworthpress.com].

KEYWORDS. Native Americans, government publications, World Wide
Web, political science–United States

Interest in Native Americans continually increases and reference librarians regularly work with people who want information on Native
American histories, cultural traditions, and the political forces that
shaped their lives. Research on Native Americans routinely includes
works issued by federal agencies and works issued by commercial publishers about United States government activities. As stated by Supreme
Court Justice John Marshall in 1831, "The condition of the Indians in
relation to the United States is perhaps unlike that of any other people in
existence."[1] Indeed, it can be argued that controversial federal perspectives, policies, legislation, and activities have more immediately affected Native Americans than the rest of this country's population. For
scholars, historians, and students, United States government documents
are major sources of primary information on Native Peoples.

The following bibliography contains a very selective list of print and
electronic sources that provide information on Native Americans and
the federal government. While most are issued by federal agencies, included are some commercially published works that provide access to
government sources or describe and interpret federal activities. These
publications and Web sites were carefully chosen based on their importance, availability, and the kinds of information they provide. Many
other Web resources were considered but were not included because of
space constraints. Fortunately, some of the Web sites described provide
extensive links to other Internet resources that are not individually described here. This bibliography is designed to help reference librarians
identify and locate important information on Native Americans in federal publications and other highly relevant resources.

The bibliography is arranged in broad subject categories. The Super-
intendents of Documents classification (SuDoc) numbers for federal
documents, used by most libraries nationwide, are included in parenthe-
ses where applicable. Many government publications are now available
electronically on the Web and annotations for them include their Uniform Resource Locators (URLs) or Web "addresses." URLs are in
brackets when they are included in the texts of annotations. Three
non-governmental Web sites are listed at the end because of their important emphases on Native American issues; two of these provide
valuable links to a wide variety of other sites that researchers will find
useful.

The amazing growth of the Internet parallels the growing number of projects that have digitized federal resources on Native Americans and mounted them on the Web, greatly increasing their availability and usability. One example is the *Native American Constitution and Law Digitization Project*, coordinated by the University of Oklahoma Law Library and the National Indian Law Library of the Native American Rights Fund. The Project's Web site includes links to the full-text of Felix S. Cohen's *Handbook of Federal Indian Law* and *Indian Affairs: Laws and Treaties* compiled by Charles J. Kappler. Other examples include the Library of Congress's *American Memory* project, *American State Papers* and *A Century of Lawmaking for a New Nation: U.S. Congressional Documents and Databases*. Descriptions of these important efforts are included in the bibliography.

FINDING TOOLS

Buchanan, William W., and Edna A. Kanely, comps. *Cumulative Subject Index to the Monthly Catalog of the United States Government Publications 1900-1971*. 15 vols. Washington, D.C.: Carrollton Press, Inc., 1975.

Provides a "single cumulative index to all publications" listed in the biennial *Document Catalog* and the decennial cumulative and annual indexes of the *Monthly Catalog* to 1971. Subject headings for Native Americans include the single word "Indian" with numerous subheadings and the names of individual tribes. Entries note the specific years the publications were included in the *Monthly Catalog*, with page numbers for volumes published before 1947 and entry numbers for later ones. It is necessary to refer to the specific *Monthly Catalog* volumes for complete bibliographical information and SuDoc classification numbers. While this can be cumbersome when researching broad topics due to the sheer number of entries, it is highly recommended for individuals doing comprehensive research. A companion set is the *Cumulative Title Index to United States Public Documents, 1789-1976*, a sixteen-volume set that is a "single-alphabet listing" of federal publication titles and SuDoc classification numbers (Arlington, VA: United States Historical Documents Institute, 1979-1983).

Checklist of United States Public Documents 1789-1909: Congressional: To Close of Sixtieth Congress; Departmental: To End of Calen-

dar Year 1909, Compiled Under the Direction of the Superintendent of Documents. 3rd ed., rev. and enl. Washington, D.C.: Government Printing Office, 1911. (SuDoc no.: GP3.2:C41/2)

Lists Congressional and department documents. This work, used to identify federal publications issued before 1900, is a copy of the Public Documents Department Library shelflist. It consists of three sections: the Congressional edition by serial number; departmental edition by the Superintendent of Documents classification number; and miscellaneous Congressional publications. The checklist includes an index of departments, bureaus, divisions, offices, commissions, and committees. This key resource has been reprinted numerous times. Another retrospective bibliography, Poore's *Descriptive Catalogue of the Government Publications of the United States, September 5, 1774-March 4, 1881*, is less complete and somewhat more difficult to use.

Frazier, Patrick, ed. *Many Nations: A Library of Congress Resource Guide for the Study of Indian and Alaska Native Peoples of the United States.* Washington, D.C.: Library of Congress, 1996. (SuDoc no.: LC1.6/4:N21)

Describes the Library of Congress's (LC) vast collections relating to Native Americans. Its arrangement is based on the seven main LC reading rooms including the Main Reading Room, the Rare Book Reading Room, the Manuscript Reading Room, and the Law Library Reading Room. These sections have instructions on how to identify and locate materials, and include clear descriptions of key resources, finding tools, and specific collections, all well placed in their historical contexts. It also has a comprehensive index.

Frazier, Patrick. *Portrait Index of North American Indians in Published Collections.* 2nd ed., rev. and enl. Washington, D.C.: Library of Congress, 1996. (SuDoc no.: LC1.2:P83/3/996)

Indexes select published portraits of individual Native Americans from seventy-five pictorial works owned by the Library of Congress. Arranged alphabetically by tribe and then alphabetically by personal names within each tribe, entries include alternate names if known, sources, and page or plate numbers. These books, or photocopies of their contents, are available on interlibrary loan from libraries around the country. It includes an alphabetical index of personal names and the tribal sections where they are found.

Hill, Edward E., comp. *Guide to Records in the National Archives of the United States Relating to American Indians.* Washington, D.C.: National Archives and Records Service, General Services Administration, 1982. (SuDoc no.: GS4.6/2:Am3)

Serves as a guide to National Archives records on Native Americans. The basic organizational unit is the record group that usually consists of the records of a single agency such as the Bureau of Indian Affairs and its predecessors. These record groups reflect a combination of chronology, relationships with Native Americans, and government organization. The text includes all information necessary to locate these materials in the Archives, including record group number, set number, and microfilm reel number when applicable, and concise descriptions of record contents. There is a comprehensive index. The National Archives and Records Service has mounted its *Archival Research Catalog* on the Web; it allows users to search by keywords, digitized images, locations, organizations, and people [http://www.archives.gov/research_room/arc/].

Hill, Edward E. *The Office of Indian Affairs, 1824-1880: Historical Sketches.* Library of American Indian Affairs. New York: Clearwater Publishing Co., 1974.

Compiled to "enable researchers to locate correspondence contained in Microcopy 234, Letters Received by the Office of Indian Affairs, 1824-1880, a microform publication of the National Archives and Records Service." Sections, arranged alphabetically by the names of specific agencies, vary in size and content. Each one provides a short agency history, geographical jurisdiction, names and appointment dates for agents, and brief descriptions of the corresponding files. Hill also provides references to related entries, an index arranged alphabetically by names of tribes, and an index arranged by jurisdiction.

Johnson, Steven L. *Guide to American Indian Documents in the Congressional Serial Set, 1817-1899: A Project of the Institute for the Development of Indian Law.* Library of American Indian Affairs. New York: Clearwater Publishing Co., 1977.

Helps researchers identify and locate the "10,649 documents on Indian affairs which are located in *Serial Set* volumes from 1817 through 1899." The massive *Serial Set* contains a wide variety of important documents and reports received by the U.S. Congress from Congressional committees, executive agencies, and numerous other sources. Entries for documents are listed chronologically and include titles, dates, citations, brief content analyses, and the *Serial Set* volume numbers where they are located. There is a detailed subject index. Many large libraries have the multi-volume *CIS US Serial Set Index*, a commercial publication by the Congressional Information Service that provides comprehensive subject access to the *Serial Set* from 1789 to 1969.

Monthly Catalog of United States Government Publications. Washington, D.C.: Government Printing Office, 1895- . (SuDoc no.: GP3.8)

Indexes print and electronic publications of U.S. government agencies each month with annual cumulations. Many of the paper titles have been routinely distributed to designated depository libraries around the country. Interfiled author, title, and subject indexes refer to specific entries that contain full bibliographic information and SuDoc classification numbers. Electronic coverage, beginning in January, 1994, is also available on the Web via GPO Access [http://www.gpoaccess.gov/cgp/index.html]. New records are added online daily and can be easily searched by date, keyword, title, and the Superintendent of Documents classification number. Many libraries subscribe to the online *GPO Monthly Catalog* that contains records from July, 1976 to date, from vendors such as OCLC.

Prucha, Francis Paul, ed. *Documents of United States Indian Policy.* 3rd ed. Lincoln, NE: University of Nebraska Press, 2000.

Contains a broad collection of sections from 238 significant government publications on federal policy affecting Native Americans from colonial times to 2000. In his preface, the author states, "For students and teachers this convenient reference work supplies in chronological order the documents they need to know when dealing with the public history of Indian affairs." Each section is prefaced by a brief explanation of that item's historical importance. A select bibliography and substantive index are included.

United States. National Archives & Records Administration. "American Indians: A Select Catalog of National Archives Microfilm Publications," rev. 1995, http://www.archives.gov/publications/microfilm_catalogs/american_indian/american_indian.html (accessed 24 March 2005).

Offers a select list of microfilm records related to Native Americans that are available in the U.S. National Archives. The catalog is divided into eight parts: an introduction; Bureau of Indian Affairs records; records of the superintendencies and agencies of the Office of Indian Affairs; census records; treaty, territory, and appointment records; civilian agency records; Fish and Wildlife Service and Adjutant General records; and military service records. The introduction states that "publications that contain the most information about Indians are listed first" in every section. Brief descriptive narratives of issuing agencies, lists of contents, and record group numbers and roll numbers are included. Initially issued in print as *The American Indian* in 1972, it was revised in 1984 (SuDoc no.: GS4.2/2:AM3) and then again in 1995 when it was mounted on the National Archives and Records Administration Web site.

FEDERAL POLICY

Commission on the Rights, Liberties, and Responsibilities of the American Indian. *The Indian, America's Unfinished Business; Report.* William A. Brophy and Sophie D. Aberle, comps. Civilization of the American Indian Series: 83. Norman, OK: University of Oklahoma Press, 1966.

Presents the final report of the Commission on the Rights, Liberties, and Responsibilities of the American Indian, created in response to the 83rd Congress's House Concurrent Resolution 108 that adopted the "policy of terminating as 'fast as possible' the special relationship" between Native Americans and the U.S. Government. The Fund for the Republic, Inc., established the Commission in response to this important policy reversal, and the work is a broad-based review of information about Native Americans. It covers such topics as tribal governments, economic development, the Bureau of Indian Affairs, education, federal policy, and assimilation. This group concluded that Native Americans should manage themselves without government supervision or involvement.

Schmeckebier, Laurence Frederick. *The Office of Indian Affairs; Its History, Activities and Organization.* Service Monographs of the United States Government: 48. Baltimore, MD: The Johns Hopkins Press, 1927.

Covers the Office of Indian Affairs history, functions, activities, organization, and personnel. Widely regarded as an important source of descriptive information on the Office of Indian Affairs, the lengthy appendixes include statistics, financial statements, a bibliography, and an index. It is a critical work for researchers focusing on this important and frequently controversial agency that so profoundly affected Native American lives.

Taylor, Theodore W. *The States and Their Indian Citizens.* Native American Legal Materials: 3324. Washington, D.C.: U.S. Bureau of Indian Affairs, 1972. (SuDoc no.: I20.2:St2/3)

Examines Native Americans and the relationship of their descendants to the "non-Indian" society around them. While federal policy is reviewed, Taylor focuses on the relationships between Native Americans and state and local governments. The discussion moves from growing state involvement beginning in the 1950s to concurrent federal activities and philosophies, and subsequent changes in relations between Native American citizens and states. An index to the work is included as one of the appendixes.

Tyler, S. Lyman. *A History of Indian Policy.* Washington, D.C.: U.S. Department of the Interior, Bureau of Indian Affairs, 1973. (SuDoc no.: I20.2:H62)

Examines the nature of Indian policy, treaties and Indian trade, tribal removal and westward concentration, tribal reorganization, and Indian policy and American life. Written at the urging of a Deputy Commissioner of Indian Affairs, this work represents U.S. Government viewpoints. These perspectives are critical to understanding how policies were developed and enacted. It includes illustrations, maps, a lengthy bibliography, a chronological list of significant policy developments, and an index.

United States. American Indian Policy Review Commission. *Final Report.* 2 vols. Washington, D.C.: Government Printing Office, 1977. (SuDoc no.: Y4.In2/10:R29)

Covers the results of a two-year investigation into federal-Indian relations. Congress directed the American Indian Policy Review Commission to conduct a comprehensive review of the historical and legal developments underlying the complex relationship between the federal government and Native Americans, and to determine how policy and programs should be revised to benefit Native Peoples. The first volume includes chapters titled "Within a Free Society" and "Contemporary Indian Conditions," and the Commission's 206 recommendations. The second volume contains appendixes on how the Commission operated, a bibliography of the materials they used, and a list of federal programs serving Native Americans. This lengthy work provides a comprehensive overview of complex federal Native American policies from the government's standpoint.

United States. Department of the Interior. Bureau of Indian Affairs, http://www.doi.gov/bureau-indian-affairs.html (accessed 20 May 2005).

Explains briefly that the Bureau of Indian Affairs' "responsibility is the administration and management of 55.7 million acres of land held in trust by the United States for American Indians, Indian tribes, and Alaska natives." This Web site's original contents are currently unavailable due to the Cobell Litigation. Elouise Cobell, a member of the Montana Blackfeet tribe, is the leading plaintiff in a massive class-action suit filed against the U.S. Government in 1996. It charges that the Bureau did not distribute ten billion dollars in royalties that the government charged for leasing non-occupied lands that were assigned to individual Native Americans as agreed upon in the late 1800s."[2] A January 24, 2003 Department of the Interior Memorandum notes that a court order was issued that prohibits all communication between everyone involved in this litigation in any way.[3] To compensate for the lack of information, the Bureau has provided numerous links that are "alternate ways to get BIA-related information." Included are links to many federal agency sites found in this bibliography such as the Bureau of Land Management, the National Park Service, and the Environmental Protection Agency. There are also links to inter-tribal organizations, U.S. Congressional sites, and several non-governmental resources. Full-text of *Strengthening the Circle: Interior Indian Affairs Highlights 2001-2004* was recently added.

United States. Department of the Interior. National Park Service. American Indian Liaison Office, http://www.cr.nps.gov/ailo/ailohome.htm (accessed 24 March 2005).

Explains how this National Park Service (NPS) division is charged with improving "relationships between American Indian Tribes, Alaska Natives, Native Hawaiians, and the National Park Service through consultation, outreach, technical assistance, education, and advisory services." The site lists primary program objectives and major activities. Links connect to "Laws, Regulations, Standards and Conventions Related to Cultural Resources," related Historic Preservation Services sites, and other NPS programs. There is also a link to the National Park

Service's Tribal Preservation Program, a multi-organizational effort that helps Native Americans protect and preserve significant sites, buildings, landmarks, and cultural traditions.

United States. Environmental Protection Agency, American Indian Environmental Office, http://www.epa.gov/indian/ (accessed 24 March 2005).

Describes how the American Indian Environmental Office (AIEO) coordinates Environmental Protection Agency efforts to "strengthen public health and environmental protection in Indian Country." AIEO's goal is for tribes "to administer their own environmental programs." This Web site provides links to: AIEO's mission and EPA Contacts; Programs; Regions; Tribal Grants; Tribal Contacts; Policies and Initiatives; Laws, Regulations and Guidance; and Publications. Other links take users to a wide variety of sites including tribal organizations, tribal environmental programs, tribal governments, and other federal departments and agencies that administer Native American regulations, policies, or activities. It also contains full-text of the 2004 *EPA Indian Program Accomplishments Report* and the *Tribal Environmental and Natural Resource Assistance Handbook*.

Washburn, Wilcomb E., comp. *The American Indian and the United States: A Documentary History*. 4 vols. New York: Random House, 1973.

Brings together a large number of significant federal publications on governmental policies and actions affecting Native Americans. It includes documents, Congressional debates, treaties, laws, proclamations, and legal decisions. Volume One and part of Volume Two contain texts from a number of Senate and House debates on key issues that occurred between 1866 and 1970. A very detailed index provides excellent subject access to the set's contents.

FEDERAL LAWS AND REGULATIONS

American Indian Civil Rights Handbook. Clearinghouse Publication: 35. 2nd ed. Washington, D.C.: U.S. Commission on Civil Rights, 1980. (SuDoc no.: CR1.10:35/2)

Reviews the Indian Civil Rights Act of 1968. The U.S. Constitution does not limit tribal government actions because Indian tribes derive their governing authority from inherent sovereignty. This 1968 law, however, selectively incorporated the safeguards of the Bill of Rights to protect tribal governments from undue interference. The publication concisely examines such issues as freedom of belief and expression, fair treatment by police and courts, federal grand juries, child custody, civil and administrative due process, voting rights, and equal employment and educational opportunities.

American State Papers: Documents, Legislative and Executive, of the Congress of the United States. 38 vols. Washington, D.C.: Gales and Seaton, 1833-1834. (SuDoc no.: Y1.1/1:)

Contains papers from the 1st through the 25th Congresses. Two volumes of the set are devoted to "Indian Affairs." The collection includes documents that cover the critical historical gap from 1789 to the printing of the first volume of the *U.S. Serial Set* in 1817. They provide valuable insight into federal perspectives, policies, and actions affecting domestic Native American tribes in the late 18th and early 19th centuries. This massive work was recently digitized and mounted on the Library of Congress's Web site as part of the American Memory Project [http://memory.loc.gov/ammem/amlaw/lwsp.html]. This site includes clear instructions on how to find information on specific topics, greatly improving access to the contents of these important documents. A related title is *The New American State Paper: Indian Affairs*, a thirteen volume set published by Scholarly Resources Inc., in 1972. It brings together all relevant materials from the original *American State Papers*, the serial volumes of the official documents of the U.S. Congress printed after 1817 and the Legislative Records Section of the National Archives.

Getches, David H., Charles F. Wilkinson, and Robert A. Williams, Jr. *Cases and Materials on Federal Indian Law.* American Casebook Series. 5th ed. St. Paul, MN: Thomson/West, 2005.

Brings together a wide variety of important information on federal Indian law. In their preface, the authors note this "field of law" has "expanded at warp speed" since their first edition was published over twenty years ago. While this book is decidedly technical, the first chapter "Introduction: Indians and Indian Law" is an excellent overview of the critical legal issues that have so profoundly affected Native Americans now and historically. Other chapters cover the "European Doctrine of Discovery and American Indian Rights," the "Federal-Tribal Relationship," and "Tribal Sovereignty and the Administration of Justice in Indian Country."

"GPO Access: A Service of the U.S. Government Printing Office," http://www.gpoaccess.gov/ (accessed 24 March 2005).

Offers an impressive wealth of electronic full-text information from a variety of recent federal legislative, executive, and judicial sources. The home page provides access to numerous sources arranged by these three governmental branches. Under these headings, there are direct links to such high-use items as the *Federal Register*, the *Code of Federal Regulations*, the *U.S. Code*, and the *Congressional Record*. A motto of the U.S. Government Printing Office is "Keeping America Informed" and this Web site truly supports that sentiment with its free, ready access to such an impressively wide range of information and materials. While searching this site's various components is quite easy, following clearly explained search protocols improves effectiveness and efficiency. It is highly recommended for finding recent legislation, laws, and regulations affecting Native Americans.

"Handbook of Federal Indian Law by Felix S. Cohen, United States Government Printing Office (1945-4th Printing)," http://thorpe.ou. edu/cohen.html (accessed 5 June 2005).

Covers the Office of Indian Affairs, Indian treaties, the scope of federal power over Indian affairs, tribal self-government, legal status and rights, and criminal and civil jurisdictions. The Native American Constitution and Law Digitization Project recently mounted the full-text of this highly esteemed monograph on the Web. In addition to breakdowns for each chapter by paging, the site offers a "Summary of the Handbook of the Layman" and a comprehensive index. This work has been reprinted several times since 1941 by both the federal government and commercial publishers, and it is repeatedly cited in bibliographies on the subject. The lengthy supporting text, with reference tables and index, clearly places a broad range of federal activities and issues in their historical contexts (SuDoc no.: I48.6:In2).

"Native American Constitution and Law Digitization Project," http:// thorpe.ou.edu/ (accessed 5 June 2005).

Provides selective full-text access to a very wide variety of "Constitutions, Tribal Codes, and other legal documents." The University of

Oklahoma Law Library, the National Indian Law Library of the Native American Rights Fund, and Native American tribes coordinate this site. Contents are arranged under subject headings such as: Indian Lands; Solicitor's Opinions; Supreme Court; and Treaties. The full-text of Cohen's *Handbook of Federal Indian Law*, as noted above, is found here. It also includes, for example, the White Mountain Apache Code, the Constitution of the Kickapoo Traditional Tribe of Texas, the *Guide to Rarick's Oklahoma Indian Land Titles*, summaries of recent relevant U.S. Supreme Court cases, and searchable full-text of *Indian Land Cessions in the United States, 1784-1894* (U.S. Serial Set Number 4015). Clicking on the 'Research Guide' link takes users to a very helpful work "Annotated Bibliography of Federal and Tribal Law: Print and Internet Sources" by Marilyn K. Nicely (2003), and the essay "Native Americans and the Law: Native Americans Under Current United States Law" by Lindsay G. Robertson and Sam K. Viersen (2001). Nicely, Robertson and Viersen are affiliated with the University of Oklahoma College of Law.

United States. Commission on Civil Rights. *Indian Tribes: A Continuing Quest for Survival: A Report of the United States Commission on Civil Rights*. Washington, D.C.: The Commission, 1981. (SuDoc no.: CR1.2:In2/7)

Provides a brief, clearly written overview of federal Indian law, civil rights, and state and tribal relations. It is included here for researchers who do not want or need the more in-depth information found in other standard sources. The title includes the Commission's findings and recommendations on civil rights violations, land claims, fishing rights, and law enforcement.

United States. Government Printing Office. "United States Code: Title 25, Indians," http://www.gpoaccess.gov/uscode/ (accessed 24 March 2005).

Contains the "general and permanent laws of the United States in force" that relate to Native Americans. The print *Code* is published every six years and cumulative supplements are published annually to ensure currency (SuDoc no.: Y1.2/5:2000/v.13). While laws concerning Native Americans are found throughout the *United States Code*, *Title 25* is the only one dedicated to them. It includes laws governing the Bureau of Indian Affairs, the constitutional rights of Indians, Indian child welfare, Indian higher education programs, Indian law enforcement reform, Indian gaming regulation, and American Indian Trust Fund management reform. GPO Access's online version contains "general and permanent laws . . . in effect as of January 2, 2001."

United States. Government Printing Office, General Services Administration, National Archives and Records Service, Office of the Federal Register, "Code of Federal Regulations: 25, Indians," http://www. access.gpo.gov/cfr/index.html (accessed 5 June 2005).

Codifies the general and permanent rules of federal executive departments and agencies. While regulations concerning Native Americans are found throughout the *Code of Federal Regulations*, this is the only title dedicated to them. Included here are regulations that govern such agencies as the Bureau of Indian Affairs, the National Indian Gaming Commission, and the Indian Health Service. Users can readily search the entire title or specific chapters by keyword or CFR citation. While the Web site's Title 25 was last revised in April, 2005, the latest print version is dated 2004 (SuDoc no.: AE2.1065/3:25/2004). The paper *CFR Index and Finding Aids* provides limited access to the entire set.

United States. Library of Congress. "A Century of Lawmaking for a New Nation: U.S. Congressional Documents and Debates 1774-1985," http://memory.loc.gov/ammem/amlaw/ (accessed 24 March 2005).

Brings together online the records and acts of Congress from the Continental Congress and Constitutional Convention through the 43rd Congress, including the first three volumes of the *Congressional Record*, 1873-1875. The search interface is easy to use and it is possible to do a keyword search in all titles or limit searches in a variety of ways including by Congress, Session, Chamber, and specific title. This impressive site provides amazing access to the contents of these key primary sources that were formerly challenging to use.

United States. Library of Congress. "Thomas: Legislative Information on the Internet," http://thomas.loc.gov (accessed 24 March 2005).

Offers electronic full-text information on the U.S. Congress. Maintained by the Library of Congress, it includes bill summaries from 1975, bill texts from 1989, major legislation from 1995, and Public Laws by number from 1975. It also provides links to "Congress in the News,"

Congressional Record text from 1989 to date, bill summaries and their status, and House and Senate Roll Call Votes. Users are urged to read the section "About THOMAS" that describes the kinds of information available and the time frames that are covered. Like *GPO Access* described earlier, this site is a landmark improvement in readily providing widespread access to U.S. legislative information. It is highly recommended for anyone interested in recent Congressional activities affecting Native Americans. Many large libraries subscribe to the commercially published paper *CIS/Index to Publications of the United States Congress* or its online counterpart Lexis-Nexis's *Congressional Universe* that provide access to Congressional publications and activities from 1970 to date.

TREATIES

Kappler, Charles J., comp. *Indian Affairs: Laws and Treaties.* 2nd ed. 7 vols. Washington, D.C.: U.S. Government Printing Office, 1904-1979. (SuDoc no.: I1.107)

Serves as the definitive research set on Native American laws and treaties. Kappler's major multi-volume work also includes executive orders. The frequently used Volume II contains treaties from 1778 through 1883 in chronological order and a detailed index. The remaining volumes include laws and executive orders from 1872 through 1970. The Oklahoma State University Library has digitized the entire set and it is now mounted on the institution's Web site as "fully searchable digitized text and as page images. The contents may be accessed from the Table of Contents or Index of each volume or through keyword searching" [http://digital.library.okstate.edu/kappler/].

Prucha, Francis Paul. *American Indian Treaties: The History of a Political Anomaly.* Berkeley, CA: University of California Press, 1994.

Reviews Indian treaties, explaining why they were established, how they were developed, and why they are unique historically and legally. This work is highly recommended for anyone who wants to understand these complicated legal agreements and how they firmly placed Native American lives under U.S. Government management. It includes illustrations, a long list of sources, and a comprehensive index.

STATISTICS

Reddy, Marlita A. *Statistical Record of Native North Americans*. 3rd ed. Detroit: Gale Research Inc., 1998.

Brings together a wide range of statistics on Native peoples from a variety of sources including federal and state government publications. Over 1,000 tables are arranged in twelve chapters covering such topics as history, demographics, the family, education, and culture and tradition. While statistics from the late 1980s are now dated, many are still the latest figures available. The historical statistics, some from the 1600s, may be particularly useful. This comprehensive, well-organized source is highly recommended for all kinds of Native American research, past and present. It includes a lengthy listing of sources and a keyword index.

Statistical Abstract of the United States. Washington, D.C.: U.S. Government Printing Office, 1879- . (SuDoc no.: C3.134:year)

Provides a broad variety of useful summary statistics on the United States that the federal government regularly compiles. Its index contains many references to tables on Native Americans under the heading "American Indian, Eskimo, Aleut population" that provide statistics on population, college enrollment, educational attainment, income, poverty, reservations, and age and sex. The U.S. Census Bureau has also mounted the *Abstract*'s full-text on the Web [http://www.census.gov/statab/www/]. Many larger libraries subscribe to the LexisNexis database *Statistical Universe* that provides subject indexing of federal and state statistical publications.

United States. Department of Commerce. U.S. Census Bureau, http://www.census.gov (accessed 24 March 2005).

Provides an amazingly wide variety of online statistical resources, much too numerous to list here, that include a great deal of information on Native Americans. The last decennial census and its statistics on Native American populations are available by clicking on the "United States Census 2000" link. Under the Newsroom heading, "Minority Links" leads to a "Facts on the American Indian/Alaska Native Population" that lists a number of full-text summary reports and figures from Census 2000. The Bureau's American FactFinder provides access to their largest "data sets" from Census 2000 that, of course, include statistics on Native Americans. The 2000 Summary Tape File 4, for example, covers social, economic and housing data for up to "335 race, ethnic and ancestry groups." Information is continually added to this site, and such changes and its comprehensiveness can intimidate users. Researchers are urged to take the American FactFinder site tour and tutorial for a quick online instruction session on how to retrieve the specific information they need. It should be noted that there have been many significant disputes about Census statistics. Bureau officials, for example, estimated that "American Indians were undercounted by 12.5% in the 1990 Census–the highest of any minority group."[4] An April 22, 2002 Associated Press wire story states that the Native American and Alaskan Native Census 2000 undercount rate was 4.64%.[5] Undercounts have serious consequences because Census statistics "help determine how and where about $200 billion in federal dollars for housing, education and other programs are spent each year.[6]

HISTORY AND CULTURE

McKenney, Thomas L., and James Hall. *Biographical Sketches and Anecdotes of Ninety-Five of 120 Principal Chiefs From the Indian Tribes of North America*. Washington, D.C.: U.S. Department of the Interior, Bureau of Indian Affairs, n.d. (SuDoc no.: I20.2:In2/27)

Contains entries from the *History of the Indian Tribes of North America, With Biographical Sketches and Anecdotes of the Principal Chiefs, Embellished With One Hundred and Twenty Portraits From the Indian Gallery in the Department of War, at Washington* that was originally published in 1838. The ninety-five items in this reprint vary in length from two to fifteen pages and include notable Native Americans from such tribes as the Seneca, Shawnee, Chippewa, Omaha, Iowa, Fox, and Cherokee. The table of contents provides subject access. In 1972, Crown Publishers issued an edition of this, edited by James David Horan, that includes "augmented versions of the biographies."

Smithsonian Institution. Bureau of American Ethnology. *Annual Report*. 48 vols. Washington, D.C.: U.S. Government Printing Office, 1880-1931. (SuDoc no.: SI2.1:no.)

Contains numerous, lengthy signed articles on field studies, written between 1800 and 1931, about various aspects of Native American tribal cultures. The first volume, for example, includes reports on Native American Indian mythology, mortuary customs, and Indian languages. It has numerous illustrations, maps, and an index. Tables of contents for these annuals, arranged by volume number, are available on the Internet [http://www.sil.si.edu/DigitalCollections/BAE/Bulletin200/200annl.htm]. The Smithsonian Institution Libraries has also mounted on the Web lists of the Bureau's *Publications of the Institute of Social Anthropology, Contributions to North American Ethnology, Miscellaneous Publications*, and an index to authors and titles for these publications and the Bureau's *Bulletin* described below [http:www.sil.edu/DigitalCollections/BAE/Bulletin200/200conts.htm].

Smithsonian Institution. Bureau of American Ethnology. *Bulletin.* 200 vols. Washington, D.C.: U.S. Government Printing Office, 1887-1971. (SuDoc no.: SI2.3:no.)

Brings together specialized anthropologic and ethnologic subjects. These monographs are sometimes the only available published information on the topics they cover. Noted Native American author Francis La Flesche, a Bureau ethnologist, contributed several volumes to this series including the *Dictionary of the Osage Language* that was issued as Volume 406 in 1932. The Bureau recently digitized two bulletins on Native Americans by John C. Ewers: "The Horse in Blackfoot Indian Culture" (No. 159) and "Hair Pipes in Plains Indian Adornment" (No. 164). As with the Bureau of American Ethnology *Annual Reports* noted above, a list of *Bulletin* contents arranged by volume number is available online [http://www.sil.si.edu/DigitalCollections/BAE/Bulletin200/200bulls.htm].

Smithsonian Institution. National Museum of the American Indian, http://www.americanindian.si.edu/ (accessed 24 March 2005).

Dedicated to the "preservation, study, and exhibition of the life, languages, literature, history and arts of Native Americans." Established by an act of Congress in 1989, this is the sixteenth Smithsonian Institution museum. This attractive, well-developed Web site reflects an appropriate sensitivity to Native American matters and is both informative and entertaining. It provides links to exhibition information, publications, events calendars, and descriptions of collections and archives for all three locations: the George Gustav Heye Center in New York; the Cultural Resources Center in Maryland; and the new National Museum of the American Indian on the Mall in Washington, D.C. Numerous online exhibitions cover such topics as Native American crafts, Mexican art, works by artist George Catlin, and Indian humor.

Sturtevant, William C., ed. *Handbook of North American Indians.* 13 vols. Washington, D.C.: Smithsonian Institution, 1978- . (SuDoc no.: SI1.20/2:vol.no.)

Examines the histories and cultures of Native Americans. Thirteen volumes of this proposed twenty-volume encyclopedic set have been issued. "Indians in Contemporary Society" and the "History of Indian-White Relations" are topics in Volume 4, and Volume 17 is titled *Languages.* The remaining ones are arranged by geographical areas and include the Arctic, the Subarctic, the Northeast, the Northwest Coast, the Southwest, the Southeast, the Great Basin, the Plains (two parts), and the Plateau. These volumes have many illustrations, extensive bibliographies, and detailed indexes.

United States. Library of Congress. "American Memory: History Collections for the National Digital Library," http://memory.loc.gov (accessed 24 March 2005).

Serves as a "gateway to primary source materials relating to the history and culture of the United States" by offering more than seven million digital items from more than one hundred historical collections. This impressive array of digitized materials includes both government and commercially produced resources. The topic heading "Native American History" provides links to: photographs from the *Chicago Daily News*, 1902-1933; photographs by Edward S. Curtis; information on Native Americans in the Pacific Northwest; notes from books on traveling in the United States, 1750-1920; and photographs from the Denver Public Library's Western History Collection. Each of these sections includes background information on their sources and their research relevance. This site provides a "Collection Finder" link that allows users to select specific collections to search; education, languages and literature, and geography are just some examples of the broad categories used. Use the "Finder Help" link to get information on how to set up effective search strategies and limit results in a variety of ways. The "Search" link allows users to search all of the collections simultaneously. A search on the keyword "Cherokee," for example, resulted in 500 hits that included maps, photographs, and some digitized reports from Abraham Lincoln's papers. The depth, scope, and range of this site are very impressive.

CONTEMPORARY ISSUES

United States. Department of Health and Human Services, Indian Health
Service, http://www.ihs.gov/ (accessed 24 March 2005).

Provides information about the Indian Health Service (IHS) goals
and mission, and area offices, management resources, and medical programs. This agency, part of Health and Human Services, is the federal
health program for American Indians and Alaska Natives; members of
federally recognized tribes and their descendants are all eligible for IHS
services. Clicking on "Press and Public Relations" leads to links for the
Native Health Research Database and numerous full-text electronic
sources as the *Indian Health Manual, Indian Health Circulars*, and the
widely-used *Trends in Indian Health.* Information on the health of Native American women can also be found in the 2002 *Women of Color
Health Data Book* issued by the Office of the Director, National Institutes of Health [http://www4.od.nih.gov/orwh/wocEnglish2002.pdf].

United States. Department of the Interior, Bureau of Indian Affairs, Office of Indian Education Programs, http://www.oiep.bia.edu/ (accessed 24 March 2005).

Covers the Office of Indian Education Program's (OIEP) mission
statement, the history of the legislation that established it, an itemized
list of its current goals, and an alphabetical list of BIA school home
pages. An agency of the Bureau of Indian Affairs (BIA), OIEP provides
"quality education opportunities from early childhood throughout life"
for Native Peoples. This Web site also offers information about programs and resources, and full-text versions of many OIEP publications
such as *Building Exemplary Schools for Tomorrow: 2002 Fingertip
Facts* that provides statistical information on a variety of educational
indicators.

United States. Department of the Interior, Geological Survey, "U.S.
Geological Survey Activities Related to American Indians and Alaska
Natives–Publications," http://www.usgs.gov/indian/pubspage.html (ac-
cessed 24 March 2005).

Provides full-text access to annual fiscal year reports from 1997
through 2002. The latest one includes sections on educational activities,
resource and environmental activities, highlights for FY 2002, technical
assistance, policy activities, and "future opportunities." The report is

"organized in the following manner: east to west, north to south . . . information about Alaska is at the end of each section."

United States. Department of the Interior, Indian Arts and Crafts Board, http://www.doi.gov/iacb/ (accessed 24 March 2005).

Describes the Board's mission to promote the economic development of Native Americans in the "Indian arts and crafts market." This Web site provides links to the Indian Arts and Crafts Act of 1990, the names of Board commissioners, a list of the three regional museums the Board operates, and information on their exhibitions. It also includes a "source directory of businesses."

United States. Department of the Interior Library, "Internet Sources on American Indians and Alaska Natives," http://library.doi.gov/internet/ native.html (accessed 24 March 2005).

Provides access to numerous Web sites that focus on Native Americans. Included are links grouped into the following categories: news; tribal governments; inter-tribal and other organizations; U.S. government organizations; legal sources; bibliographies; digital libraries; and directories of Internet sites on Native Americans. The section on legal resources contains links, for example, to eighteen related sites including the Cornell Legal Information Institute, the American Indian Law Review, and the Indian Law Resource Center. The scope of this massive site highlights the impressive amount of information on Native Americans now available on the Web. While some of these sites are included in this bibliography, many others were not due to space constraints. This resource will be particularly useful to researchers who want an overview of information on Native Americans available on the Internet.

United States. "First Gov.gov: The U.S. Government's Official Web Portal: For Tribal Governments and Native Americans," http://firstgov. gov/Government/Tribal.shtml (accessed 24 March 2005).

Provides access to numerous U.S. Government Web sites created for Native Americans. Included are links to such sites as the National Park Services American Indian Liaison Office, Federal Grant Resources, the Federal Interagency Task Force on Older Indians, and the Indian Health Service Facilities Locator. These links are grouped into broad categories including: education, jobs, and economic development; family and health; housing; land and the environment; legal resources; and other resources. While some of these Web sites are described in this bibliography, many others were not included due to space constraints.

United States. National Indian Gaming Commission, http://www.nigc. gov/nigc/index.jsp (accessed 13 May 2005).

Describes the responsibilities and activities of the National Indian Gaming Commission (NIGC). This "independent federal regulatory agency" was established by the Indian Gaming Regulatory Act of 1988 (IGRA). This Web site provides a great deal of information on all aspects of tribal gaming including full-text of the enabling legislation, Commission regulations, lists of casinos arranged alphabetically by tribal name, statistics on tribal gaming revenues, and answers to frequently asked questions on sovereignty, tribal-state compacts, and gaming applications.

NON-GOVERNMENTAL WEB SITES

Harvard University. John F. Kennedy School of Government, The Harvard Project on American Indian Economic Development, http://www. ksg.harvard.edu/hpaied/ (accessed 12 May 2005).

Describes the Harvard Project's focus on the "systematic, comparative study of social and economic development on American Indian reservations." This valuable resource includes a wide array of information, including full-text research publications. Issued in January, 2005, *Native America at the New Millennium*, for example, covers a broad range of current issues affecting Native Americans including tribal government, political activism, economic development, housing, and health and welfare. It offers extensive, detailed footnotes and references useful for serious researchers. This site also provides links to Joint Occasional Papers on Native Affairs, "testimony and speeches" by Harvard Project personnel, and current events and news.

Mitten, Lisa. "Native American Sites," http://www.nativeculturelinks. com/indians.html (accessed 24 March 2005).

Provides access to many other relevant Web pages. These links are arranged in such categories as "Information on Individual Native Nations," "Languages," "Sources for Indian Music," and "Powwows and Festivals." Maintained by Lisa Mitten, a *Choice Magazine* social sciences subject editor and librarian who is a "mixed-blood Mohawk urban Indian," this meta-site provides access to home pages of "Native American Nations and organizations, and to other sites that provide solid information about American Indians." It is also the home of the American Indian Library Association. Mitten updates the site frequently, and it is valuable, comprehensive, and very easy to use.

"NativeWeb," http://www.nativeweb.org/ (accessed 24 March 2005).

Provides "resources for indigenous cultures around the world." The site offers numerous links to other relevant Web sites that cover a wide variety of topics. The home page includes full-text links to recent newspaper articles on Native American issues, a link for books and music, a link to community listings, and the "Resource Center" with its groups of such sub-categories as: anthropology and archeology; genealogy; elders, and native businesses and products. A search on the word "Sioux," for example, led to a list that included treaties, tribal industries, and the Cheyenne Sioux Tribe's official Web site. Since this covers indigenous cultures worldwide, it is suggested that researchers use specific terms such as Native American tribal names or locations. NativeWeb is included in the Institute for Scientific Information's "premium collection of evaluated scholarly Web sites" and in the Social Science Information Gateway of the UK Resource Discovery Network's list of "trusted sources of information."

REFERENCES

1. Francis Paul Prucha, *American Indian Treaties: The History of a Political Anomaly* (Berkeley, CA: University of California Press, 1994):1.

2. "Justice for Indians." *Economist* 3623 (23 March 2002): 33.

3. United States Department of the Interior Memorandum. "Subject: Important Court Order on Communicating With Class Members in the Cobell v. Norton, Civ. No. 96-1285," http://www.fws.gov/policy/m0204.html (accessed 4 June 2005).

4. Tim Talley, "Census Presses for More Accurate Count of Indians," *Fort Collins Coloradoan* (July 21, 1999): A9.

5. Genaro C. Armas, "Preliminary Census Estimates Show Revised Undercount for Several Minority Groups," Associated Press Washington Dateline, April 22, 2002. Database on-line. Available from Academic Universe, http://web.lexis-nexis.com/universe/document?_m=5075931bba9f411f . . .], accessed 14 August 2003.

6. Talley, *Fort Collins Coloradoan*, A9.

Going Local:
Environmental Information on the Internet

Margaret M. Jobe

SUMMARY. The United States federal government provides an increasing amount of state local environmental information via the Internet. This proliferation of information provides libraries of all types and sizes with service opportunities. An informed citizenry can contribute to the debate on environmental policy. The article identifies key sites that can be useful in providing local environmental information. *[Article copies available for a fee from The Haworth Document Delivery Service: 1-800-HAWORTH. E-mail address: <docdelivery@haworthpress.com> Website: <http://www.HaworthPress.com> © 2006 by The Haworth Press, Inc. All rights reserved.]*

KEYWORDS. Environmental information, state and local information, environmental policy, library services

INTRODUCTION

When the Gallup Organization polled a sample of adult Americans in 1998, sixty-eight percent of the respondents were of the opinion that

Margaret M. Jobe is Faculty Director, Gemmill Engineering Library, University of Colorado at Boulder, 184 UCB, Boulder, CO 80309-0184 (E-mail: Margaret.Jobe@Colorado.edu).

[Haworth co-indexing entry note]: "Going Local: Environmental Information on the Internet." Jobe, Margaret M. Co-published simultaneously in *The Reference Librarian* (The Haworth Information Press, an imprint of The Haworth Press, Inc.) No. 94, 2006, pp. 257-276; and: *The Changing Face of Government Information: Providing Access in the Twenty-First Century* (ed: Suhasini L. Kumar) The Haworth Information Press, an imprint of The Haworth Press, Inc., 2006, pp. 257-276. Single or multiple copies of this article are available for a fee from The Haworth Document Delivery Service [1-800-HAWORTH, 9:00 a.m. - 5:00 p.m. (EST). E-mail address: docdelivery@haworthpress.com].

protection of the environment should be given priority even at the risk of curbing economic growth. Twenty-eight percent felt that economic growth should be given priority and eight percent refused to answer or did not know.[1] When Gallup asked a similar question in 2004, the aftermath of the war in Iraq and economic uncertainty had taken its toll. Forty-nine percent of the respondents favored protection of the environment over economic growth, forty-four percent favored economic growth, and four percent of the respondents thought that the issues should be given equal priority.[2] Although the percentage of respondents who gave higher priority to the environment than to economic growth dropped significantly, these data suggest that Americans remain interested in environmental issues. If Tip O'Neill's famous maxim that "all politics are local" is valid in the environmental arena, then Americans are likely to be very interested in the local environment. The Environmental Protection Agency (EPA), other federal agencies, and third party suppliers of federal information now provide access over the Internet to a broad array of local environmental data, introductory materials, bibliographic databases, and specialized technical publications that can be used to research local environmental issues.

In the not too distant past, most of this information was available only in depository libraries. At the present time, any library with Internet access can provide detailed information about local environmental conditions. Although providing access to highly technical information can challenge libraries, Michael Zimmerman makes a strong case for environmental literacy and access to information. He argues, "The more people know about the world around them, the more likely they are to make rational policy."[3] Although Zimmerman argues for access to information, this topic has been the subject of contentious debate between environmental groups and industry. Environmental groups favor public disclosure of information while industry representatives generally oppose disclosure of detailed information. These industry officials have argued against the public release of environmental data because of its highly technical nature and the problems inherent in understanding the potential risks associated with exposure to polluted air, water, and toxic chemicals. In answer to critics of broad-based access to industry and company-specific environmental data, Zimmerman also observes that there is a "purposeful confusion about the difference between information and interpretation. In an ideal world, the former should be value-free and shared as widely as possible. In such a world, it is the interpretation of data, rather than the data themselves, which engenders lively scientific debate."[4]

Broad-based access to information via the Internet has raised questions about the appropriate roles for libraries. In light of this policy analysts in academic libraries are beginning to rethink the role of libraries in providing information. In their 1999 article in *Journal of Government Information*, Joan K. Lippincott and Joan F. Cheverie perceive a blurring of the distinctions between federal information and services as they apply to academic libraries. In the "blur" model, artificial distinctions between a product and services disappear. In their view, in the past libraries acquired content and created services (reference and instruction), which related to the content. Lippincott and Cheverie view content and service as closely intertwined in the electronic era. For them, "The new climate will demand that information professionals . . . develop a skill set that includes capabilities to assist users to manipulate, organize, relate, and filter content of various types."[5] A librarian who helps a patron access local environmental data certainly needs a diverse set of skills. The information can be highly technical. In addition, much of the information are data that require specialized software for access and manipulation. In addition to the challenges posed by software applications, the structure and content of the data relate to the mission of an agency and its governing legislation. In order to provide effective service, the librarian needs to understand the structure of the government and the overlapping functions of individual agencies as these structures and functions relate to environmental regulation and collection of data.

The information, however, is there and available for use and interpretation. A combination of technological developments and an environmental disaster helped shape the information landscape that exists today. Technology, in the form of the Internet, has enabled federal agencies and others to deliver detailed data, bibliographic databases, and publications in a cost effective manner. The first significant environmental database, however, was created as a reaction to the Bhopal, India, disaster in which over 2,500 people lost their lives after an accidental release of methyl isocyanate gas from a Union Carbide plant. Responding to citizen concern about the potential for catastrophic chemical releases in the United States, Congress passed the Emergency Planning and Community Right to Know Act (EPCRA) as Title III of the Superfund Amendments and Reauthorization Act of 1986 (SARA). Among other things, EPCRA included a requirement that the EPA establish a database containing information about toxic chemical releases to air, land, and water by manufacturing facilities. This database, known as the Toxics Release Inventory or TRI, was the first database mandated by law. When it passed the EPCRA legislation, Congress anticipated that access to data would provide communities with a powerful tool. As an EPA pamphlet explains:

> Local communities and states have the basic responsibility for understanding risks posed by chemicals at the local level, for managing those risks, for reducing those risks, and for dealing with emergencies.[6]

Although the data has limitations, both the EPA and outside observers have credited the TRI with significant pollution reductions. Learning from the TRI experience, the EPA has expanded the suite of environmental databases that it makes available on the Internet and has integrated the data with a variety of explanatory and complementary materials. Private citizens, activist groups, and industry can use the databases as tools to promote dialogue on the long-term future and health of the environment.

With training and commitment, libraries can provide their patrons with data and information that empowers them as citizens and enables them to contribute to the policy debate. The Internet provides libraries with unprecedented opportunities. If the surveys are correct, people are very interested in the environment. It follows that local environmental issues are of particular concern. Although the undertaking is by no means trivial, libraries can advance to new levels of information service if they embrace the challenge.

What follows is a selective list of government and related resources useful to libraries of all types. The sites were chosen because they are important sources of state and local environmental information. With the possible exception of the bibliographic databases, all include information for states and other geographic units such as cities, counties, watersheds, and zip code areas. To illustrate these points, many of the annotations include specific examples of state and local information available at a site. The selected resources fall into four broad groups:

- Integrated sites that provide data from a variety of federal programs.
- Non-governmental sites that provide selective access to data collected by the EPA and others.
- Topic specific sites.
- Bibliographic databases.

SELECTED INTERNET SITES

Integrated Sites: Data from Multiple Sources

Envirofacts
http://www.epa.gov/enviro/index.html

Envirofacts is the EPA's most extensive and ambitious environmental data warehouse. It provides a single point of access to major EPA databases (see Table 1). The databases contain information on stationary sources of air pollution; hazardous waste; releases of toxic chemicals to air, land, water; underground injection; transfer of toxic chemicals to off-site locations; wastewater dischargers; compliance status of water suppliers with safe drinking water regulations; data on the presence of physical, chemical, microbial and radiological contaminants in drinking water; Superfund sites; regulated facilities; grant programs; and compliance status of regulated facilities. The databases can be queried singly or in combination. Although the access points vary by database, users can access most databases by facility name, geography, or Standard Industrial Classification (SIC) code. The EPA plans to use the North American Industrial Classification System (NAICS) for newer data. The site has several points of access. The Quick Start! area on the left enables the user to query by zipcode, city and state, or county and state. The Topic area presents the user with an overview of databases by type, such as air, water, or hazardous materials, and a geographic search similar to Quick Start! The Advanced Capabilities area includes drop-down lists of databases available for query, map tools, and batch report options. Since the databases are listed by their sometimes cryptic initialisms, novice users will probably want to start with the Quick Start or Topic sections of the site.

Envirofacts integrates a number of complementary databases (see Table 2). For example, Envirofacts includes a suite of mapping applications that enable the user to create custom maps. An overview and links to the EnviroMapper applications is available at http://www.epa.gov/enviro/html/em/. In addition, when a user queries an individual database, such as the Toxics Release Inventory, Envirofacts presents the user with links to the appropriate mapping application or applications and transfers mapping data, such as coordinates and facility name, to the map tool. Many of the applications enable the user to select layers of geographic data from a menu of choices.

TABLE 1. Partial List of Envirofacts Databases

DATABASE NAME	DESCRIPTION
Air Releases (AIRS/AFS)	Information about stationary sources of air pollution such as power plants and factories.
Biennial Reporting System (BRS)	Data on generation of hazardous waste from large quantity generators and data on waste management practices from treatment, storage, and disposal facilities.
Enforcement and Compliance Online History (ECHO)	Indicates whether EPA or state/local governments have conducted compliance inspections, violations were detected, or enforcement actions and penalties were taken in response to environmental law violations.
Grants Information	Information about EPA's federal grant programs.
Master Chemical Integrator	Acronyms, chemical identification numbers and chemical names included in Envirofacts.
National Drinking Water Contaminant Occurrence Information (NCOD)	NCOD contains regulated and unregulated contaminant data for public water systems. Includes physical, chemical, microbial and radiological contaminants.
Permit Compliance System (PCS)	Contains data on permits of wastewater dischargers, industrial point sources, and animal feeding operations that discharge into wastewater collection systems or directly into receiving waters.
Radiation Information Database (RADINFO)	Contains information about certain facilities that the EPA regulates for radiation and radioactivity.
Resource Conservation and Recovery Information System (RCRIS)	Information about generators, transporters, treaters, storers, and disposers of hazardous waste.
Safe Drinking Water Information	EPA collects data about how well water utilities comply with drinking water regulations and whether any enforcement actions were taken against utilities. Includes ten years of violations and enforcement actions.
Superfund (CERCLIS)	Hazardous waste sites such as abandoned warehouses, landfills, and industrial facilities that dumped waste before it was regulated by federal law. The EPA locates, investigates, and cleans up the worst sites.
Toxics Release Inventory (TRI)	Data on air emissions, surface water discharges, release to land, underground injection, and off-site transfer of more than 600 toxic chemicals by manufacturing and other facilities.

Envirofacts also integrates chemical information in a user-friendly fashion. If the user is searching for information on the toxic releases of a specific chemical, the online report includes links for additional information on that chemical from other databases such as the Integrated Risk Information System (IRIS), information on the health risks associated with specific toxic chemicals, and Chemical Fact Sheets, information on the environmental and health risks, regulatory status, and associated with exposure to toxic chemicals.

TABLE 2. Partial List of Databases Integrated into Envirofacts

DATABASE NAME AND URL	DESCRIPTION
Integrated Risk Information System (IRIS) http://www.epa.gov/iriswebp/iris/index.html	IRIS is a database of human health effects that may result from exposure to various substances found in the environment.
EnviroMapper http://www.epa.gov/enviro/html/em/	Interactive mapping applications by geography or facility. Includes variable data layers.
OPPT Chemical Fact Sheets http://www.epa.gov/opptintr/chemfact/	The Fact Sheets cover each chemical's identity, production and use, environmental fate, and health and environmental effects.

In 2000, the EPA launched the TRI Explorer, an alternate version of the Toxics Release Inventory. The Explorer <http://www.epa.gov/triexplorer/> features easy-to-use pull-down menus. In contrast to the Envirofacts TRI, which focuses on individual facilities, the Explorer provides tools for the user to study a particular industry, a particular facility, all of the facilities in a state or county, releases of a specific chemical, or to examine emissions trends with time-series data. The Explorer includes an option to download data in a format suitable for spreadsheets.

Enforcement Compliance History Online (ECHO)
http://www.epa.gov/echo/

Drawing on data from the EPA's enforcement system and other databases, ECHO provides a "snapshot of a facility's environmental record, showing dates and types of violations as well as the State or Federal government's response"[7] for over 800,000 regulated facilities. With a search of ECHO, the user can quickly locate inspection, violation, enforcement, and penalty actions for individual facilities within the last three years under the Clean Air Act, Clean Water Act, and other environmental laws. ECHO also provides basic demographic data for the area surrounding a facility with links to a mapping application and to the Environmental Justice Assessment Tool.

Environmental Justice Geographic Assessment Tool
http://www.epa.gov/Compliance/environmentaljustice/assessment.html

The EPA defines environmental justice as "the fair treatment and meaningful involvement of all people regardless of race, color, national origin, or income with respect to the development, implementation, and enforcement of environmental laws, regulations, and policies."[8] The tool integrates information on regulated facilities with social and economic data from the U.S. Census Bureau, health data from the National Center for Health Statistics, and interactive maps. The health data, derived from the *Atlas of United States Mortality*, include death rates by county for heart disease, cancer, chronic obstructive pulmonary disease, pneumonia and influenza, and liver disease. Data are available by gender and race for black and white populations. Most significantly, the data reveal whether or not the county-wide death rates from any of these causes differ from the rates for the United States as a whole. The site can be used to investigate the racial makeup, educational attainment, poverty levels, and mortality rates for areas that surround sites such as coal-fired power plants and other industrial facilities.

Window to My Environment
http://www.epa.gov/enviro/wme/

Like Envirofacts, Window to My Environment (WME) presents data from a wide variety of sources. Search options include zipcode or city or town and state. Search results include an interactive map several data layers, geographic and demographic information, and a wide variety of environmental information grouped into five topic areas: Air/Climate, Land, Water, Cross Media, and What Is Being Done About My Environment? Because of its user-friendly interface and avoidance of overly technical jargon, WME is a good access point for lay users seeking local environmental data.

EPA Data from Alternate Sites

The Right-to-Know (RTK) Network
http://www.rtk.net

RTK has collaborated with the EPA to distribute several agency databases and datasets including the Toxics Release Inventory. RTK provides the information in several formats including plain text and database import versions. The RTK version of the TRI enables the user to download and manipulate large amounts of data on a specific location, industry, company, or chemical.

Chemical Scorecard
http://www.scorecard.org/

This site from the Environmental Defense Fund integrates data from the Toxics Release Inventory, AIRS Data, and other sources with models of risk assessment. For example, EPA version of the Toxics Release Inventory can be used to identify the toxics released by a specific site. The companion Integrated Risk Information System files can inform the user about the known health risks from each toxic chemical. However, the EPA does not attempt to assess the risks to individual and community health caused by such facilities. In contrast, the Chemical Scorecard offers local community assessments of the increased health risks that can be expected from releases of toxic chemicals. Scorecard employs risk assessment models developed by the EPA and others. Various industry groups have criticized the scientific assumptions upon which the risk assessment is based. In response to industry criticism, the site has extensive explanations of its methodology, data, and interpretations.

Sites on Specific Topics

Air

AirData
http://www.epa.gov/air/data/index.html

In late 1997 the EPA launched the new AirData service to provide online access to selected data on air quality and pollutant emissions estimates for six principle pollutants regulated under the Clean Air Act (CAA). The act required that the EPA establish air quality standards for pollutants considered harmful to public health and the environment. These "criteria" pollutants are: CO–carbon monoxide; NO2–nitrogen dioxide; O3–ozone; SO2–sulfur dioxide; PB–lead; and PM10–particulate matter (particles smaller than 10 micrometers). With AirData, users can identify sources of air pollution, locations of pollution monitors, and pollution amounts at national, state, and county levels. The site provides access to multiple years of data. In addition, the site has online maps of areas that consistently fail to meet air quality standards for each of the criteria pollutants, the locations of monitors, and the sources of pollutants. Users can also create custom maps. Data can be viewed online or downloaded in spreadsheet format. Using AirData, the user can find out the address of the nearest monitor that measured a criteria pollutant such as ozone and the number of times that the measurements exceeded the national standards within the past six years. In addition, that same user could determine how many days the air quality in a county was good, moderate, or unhealthful under the Air Quality Index. The user could also determine the point sources for each of the principle pollutants in his or her state and the total emissions. Although this is technical material, AirData includes a number of explanatory publications that help put the data into context.

AIRNOW–Real Time Air Pollution Data
http://cfpub.epa.gov/airnow/index.cfm?action=airnow.main

This EPA site provides links to real time air pollution data provided by state and local pollution agencies. In addition, the site provides access to online ozone forecasts, maps, and the Air Quality Index, a numerical index for reporting overall levels of ozone and other pollutants. Currently the site focuses on ground-level ozone pollution (smog) and particulate matter. Data, maps, and the Air Quality Index are available for selected areas of the country. The EPA intends to expand the geographic mapping coverage and to include information on additional pollutants. The site includes a number of publications that explain the health risks associated with smog, steps to reduce potential exposure, and measures that can help reduce ozone pollution.

Climate Change and Related Topics

EPA Global Warming Site
http://yosemite.epa.gov/oar/globalwarming.nsf/content/Impacts.html

The site includes an overview of the issue as it relates to health, water resources, selected ecosystems, agriculture, fisheries, national parks, and individual states. The State by State Impacts page provides a discussion of potential local climate changes and the impacts of these changes. The discussion is enhanced by the addition of charts, maps, and possible scenarios that attempt to forecast conditions for each state. For example, the report for California posits the idea that heat-related deaths could double in the Los Angeles area if the temperature rose 3°F. In Colorado a 5-9°F rise in temperature could lead to an increase in insect-born diseases such as equine encephalitis. This site also provides information on state emissions of greenhouse gases, state action plans and actions to reduce emissions, county level information on non-attainment areas for ozone and particulate matter under the National Ambient Air Quality Standards, emissions from fossil fuels, and data on the population and economy.

EPA Green Book
http://www.epa.gov/oar/oaqps/greenbk/

The Green Book lists non-attainment areas for the "criteria pollutants" regulated under the Clean Air Act (CAA). These pollutants include ozone, carbon monoxide, nitrogen dioxide, sulfur dioxide, particulate matter, and lead. Although the data varies by pollutant, most pages provide a list of states and counties (and parts thereof) that are not in compliance with standards, a description of the area covered, and an assessment of the level of severity. Many pages include maps.

National Atmospheric Deposition Program
http://nadp.sws.uiuc.edu/

This site is a cooperative program between state agencies, several federal agencies, and a group of private organizations. The program collects weekly data on the chemistry of precipitation from sites throughout the United States. It analyzes the data for acidity (pH) and concentrations of sulfates, nitrates, ammonia, chloride, magnesium, potassium, and sodium. In addition, it maintains two smaller data networks: deposition of mercury and daily collection of precipitation data. From the data access menu, users can select a geography and collection station. After registration, a user can retrieve detailed chemistry of precipitation data for that site. Casual users may choose to view the isopleth maps. The maps, available from 1994 forward, graphically illustrate the distribution of pollutants that cause acid rain and other environmental problems. For example, on the 1999 map of pH (acidity) as measured at the collection stations, areas in the west are generally shaded green (less acid) while the northeastern region of the United States is shaded from yellow to red (more acid).

Energy

Department of Energy (DOE) Energy Information Administration (EIA) State Energy Data
http://www.eia.doe.gov/emeu/states/_states.html

Production of carbon monoxide and other greenhouse gases is closely related to energy consumption. The site includes data on overall consumption of energy by type, consumption of petroleum, and consumption by sector (residential, commercial, industrial, transportation, and electric utility use). In addition the site includes data on prices and expenditures and state rankings in consumption, prices, and expenditures. For example, Alaska, with its small population, had the highest per capita energy consumption in 1996. Texas, with its much larger population, led the nation in total consumption of oil, coal, natural gas, and electricity.

DOE Office of Environmental Management
http://www.em.doe.gov/index4.html

The Office of Environmental Management is charged with the assessment and cleanup of inactive nuclear-related facilities, including weapons plants and uranium mining operations. The site provides state-by-state news on cleanup operations, a database of site-specific documents, budget and background information, congressional testimony, an image archive, a glossary of terms, and other information. Use the search feature to locate information on individual sites. Because of a site redesign by the Bush administration, pages often link to dead ends. In addition, materials prepared by the Clinton administration are usually labeled "Historical Document."

International Nuclear Safety Center
http://www.insc.anl.gov/

This site provides information about nuclear reactors used for research and power generation. Although much of the site is password-protected, public users of the site can view basic plant information and a general map of the area in which the plant is located. Since 9/11 most general facility information, including evacuation plans and routes, system data, and other information, are no longer available from the site.

Nuclear Regulatory Commission
http://www.nrc.gov/

The Nuclear Regulatory Commission regulates U.S. commercial nuclear power plants and the civilian use of nuclear materials. The site provides information about nuclear reactors, materials, and radioactive waste. The Electronic Reading Room includes the Adams document system, a collection of declassified documents, including congressional testimony, technical reports, public comments, and other information. Access to the Adams system is available via the Web or with custom client software.

Flora and Fauna

Fish and Wildlife Service (FWS) Endangered Species Site
http://endangered.fws.gov/index.html

The site provides text and overview of the Endangered Species legislation, frequently asked questions, lists of proposed and candidate species and information on listed species. The species information is arranged by FWS region and state or by major group (vertebrate or invertebrate animals, flowering or non-flowering plants). Although the amount of information varies, the species information often includes links to fact sheets, press releases, and other information. In addition the links provide information on the status of the endangered plant or animal, such as the date it was first listed, relevant citations to the *Federal Register (FR)*, the existence of an approved species recovery plan, and other information. The site is also posting the final species recovery plans online. For those plants and animals recently designated as endangered species, the species page includes links to the proposed and final regulations published in the *Federal Register*. The *Federal Register*, a daily publication that includes announcements and proposed and final regulations, can be a rich source of background information on a specific species. For example, the recent threatened species listing for the Sacramento splittail (*FR*, February 8, 1999) included an overview of the species, threats to habitat, traditional range, habitat requirements, and agency responses to comments made within the public comment period.

Northern Prairie Wildlife Research Center (USGS)
http://www.npwrc.usgs.gov/resource/resource.htm

The site publishes numerous online resources arranged by type (such as checklists, species accounts, distribution, and trends), taxon (such as waterfowl and mammals), and geography. For example, under "Checklists," a person interested in birds could find "Bird Checklists of the United States." Although the site emphasizes the prairie states, it provides many national resources. For example, if you were planning a visit to Georgia's Okefenokee National Wildlife Refuge, you could print a checklist of birds that visit the site. The distribution menu provides access to, among other things, "Butterflies of North America."

Arranged by state, the online atlas provides photos, background information, and distribution maps.

North American Breeding Bird Survey
http://www.mbr-pwrc.usgs.gov/bbs/bbs.html

The North American Breeding Bird Survey is an extensive Web site that documents thirty years of research on all North American breeding birds. For the study, birders made an annual survey of birds on 2,900 routes during the peak of the nesting season (usually June). The site provides species accounts that include life history, identification tips, photographs, songs, breeding distribution maps, and winter distribution maps. In addition, the site provides access to trend estimates, annual indices, distribution maps, and trend maps for regions and species. For example, a user in Minnesota could determine whether the observed population of wood ducks in Minnesota had increased or declined from 1967-1995. The site also includes a number of tools for analysis of bird population trends by region or route.

PLANTS Database
http://plants.usda.gov

This database of the Natural Resources Conservation Service (USDA) includes information about all native and naturalized vascular and nonvascular plant species known to occur in the United States. It can be queried in a variety of ways, including common name, scientific name, symbol, family, and genus. Although the data available for individual plant species varies, each record typically includes names, family, symbols, federal status, origin, synonyms, distribution information, wetlands information, and bibliographic citations. Selected records contain photographs or county-level distribution maps. Some searches can be limited by state. For example, the database reveals that the Mesa Verde fishhook cactus, found in Colorado and New Mexico, is a native species included in the list of threatened species.

Hazardous Waste

Environmental Protection Agency Superfund Program
http://www.epa.gov/superfund/

In 1980 Congress established the Comprehensive Environmental Response, Compensation, and Liability Act (CERCLA) to clean up uncontrolled or abandoned hazardous waste sites. This legislation and its programs are more commonly known as Superfund. The Superfund site includes an overview of the issue, laws, regulations, policy, data, and information about properties or locations considered for cleanup. After intensive study, the EPA identified the sites that required remedial action and placed them on the National Priorities List (NPL). The user can choose facilities on the list from a map or basic and advanced query functions. Depending on the method of access, the user finds a wide variety of site-specific information that may include site status, background narrative, alternate site names (aliases), a listing of all actions, financial data, and abstracts and full-text of relevant Records of Decisions (RODS) publications. An individual ROD details the rationale for the selected cleanup options. RODs also include a detailed site history and description, information on contaminants, enforcement activities, community participation in the decision process, and other information–in short a treasure trove of information.

Agency for Toxic Substances and Disease Registry's (ATSDR)
HazDat Database
http://www.atsdr.cdc.gov/hazdat.html

The HazDat Database contains information on the release of hazardous substances from Superfund sites and chemical emergencies. In addition, it includes health information for individual toxic chemicals. Users can query the database by site map or name. The results include site information, including data from tests for specific chemicals in various media such as soil, groundwater, and air. Chemical names are linked to information on regulatory status and may include toxicological profiles with information on the health risks associated with a chemical. Using HazDat, a user could determine that a site on the National Priorities List contained measurable amounts of a chemical such as toluene and then read about exposure limits and health consequences from the toxicological profiles. HazDat also includes links to a database of ATSDR documents, including public health assessments (evaluations of specific sites for specific contaminants and media), congressional testimony, and toxicological profiles. Direct search of these documents is available at http://www.atsdr.cdc.gov/HAC/PHA/. The complete list of toxicological profiles, which ATSDR identifies as "Frequently Asked

Questions About Contaminants Found at Hazardous Waste Sites," is available at http://www.atsdr.cdc.gov/toxfaq.html.

Resource Conservation and Recovery Information System (RCRIS)
http://www.epa.gov/enviro/html/rcris/rcris_query_java.html

The Resource Conservation and Recovery Act of 1976 (RCRA) gave the EPA the ability to regulate hazardous waste from cradle-to-grave. RCRA data is reported in two databases available from the Envirofacts Data Warehouse. The Envirofacts RCRIS database (above) includes some basic information on generators, transporters, treaters, storers, and disposers of hazardous waste. The companion Biennial Reporting System (BRS) at http://www.epa.gov/enviro/html/brs/brs_query.html provides more detailed information on these same facilities. A detailed BRS report will include information on the waste generated or handled, including total amounts and type of waste stored onsite, total amounts and types of waste transferred offsite, disposal methods, and other information. Both databases can be queried from a wide range of variables, including geography (state, city, county, or zip code).

Land Use

National Resources Inventory
http://www.nrcs.usda.gov/technical/NRI/

The site provides reports, data, and maps that document the use of non-federal lands in the United States. The inventory is a major data component of the National Resources Conservation Service (U.S. Department of Agriculture) State of the Land site.

State of the Land
http://www.nrcs.usda.gov/technical/land/

State of the Land provides data, maps, and publications on land use topics such as agricultural productivity, cropland, grazing land, irrigation, private forest land, soil erosion, soil quality, water quality, water supply, wetlands, and wildlife habitat. The State of the Land site presents an overview of each topic, maps in various formats, and the data used in the preparation of each map. The rich map descriptions include interpretations, brief discussions of potential uses, and disclaimers about the limitations of each map and its accompanying dataset.

Water

Ground Water Atlas of the United States
http://capp.water.usgs.gov/gwa/

This publication contains describes the location, extent and geologic and hydrologic attributes of the principle aquifers of the United States, Puerto Rico, and the U.S. Virgin Islands. The atlas provides a good introduction to regional ground water issues. Individual chapters contain descriptions, discussion of major issues and impacts, maps, and other information.

National Water-Quality Assessment (NAWQA)
http://water.usgs.gov/nawqa/

NAWQA is a USGS program to assess water quality in freshwater streams and aquifers and to identify factors that influence water quality. The program identified geographic areas, called study units, which account for 60 to 70 percent of the water use in the United States. The long-term goals of the program are to answer basic questions on the safety of water resources for recreational use, freshwater fish consumption, human consumption, and pollution of ground waters. NAWQA also plans to evaluate the long-term effects of water pollution control and cleanup programs. Currently the site offers national overviews and data on pesticides, nutrients (such as nitrogen), volatile organic chemicals, and surface water quality modeling. These national overviews contain a broad range of materials, including publications, maps, data, and educational materials. In addition, the local study units provide specific information for parts of the country. Although the work of the study units is not complete, many units have significant resources available online. For example, the site for the South Platte River Basin (parts of Colorado, Nebraska, and Wyoming) has numerous full-text reports and fact sheets available online. The site also provides access to detailed water quality data collected for the study. Users can select a study unit by clicking on a national map or by selecting a unit name. When the program is complete, NAWQA will provide a rich body of local water quality information for those areas included in the study units.

Water Use in the United States
http://water.usgs.gov/watuse/

Every five years, the U.S. Geological Survey (USGS) estimates surface, ground, and saline water withdrawals and how it is used. The site provides data on water use by county, state, or watershed for the years 1985-2000. Water uses include: public supply, domestic, commercial, irrigation, livestock, industrial, mining, thermoelectric power, hydroelectric power, and wastewater treatment. The site also includes explanatory materials, a glossary of terms, and other information.

Bibliographic and Full-Text Databases

AGRICOLA (AGRICultural OnLine Access)
http://agricola.nal.usda.gov/

AGRICOLA is the bibliographic database of the National Library of Agriculture. The database includes the Online Public Access Catalog for books, serials, and other materials in the collections and of the library and a Journal Citation Index with citations to journal articles, book chapters, and other materials in the collection of the library. Abstracts are available for some materials. The database could be used to identify materials on the persistence of pesticides in soil and water and other topics related to agriculture and its allied disciplines such as plant and animal sciences.

EPA (Environmental Protection Agency) Publications Search
http://www.epa.gov/epapages/epahome/pubsearch.html

Recognizing that its Web site has not provided access to online publications in a consistent manner, the EPA developed this special search interface for full-text publications available on its Web site. Search options are available for report number, exact title, and words within the title.

National Environmental Publications Internet Site (NEPIS)
http://www.epa.gov/nepis/

NEPIS contains the full-text of over 10,000 EPA technical publications. Access is available by simple search or enhanced search. From the simple search page, NEPIS displays results as individual pages in image format only. The results list includes navigation options within documents or to the next document in the results list. The simple and enhanced searches also include an option to generate a printable version of a document in image format. Since the reports can be quite lengthy, the enhanced search page is recommended for most needs. Use the enhanced search to access to a list of results in short format. After choosing a title for display, the user is able to select the complete text for online display as "formatted text." Once the complete text is available in the web browser, it is possible to use the "find" tool of the Web browser to find relevant sections of the text. After finding relevant portions of the text, the user can then display and print the image version of selected pages, which include any illustrations, tables, and graphs that cannot be displayed in the text version. The NEPIS database is useful when the patron needs mention of specific local issues and places. For example, a resident of Pennsylvania could search for references to Three Mile Island that occur within various EPA reports.

PubMed (MEDLINE)
http://www.ncbi.nlm.nih.gov/entrez/query.fcgi

The bibliographic database of the National Library of Medicine includes citations, many with abstracts, to medical literature published from 1966 to the present. Search by author, keyword, medical subject heading, journal title, and other characteristics. PubMed includes a feature to limit searches by language, publication date, publication type, gender, age, human or animal studies. The Preview/Index feature enables the user to add terms to an existing search or search an index of subject headings. The site provides a tool to search for related articles and books. In addition, it provides links to free and fee-based electronic editions for over 1,800 journals. The site provides a tutorial on its use. MEDLINE can be used to research the health effects of environmental variables, chemicals, and other factors.

REFERENCES

1. "Gallup/C.N.N./U.S.A. Today Poll, April 17-19, 1998. Question ID USGALLUP. 98AP17R42," in *Polls & Surveys* (Storrs, Conn.: Roper Center for Public Opinion Research, 1935-), LexisNexisAcademic, via Chinook http://libraries.colorado.edu.

2. "Gallup Poll. March 8-11, 2004. Question ID USGALLUP.04MARH8R19," in *Polls & Surveys* (Storrs, Conn.: Roper Center for Public Opinion Research, 1935-), LexisNexisAcademic, via Chinook http://libraries.colorado.edu.

3. Michael Zimmerman, *Science, Nonscience, and Nonsense: Approaching Environmental Literacy* (Baltimore and London: Johns Hopkins University Press, 1995), 6.

4. Ibid., p. 54.

5. Joan K. Lippincott and Joan F. Cheverie, "The 'blur' of federal information and services: Implications for University Libraries," *Journal of Government Information* 26, no. 1 (1999):26.

6. U.S. Environmental Protection Agency, Office of Solid Waste and Emergency Response, *Chemicals in Your Community* (Washington, D. C.: Environmental Protection Agency, 1999): 6. http://yosemite.epa.gov/oswer/ceppoweb.nsf/vwResourcesByFilename/chem-in-comm.pdf/$File/chem-in-comm.pdf (accessed 19 May 2005).

7. U.S. Environmental Protection Agency, "About the Site," U.S. Environmental Protection Agency, November 15, 2004. http://www.epa.gov/echo/about_site.html (accessed 16 April 2005).

8. U.S. Environmental Protection Agency, "Basic Information, " U.S. Environmental Protection Agency, http://www.epa.gov/Compliance/basics/ej.html (accessed 16 April 2005).

Index

Page numbers followed by the letter "t" indicate tables.

BOOK ORDER FORM!

Order a copy of this book with this form or online at:
http://www.HaworthPress.com/store/product.asp?sku= 5763

The Changing Face of Government Information
Providing Access in the Twenty-First Century

___ in softbound at $29.95 ISBN-13: 978-0-7890-3156-3 / ISBN-10: 0-7890-3156-6.
___ in hardbound at $49.95 ISBN-13: 978-0-7890-3155-6 / ISBN-10: 0-7890-3155-8.

COST OF BOOKS _____

POSTAGE & HANDLING _____
US: $4.00 for first book & $1.50
for each additional book
Outside US: $5.00 for first book
& $2.00 for each additional book.

SUBTOTAL _____

In Canada: add 7% GST._____

STATE TAX _____
CA, IL, IN, MN, NJ, NY, OH, PA & SD residents
please add appropriate local sales tax.

FINAL TOTAL _____
If paying in Canadian funds, convert
using the current exchange rate,
UNESCO coupons welcome.

❏ **BILL ME LATER:**
Bill-me option is good on US/Canada/
Mexico orders only; not good to jobbers,
wholesalers, or subscription agencies.

❏ **Signature** _____

❏ **Payment Enclosed: $**_____

❏ **PLEASE CHARGE TO MY CREDIT CARD:**
❏ Visa ❏ MasterCard ❏ AmEx ❏ Discover
❏ Diner's Club ❏ Eurocard ❏ JCB

Account #_____

Exp Date_____

Signature_____
(Prices in US dollars and subject to change without notice.)

PLEASE PRINT ALL INFORMATION OR ATTACH YOUR BUSINESS CARD

Name

Address

City   State/Province   Zip/Postal Code

Country

Tel   Fax

E-Mail

May we use your e-mail address for confirmations and other types of information? ❏Yes ❏No We appreciate receiving
your e-mail address. Haworth would like to e-mail special discount offers to you, as a preferred customer.
We will never share, rent, or exchange your e-mail address. We regard such actions as an invasion of your privacy.

Order from your **local bookstore** or directly from
The Haworth Press, Inc. 10 Alice Street, Binghamton, New York 13904-1580 • USA
Call our toll-free number (1-800-429-6784) / Outside US/Canada: (607) 722-5857
Fax: 1-800-895-0582 / Outside US/Canada: (607) 771-0012
E-mail your order to us: orders@HaworthPress.com

For orders outside US and Canada, you may wish to order through your local
sales representative, distributor, or bookseller.
For information, see http://HaworthPress.com/distributors

(Discounts are available for individual orders in US and Canada only, not booksellers/distributors.)

The Haworth Press Inc.

Please photocopy this form for your personal use.
www.HaworthPress.com

BOF06